TO ROMANIA WITH LOVE

To Romania with Love

TESSA DUNLOP

QUARTET

First published in 2012 by
Quartet Books Limited
A member of the Namara Group
27 Goodge Street, London W1T 2LD

A catalogue record for this book
is available from the British Library

ISBN   978 0 7043 7257 3

Typeset by Antony Gray
Printed and bound in Great Britain by
T J International Ltd, Padstow, Cornwall

Though this book tells a true story, various
individuals have had their identities
disguised to protect their privacy.

1

Acknowledgements

I have tried the patience of many while writing this book; however, special thanks must go to all at Quartet in particular my editor Gavin James Bower and fantastic agents Charlotte Robertson and Hilary Murray. For wading their way through early drafts a big thank you to Izzie Woodliffe, Michelle Henery, Lara Legassick and James Marshall and thank you Paul Andrei Lungu, Radu Stancu and Cristian Bândea for vital Romanian input.

It goes without saying that there would be no story without my amazing family and friends both here and in Romania – thank you all. Elena, Mum and Cathy I owe you for the rest of time and ditto dear husband for turning a blind eye to my lack of discretion. And finally I'd like to thank Dad for always listening – I'm just sorry he isn't here to see the book in print. How we miss him!

Prologue

If you look for all the little accidentals that lead you to an end point (or another beginning), it's possible to believe there's a force behind each one linking unavoidably to the next. What follows is a story about a boy and his country and how together they changed my life.

Of course, back in the autumn of 1991 I wasn't looking for love and certainly had no plans to go to Romania. I was in my last year at school and busy trying to get into Oxford University to read History; that is, until the postman delivered a three-line letter just in time for Christmas. Despite my best efforts it appeared Oxford didn't want me. I was inconsolable. Rejected outright I craved what I couldn't have with the compulsive throb of a teenage addict. I had to re-apply and with additional strings to my bow. I needed to do something extraordinary.

It was my father who suggested Romania. He'd read about Ceauşescu's grizzly end in the *Glasgow Herald*, and after the Revolution orphan stories were everywhere; images of shorn heads and neglect entered our sitting room in the Scottish Highlands sometimes on a nightly basis. It was a church contact of Mum's who tipped me off about a voluntary scheme in one of the remote children's hospitals. I had never done any charity work but Romania sounded wild. I applied and was duly accepted without an interview.

And so it was that, aged eighteen – a few months after my A-levels and shortly after Romania had been returned to the world – I left home with a pack on my back and a spring in my step, blissfully unaware of what lay ahead.

CHAPTER ONE

Romania, January '93

Taking a school friend reassured my parents. Alice was a fellow Oxford reject. We flew together early in the New Year armed with felt-tip pens, Christmas chocolates and crisp dollar bills.

When we landed in Bucharest it was dark and the contrast with the world we knew sudden and stark. I remember holding Alice's hand in the Dacia cab as we crossed the capital, our noses pressed against the window, astonished and appalled by the sinister black city. The train station was its own particular hell. Feral boys came at us and clung to our buff rucksacks, mewling and pulling our fleecy arms. I cried out – we both did. People stared but no one helped. Then a man in uniform kicked at them with the toe of his boot. The smallest yelped like a dog and they melted away.

'Gypsies!' He spat on the ground and walked off.

We booked an overnight train to Suceava in the Moldavian north. There were dogs everywhere, guards standing beside their numbered wagons in official caps and buckle boots, and tired men hanging from windows smoking. A fat woman with a string bundle was pushed up the steps in front of us. Inside, the carriage compartments had sliding glass doors and large dusty seats, each squatting opposite the other.

'It's like going back in time, isn't it?'

'Tessa shh!'

I didn't sleep that night. Instead I tasted small country apples, learnt *please, thank you* and *I want* in Romanian and pocketed several random addresses that all looked the same. I thrilled an old woman with a Murray Mint. Her naked gums contorted with joy and for a brief second she was a child again. I talked all night with no language; soon I was showing a young woman the contents of my bag. I held up a box of Tampax. She nodded sagely and pocketed two wrapped tampons as souvenirs.

'Tessa, we need to get some sleep.' Alice was sharp. 'I can't sleep if you're going to show off all night.'

'I'm not showing off. I'm being friendly.'

We found a solitary taxi at Suceava station and arrived in Siret early the following morning, taking the volunteers by surprise. First impressions were sealed when Sue, a Kiwi in hiking boots, complimented Alice on her tan.

'Hey kiddo, nice tan. Have you been skiing?'

No,' replied Alice. 'It's fake.'

There was an uncomfortable silence around the induction table. Our arrival looked like an inappropriate accident – two trussed-up teenagers who'd been sent with no vetting from the charity's Christian headquarters in Hull. And there was nothing any of us could do about it.

Sleep deprived and scared, on that first day we didn't enter the hospital but we could see it – you couldn't miss it; a huge carbuncle amid the scramble of cement blocks and simple housing, with bars in the windows and a wall that partially obscured our view. Alice turned away first, focusing on the dirt track flanked by naked chestnut trees and two churches. We were in Suceava country and that, according to a man on the train, was the Land of God.

'There are more churches here than anywhere else in Romania. God welcomes you!'

Dave, a British volunteer, showed us to our living quarters. We walked behind his bowed frame through Siret, a small border town minutes from Ukraine. It was brutally cold – the wind blew off the frosted plains at a bitter minus-twenty-five degrees. I stopped worrying about whether my thermal underwear made me look fat. I reckon Alice had, too.

The charity organised the accommodation. I think we'd expected our own rooms, or at least our own beds, so the small pull-out mattress in an unheated room shocked us. And so did our hostess. Landlady Ana was inexplicably old; she lived and slept in the kitchen on top of her ceramic stove. Her face was sugared with white whiskers and she never got undressed. What was the point? Her son killed their cow in our first week. Severed body parts lay in large frozen bowls in the icy bathroom and when we bent to pee half a head eyed us from the floor. Alice pretended she was a vegetarian but Ana didn't understand our Romanian phrase book. She was Ukrainian.

'I want to go home.'

'I know but we can't go yet, because everybody will say *I told you so.*'

Alice was right, of course, so we stayed. And after a few days it got easier until it became almost normal and I began to enjoy myself. (Apparently this ability to adapt is common; it explains why so many atrocities go unnoticed. But in this case the atrocity had already happened.)

Nothing prepared me for the smell in the hospital: urine, potato, faeces, wet stone, breathed air. I never fully got used to it. I tried to imagine what it was like before the children came, when the building had been an army barracks. Four floors high, solid and conveniently far away from the capital, it was soon converted into the largest dumping ground for children in the country. Communists didn't cope well with deformity, nor indeed with unwanted infants, but that hadn't deterred their leader.

'Breed comrade women! Breed!' Ceaușescu insisted and proceeded to remove all the contraceptive options available on the market. Future socialist workers began arriving in their multitudes. Home-made efforts at abortion and a paucity of food to feed growing families meant things soon got ugly. Ceauşescu called his hungry population greedy and the state duly took over the care of the most vulnerable. Thousands of abandoned and malformed children were locked up and left to fester. Hepatitis and HIV rates soared; Romania's stray dogs had better lives. And then the Revolution came and with it the TV cameras and Western opprobrium.

How could this have been allowed to happen? Before I arrived the institution had been the subject of a British TV programme hosted by Anneka Rice, a blonde presenter with a gash for a mouth. Her challenge was to improve the living conditions for the orphans. Ha! No problem a girl in a jump suit couldn't solve. One year on and the pastel cartoons painted onto the walls were still visible. Prior to that no one had bothered. All this in a country where babies had their bottoms washed in camomile tea, little girls were dressed up as if china dolls and boys cooed over like princes. Romanian culture was besotted with children and then there were the orphans. The only way to deal with them was to pretend they didn't exist.

And yet despite the horror stories the first time I entered the hospital and met the children – over-excited at the prospect of fresh prey and friendship – I knew instinctively it was going to be OK. Manageable. Dare I say it (once I got my ponytail back), even fun. They needed me and, in a foreign land with a frosty roommate, I needed them.

'Bună ziua, mă numesc Tessa!'

More than that I couldn't say.

Within a month I was put in charge of entertaining 'Salon Sixteen': twenty-six teenage girls who lived on the top floor in one room. I found them easier than the very young children who struggled to speak or walk and occasionally doused me in pee. I was in a Romanian orphanage but I had no experience with toddlers. On my second day I tried to help a small boy negotiate the stairs.

Perhaps unnerved by the foreign girl in front of him, perhaps scared of the heights he had to scale, he went berserk. He flipped and bit and kicked as I gingerly tried to calm him and he cracked his head against the wall and then the floor. There was blood – his and mine. Eventually two women in white took him away and stuck a needle of diazepam into his little leg to stop the hoo-ha. I watched on, the helpless fool, as his body went limp.

Sometimes foreigners made things worse. Marianne, our charity leader, assured me sometimes things had to get worse before they got better.

I spent most of my days with the teenage girls – the ones who hadn't made it into the hospital school. Among them were those so damaged there was no way in. Petrea (no one seemed to know her first name) was pale and pretty with a neat nose and stood, in the same unlit corridor, against the wall where she swayed gently backwards and forwards, a short stick the length of a ruler held in her two hands and a little smile in the corners of her eyes. Petrea and her stick – after ten months I couldn't tell you any more about her. She didn't speak and nor did Andreea, who was the oldest in the hospital at twenty-eight and, rumour had it, the daughter of an important communist functionary. Not that it'd done her any favours. Andreea hit herself so frequently that a large blue-red ridge protruded permanently from her forehead.

'Poc poc,' she said and crashed her bony hand over and over into her head, unless there was a wall nearby. 'Poc!' I tried to hold down her arms but she was as strong as an ox. 'Poc! Poc!' She continued to hit at the devils in her head.

In time I learnt the only way to stop the hitting was to distract her with simple sewing or fast, demented walking in a semi-circle. That was where we were, walking in a semi-circle, when Marius slid silently into the room and shut the door behind him. Marius – spookily beautiful, lean, large-eyed and reckless, the chief among the children.

'Hello Marius.'

'Hello blonda.'

He charmed with his few English words, touched my cheek and took mad Andreea's hand and we walked together in the same semi-circle – and all the while I cursed that I should have been so stupid as to let myself be caught alone. He bided his time, continued to smile his beautiful smile and then quite suddenly, just when I began to think people talked ill of him for no good reason, he pounced.

Marius took me by my hair and pinned me against the wall. He laughed to see me squirm. Just like that I was his. He pulled my head down so I was facing the floor, bent double, every bit the foreign idiot.

'Marius let go!' My voice a pathetic squeak.

He violently pulled me back up by my hair and looked into my face laughing and then, quick as a flash, his time for fun over, he whipped out a free hand and tugged violently at the gold chain around my neck, thrusting his prize swiftly into his pocket before turning, leaping across the desks and back out the way he came.

I sat stunned, sobbing silently on the stone floor. 'Poc poc,' said Andreea on the other side of the room, hitting hard at her head.

Goddamn it! How often had the volunteers told me not to wear jewellery in the hospital?

Of course I had my favourites. I tried to hide this but couldn't help myself. There were girls who I could understand and so reach out to more easily.

Vasilica had been abused. I had no training but it was the way she got my attention, punching me hard between the legs, smacking and aiming where she knew was naughty. When I protested she cursed and spat. My limited language protected me from her fury; it was month three before I discovered I was a *cunt* and a *big cow* and by then Vasilica was my friend. I comforted her when she mourned the loss of her treasured hair (their heads were shaved every eight weeks). And I bathed her septic ears after she punched holes in

14

them and tied coloured thread through the sores. She was a young woman and all she had to show for it was some pink thread and a monthly bleed. We grew mustard and cress on small trays with the other girls and in the spring I helped her negotiate a slope outside the hospital for the first time, and we cried together once when she hit me.

Vasilica was friends with moon-faced Mariana who poked her finger in my eye when things weren't going her way. But she could laugh! An infectious ripple that included everyone. Mariana was given up to the communist state when she was just six weeks old. She learnt to suckle from a machine strapped to the side of an iron cot.

That summer the three of us with the rest of the salon sewed and played and danced. I cooked pancakes and they ate their first meal that wasn't served in a bucket. We went on walks outside the hospital and they braided and re-braided my hair. Best of all, they loved to rummage in my make-up bag. Mariana painted huge red lips on her round brown face and couldn't bear to wipe them clean when summoned back to her room. Vasilica tried to steal my mirror. She refused to give it back. We argued and she won (stuffing it down her pants). As a punishment I left her in the salon the following day and then burnt inside with guilt.

'Watch out,' said Dave one night in the Snack Bar, where volunteers gathered each evening to drink and watch MTV. 'You only have a few bullets in life and you don't necessarily want to fire them all into this country.'

Dave washed dishes in Britain and when he saved up enough money came back out to Romania with his guitar where he could live for many months on cheap vodka and unconditional love. And then he went back home again to wash more dishes. No one in Siret could believe he lived in a country where washing dishes might pay enough money to fund a flight and a life in someone else's country.

'I'm OK. I've got into Oxford to read history. I'm going up in October.'

But I knew even then, after a couple of months, that Oxford wouldn't be the same. Not after this.

We'd agreed to work in Siret for four months, and all too soon it was time to leave. Alice departed as planned to travel around the rest of Eastern Europe but I decided to stay on with old Ana. I no longer wanted to scratch the surface of other countries. I wanted to continue living in this one. Like Dave said, I only had so many bullets.

In Siret every day mattered in a way it never had done before and for all the hardships (ringworm pacing its way across my neck, no hot water, scuzzy food) there were many highs. Maybe madcap gap year schemes made sense after all. Surely only a green teenager with no experience of life's vulnerability, cushioned by the splendid optimism of youth, could crash through such injustice and plant seeds and dance and then laugh like everything was OK. And years later remember the good first and then the bad.

In fact there was only one girl who was rotten right through, and how much of that was her fault? Dana was wild like a cat and she would always be hovering in the toddlers' rooms where she wasn't allowed; bending over the cots, a guilty glance over her shoulder, mewling and prodding.

'By Christ, Dana! Get out of this salon. Back to room sixteen. Now!'

And she would leap for me that I wouldn't let her at the little ones, scratching and pulling and twisting. Under the beds she went writhing with hate, implanted with wrongs and filth that she could only pass on to those smaller, less able than herself.

Why the hell were the most damaged girls charged to look after, to change and to wash the youngest children?

And the one morbid hospital carer who stood at the infant's door all day and got the delinquents to do her job, she shook her head that I let it upset me so. 'Vai dolly,' she said, twisting my pink cheek. 'It doesn't matter. You must remember these mad children are a punishment from God.' She pointed to the sky and bared her fist to make sure I understood. 'God was angry with their parents. That's why they're here.'

In Siret God was, it seemed, a very angry man. What hope was there for the children who'd arrived as a black mark against their parents? Orthodox awe for this active God was everywhere; in the end the Lord had even crushed the communists.

There were very few exceptions. Irina was young with purple hair but she too believed in a punitive God – although as one half of the best looking couple in Siret Irina was clearly blessed. Her husband was called Valentin, which I thought very romantic. Valentin ran the Snack Bar. He was tall and silent. Sometimes I had to resist the urge to reach up and touch his thick black moustache. Irina wanted me in their flat with my tinted lips and Gap polo neck as often as possible and for the same reason the volunteers were wary. She decided early on that Alice and I looked like her idea of proper Westerners. And she was keen to improve her English.

'Taysa, Taysa,' she would murmur, and stare at me through spell-binding aqua eyes.

There wasn't much else to say so we watched *Dallas* together and giggled over glasses of chilled red wine.

'Taysa, why you bother with these orphans? Eh?' And we continued to sit hand in hand, her one small son obediently playing in the corner.

Mariţa was my favourite hospital carer. She was fat and poor and quite different from many of the others, rough-tongued and too quick with their hands. Mariţa had a heart so big she had nothing left that was her own. She squeezed my cheek and watched me leap among the orphans.

'Me, I adore the children,' said Mariţa – and it was true, she really did. Especially the naughty ones like Vasilica and Mariana who weren't cute.

'And you know, Tessa, everyone complains at you people in the hospital. But not me. I am not complaining! They were vegetables

17

and then the foreigners came and they learnt how to cry and mis-
behave, as it should be.'

At the end of every day Mariţa walked up the hill to the top of the
town, back to her boys and her big husband who looked like a
friendly elephant, thankful that when she lost her factory job after
the Revolution the Lord had provided and given her a new one as
a carer in charge of Salon Sixteen.

In fact it was Doina who found Mariţa her job. Doina was
educated and chic with high, wild cheekbones and a shaggy-dog
husband. She worked as the hospital pharmacist and suffered from
thinking too much. Huge tears would roll down her exotic face
once the country wine had its way.

'There were over one thousand children in that hospital and then
one night in '86 over half of them were bussed away.'

'Who? Why?'

She shrugged and pulled on her cigarette. There was a pause for
more tears.

'The most sick. The really damaged ones.'

'Where did they go?'

She shrugged again. The silence was ghastly.

'I saw them the night they left, squashed against the windows.
And then we never saw them again. You must understand, Tessa,
you didn't ask questions. This was not something you did.'

I nodded but I didn't understand. How could I possibly? Maybe
one day we would know where the missing children went, but I
doubted it would be in Doina's lifetime.

And as quickly as it began, our conversation was over and little
Olivia pushed her head under the crook of her mother's arm.

'Hello Taysa! You want to stay for some food with us?' Olivia
was the sweetest thing. She had a beautiful cooing child's voice and
delicate manners.

I returned to Ana's house that same night, my belly full of meat-
loaf and plum brandy and my head full of Romanian songs and
stories. I walked past the hospital where knickers and socks hung

from the barred windows and shouted up at my room as I went.

'Hey Vasilica, Mariana! It's me, Tessa! See you tomorrow! Noapte bună!'

Like I said, if enough time passes things become almost normal.

'I'll come home soon, Mum, don't worry. I just want to stay as long as possible. I'll be back sometime in October.'

'Darling, your father's very keen you shouldn't go up to Oxford late . . . '

The line from Siret to Scotland went dead and I couldn't face the wait to be reconnected. Anyway I didn't want to leave, not yet. Not until I had to. The chill of autumn was in the air and things had calmed down at last. The summer hadn't been as much fun as I thought it might be. The weather was relentlessly hot and the charity swamped us with short-term volunteers arriving from Britain. Our team of six swelled to nearly thirty; orphan tourists, often sponsored and on the hunt for an alternative holiday. They brought their cameras to take pictures and pockets full of sweets to tempt the children. Few stayed for longer than two weeks. I spent more and more time sitting with Marița or Irina in their flats, avoiding the mobbed Snack Bar. Occasionally I would sneak into the hospital at the weekends so I could be alone with the girls.

I ran from school with my arms waving in the air and never looked back, but when I got ready to leave Siret I felt no jubilation – I was sad to go. I was tired, though, after ten months and there was a large, septic boil on the back of my hand that Mariana would keep prodding. And I didn't want to become like Dave, a stranger in my own land.

So I packed my bag and took the girls down to the river for the last time. I told Mariana I was going home; I spread out my arms as if an aeroplane.

'Is there room for me?' she asked with dolorous brown eyes.

It was the first time I properly understood anything she said and

19

I didn't know how to reply so instead I hugged her, until she pushed me away.

On that last evening when Doina's husband Radu drove me across the Moldavian plains to the station, swinging past the horses and carts under the pink autumn sky, my tears were hot and guilty. I was doing what everyone did; I was fucking off back to my world, leaving the odd, bald girls and Siret behind.

'Pa! Pa pa!'

'Bye bye, dolly foreigner, come back won't you? Come back!'

CHAPTER TWO

Iaşi, Romania, Toma Apartment, July '94

Elena was standing at her kitchen window on the second floor when she saw me – or did she hear me first? – as I bounced towards the entrance of her block. She was struck immediately by my size and the luminous white of my skin. I was laughing noisily with her son as we walked through the metal door. Elena didn't move. She stayed where she was and continued to work the meaty putty in her hand, dabbing the ball in flour and dropping it, just so, into the pan. Her sister had wanted to come and have a look, too, but Elena dissuaded her. She didn't like a fuss. And she knew today was important to her son.

Marcel rarely bothered his mother for a favour. That said, there was nothing she wouldn't do for him – her first born and most beautiful boy. He'd arrived into the world screaming, twenty-two years earlier in the month of St Maria, all pink and perfect with a shock of dark hair and cherry lips. Immediately he became and remained her primary love, his consistent adoration of his mother protecting her from the repetition of her work and the pitfalls of her marriage. There was surely something magnificent about her husband if he had given her Marcel.

So when he came back from town one evening in an uncharacteristically good mood, volunteering conversation and finally requesting that a foreign girl might join them at their table, how could Elena possibly refuse? Foreign was, after all, a byword for quality.

For my part, I was touched by the invitation and accepted promptly. I hadn't found my return to Romania easy. On leaving the orphanage I'd found nothing easy. Especially not Oxford. (So much

21

for teenage dreams.) I crossed the days and weeks off a calendar and I longed for the stretch of summer that would separate me from the pomposity of college life so far from home, so far from the country I'd learnt to love.

But I didn't return to the orphanage. I couldn't face it, not for two short months. Instead I applied to teach English in Moldavia's biggest city. I'd had sweet memories of celebrating my nineteenth birthday in Iaşi the year before but as soon as I arrived with three (Oxbridge) volunteers I knew I'd made a mistake. I ached for the intimacy of Siret and I wasn't a very good teacher.

It was as I stumbled along in one of my many classes that I first noticed Marcel. He was a dignified presence at the back of the room, poised in the heat, always meticulously note-taking even when I was talking nonsense. His faltering English and gentle eyes drew me in; I looked out for him every morning and smiled at his shy acknowledgements. He was cute, I decided, but too small and way too earnest to be sexy. Still, I welcomed the invitation to take a meal in his flat; anything to escape my English colleagues and the disappointing, alien monotony of the city. Not at all what I had remembered.

Eager to please, the morning of my visit I rose early to buy flowers and coffee and these I handed to Elena as I entered her flat. It was a relief to be out of the heat.

'Hello, sunt Tessa. Hot outside! Cald!'

We stood opposite one another in the gloomy hall; I stooped to make way and Elena stepped forward to look up at me, through the red gladioli spears in their crinkly paper. She had a perfectly oval face, dark hair cropped short, and I noticed her bowed mouth that didn't move. There was a long blonde girl in her flat with whom she could not speak – she had no reason to move her mouth. Instead she bobbed and turned, keen to return to the familiar business of food.

In the main room stood a wooden sofa and a lace-covered table waiting for its guest with sweet, dusted morsels on an aluminium cake stand, a Tango bottle full of wine and mashed potato in a bowl.

Marcel wiped a thin film of sweat from his upper lip. It was thirty-eight degrees outside.

'So Tessa, welcome to my house!'

His evident anxiety left me feeling conspicuous. As did his silent mother who worked around us, wondering who I reminded her of. Certainly not someone she had ever met before. (Maybe a girl in that new soap, *The Young and the Restless* – but she wasn't sure.) And why, she wondered, was I smiling all the time? Was I laughing at my luck? Were they born with a laugh in their throats, these English people, all over-grown and happy? And because I couldn't trust my Romanian I kept smiling as she continued putting and placing with her face as before, serving warm meatballs in moats of pureed potato.

'Tess, what music are you liking? Have you a favourite group?' Marcel sat on his stool, legs crossed at the ankles.

'No. Not really. I'm afraid I'm tone deaf.'

He was not familiar with 'tone deaf' so he excused himself briefly to fetch a pocket-sized notebook filled with precise rows of English words. *Comb, brush, playmat, klutz.* I added *tone* and *deaf.*

'I get them from the American films.'

'Of course. Good idea.'

'I like Iron Maiden. They are very popular in my country.'

His mother reappeared from the kitchen. She was holding two plates of steaming maize, the colour of custard.

'Polenta! How lovely. Mulţumesc!'

I struggled through the mound of corn – twice Marcel tried to relieve me of my plate and twice I resisted. Elena would later marvel at my appetite (all the maize and the meatballs, salami on bread, and finally spaghetti in sweet, warm milk). Some days later Marcel told her the truth: I thought leaving food on a plate was rude.

Marcel was unable to hide even the smallest truth from his mother and she loved him all the more fiercely for his honesty. It was, Elena believed, no coincidence her eldest son had retained into adulthood the face of an angel; heart-shaped with long dark lashes and a generous mouth. He was diligent, too, rising early every morning to study engineering in the city centre, returning to the family apartment at nightfall where he shared a room with his brothers. It was on their bedroom door that I saw the faded Iron Maiden sticker.

'Wow, you *do* love Iron Maiden!'

'It won't come off,' he protested. We were in the narrow hall putting on our sandals. 'Besides is Vlad's room also.'

'Vlad?'

'My small brother.'

'The one doing National Service?'

'No. That's Dumitru. Vlad is smaller.'

His mother watched as we readied to leave, noting the superior cut of my blue cotton skirt and my fancy fabric sandals.

I could feel the heat of her gaze but there was no way in. 'Nice names,' was what I wanted to say. 'Vlad, Marcel, Dumitru! Good choice.' But I couldn't remember how. (Did I ever know?) So instead I said thank you.

Elena remained silent as I took her hand in mine. She looked up at my rosy, puppy-round face and felt exhausted.

Maybe it was my rueful state that made me susceptible to Marcel's unassuming charm. And the meal, his apartment, the block with its attempt at a honeysuckle façade – it all had a whiff of the familiar, although his mother was closed off, nothing like the Siret women accustomed to crowds of foreign volunteers. In Iaşi there was an altogether more terrifying, suppressed desperation. I felt it as a summer visitor; Marcel, meanwhile, lived it. The cloying need for escape explained the heady numbers of students who swarmed into our amateur English classes and sat and stared and afterwards stood in cooing pairs holding on tight to their special one.

Marcel sat alert and upright, and when he saw me he waved with an energy that surprised him. I was half an hour late and distracted but that was OK. I was his new foreign friend, a concept he was still coming to terms with. It hadn't even been Marcel's idea to join my classes. It was his post-graduate neighbour Lili who'd alerted him to the small pin-up on the college notice board. In truth, Marcel was a little self-conscious of his fumbling English, but Lili had explained on several subsequent occasions that the way out of Romania was with the English language.

'Hello! I didn't know which café you meant. They all have Coca Cola umbrellas!'

Marcel flushed pink at my loud voice and stood to offer me a red plastic stool. 'We love Coca Cola in my country.'

He was with his girlfriend Simona and when he sat back down he reheld her hand beneath the table. They were sharing a cigarette and coffee in a Styrofoam cup. He'd been waiting for me after class like he said he would. During the lesson Marcel had made up his mind that soon he would stop coming to my lectures. They lacked rigour (surely he could learn more from the TV?) and some of his Romanian colleagues embarrassed him. He was too polite to tell me his intentions. He simply wouldn't turn up one day but he would carry on meeting me. He liked speaking English and, in his opinion, I was a bit crazy for a girl. It helped that Simona was impressed he had a Western friend.

She smiled and looked at me through thick lashes. Her hair was painted flame red – an astonishing chestnut frame around kohl-rimmed eyes. It was hard to know how pretty she was. Marcel's fingers remained linked through hers. I wanted to ask them if they'd like some of my condoms. There were thirty back in my room and I had no plans to lose my virginity, but I didn't quite know how to drop Durex into the conversation.

'Hey Tess, do you want to come to my apartment again for dinner?'

'Won't your mum mind?'

'No. She's fine. She's working late this week.' Marcel smiled at Simona and insisted on paying for their Styrofoam coffee.

Elena had been drafted onto a rare late shift at the textile factory. It was a different factory from the one she'd worked in for the last thirty years. There, behind a red and black panelled exterior a short walk from her apartment, she'd been worker 4593. Every day she inserted the elastic waistband into one thousand, two hundred pairs of pants after her colleague had run up their sides and another sewed in the cotton base. If she didn't reach her target her salary was cut. Her personal record was one thousand, four hundred and thirty-two, when her eyes were still sharp and her hands quick. Elena rose in the dark at four each morning to clock-in for five; that is, until the factory closed down without warning two years after the Revolution, when the demand for white cotton men's Y-fronts plummeted. Now Elena sewed pyjamas – she liked the more varied work and the colourful man-made textiles. Whenever she passed the old factory her stomach tightened. She tried not to think about her time there.

That evening and with an expert touch she ran up a sleeve the colour of candy floss and tossed the finished garment onto her pile. And as she worked she couldn't help but feel a little sorrowful. If only Marcel had given her more warning about his guest. She could have baked walnut bread or a snow cake – the English girl definitely liked her food.

As it was Marcel stood at his mother's place in their kitchen, savouring the sense of anticipation that came with playing host in a flat minus parents. Simona sat against the long net curtain watching her boy tend the cabbage stew as she flicked and shuffled a pack of cards. They were so young and foreign it surprised me they played bridge.

Marcel offered to teach me the first week we met, but his note-book didn't stretch to trumps and tricks. I slowed things down and made five. He had to sit on the wooden arm of the bench while I tried to grasp a game in ten minutes that my parents were still

26

perfecting. I quietly hoped it wouldn't be a bridge night. I wanted it to be just the three of us for chats and jokes. I wasn't so sure about their bridge mates Lili and Alex. They were proper grown-ups. Lili had orange hair and Alex had a handle-bar moustache that was too old for him and a marbled denim jacket.

'Lili should be here soon.' Simona had put down the cards and was painting her nails from a plastic bottle. The smell did not mix well with the cabbage.

'Hi guys! Hiya Tess!'

Cable TV had given Lili a particularly pronounced American accent.

She leant in to kiss me through the steam. 'Great to see *you*, Tess! How are you? Alex and I have got a favour to ask you. Huh. If you don't mind?'

Marcel never asked me for a favour.

Alex pulled out a cigarette and moved towards the gas stove. 'I'm looking for a book.' He paused to inhale. '*The Quantum Self: A Revolutionary View of Human Nature and Consciousness Rooted in New Physics.*' He exhaled. Alex took himself very seriously.

'I haven't heard of it.'

'No, you would not have. This is something new.' He bent over the table and started writing the full title down on a scrap of paper.

I felt foolish and slightly homesick. Why had I brought the condoms? Simona placed a jar of soured cream on the table and began spooning cabbage into bowls. Marcel poured translucent liquor into a small engraved glass.

'It's my father's. Drink it! You will do him a favour.'

He smiled gently. He liked having me in his flat. Alex didn't drink, resisting in a country where all men did. Simona didn't drink either and Marcel was more interested in his cigarette, which he knew he shouldn't be smoking in his mother's kitchen. His exhaled fug hung in the air. Like liquid fire the *ţuică* hit my stomach. I longed to leave the kitchen, too small for five.

*

27

I suppose at the time I knew I shouldn't – after all it was not my flat to poke about in – but I couldn't resist.

Quietly I excused myself from the kitchen and, having taken stock in the hall mirror, gently pushed open the bedroom door (the one with the faded Iron Maiden sticker). Inside, the room was painted in the same cool blue as the rest of the apartment. Between the ceiling and the walls there was white decorative piping that resembled the icing on a wedding cake. The evening sun was spattered over the blue and white, throwing the image of the lace mosquito net on the back wall where a framed photograph was hung a little too high. Two small boys with bobbed haircuts, matching sailor suits and big eyes looked out of the colourless picture – unsmiling and respectful. The older and prettier of the two was Marcel; the younger, I surmised, the absent Dumitru.

I passed the picture and had stepped fully into the narrow space between the door and the bed when I saw him: another little boy, not pictured in the photo-frame but not entirely dissimilar, perched modestly on the edge of the bed with one bare knee drawn up to his chin.

'Oh . . . ce faci? Mă numesc Tessa.'

The sound of my voice appeared to startle him. Maybe he flinched – if so he recovered quickly, reaching out a narrow arm to push a button on the cassette player by his side. He removed the headphones and turned to look at me.

'Hullo. I'm Marcel's friend, Tessa.'

'I know, my brother told me.' The boy was now staring directly at me and there was a pause when neither of us said anything.

'I can understand English, you know,' he finally added then, averting his gaze, replaced his sponge headphones and pushed play on the tape recorder. It was my cue to leave. I had been dismissed in my own language by a boy as thin as a pencil.

'Ah, you met Vlad,' said Marcel when I re-entered the kitchen.

'Yes, I hope I didn't disturb him.'

'No no, he's just discovered Metallica. Nothing can disturb him.'

Marcel told me how he heard Scotland was full of mean people in skirts. I told him I'd heard Romania was full of orphans and vampires. I'd found the orphans but not the vampires.

It didn't get a laugh. Marcel said I wouldn't find vampires in Moldavia. I wanted to talk about where I had worked the year before but no one wanted to talk about Siret, and they didn't ask me about my time there. No one ever did. Alex took another sip of squash and I forged on regardless.

'What happened over here was big news in Britain.' I took a swig of *ţuică*. 'It was a major scandal. Siret's still bad.'

'It was a shock for us, too. We know about shocks.' Lili poked at a pulled thread in the carpet with the toe of her shoe. She couldn't understand why I kept bringing up the orphans. Didn't I realise most of them were gypsies?

'The children really grew on me. I missed them. I still do.'

'So why you come to Iaşi this summer and not Siret?' Alex smacked his lips together.

It was not a question I could answer and I was glad I didn't have to for just then little Vlad pushed his head around the door.

'Ce faci eh?' Marcel cuffed his brother over the head.

'Shh, I'm huntin' wabbits.'

Well, what else do you say if you're eleven years old and faced with a room of adults who've all gone quiet? Vlad hid behind Elma Thud, put his finger to his mouth, smiled at his brother and pulled back out of the room as quick as you like – giving himself just long enough to have a good look, and immediately wishing he hadn't. All Marcel's friends and the foreign girl crammed in the kitchen, under a cloud of smoke, staring at him. He went into the next room and sat down in front of the TV to recover. He didn't have a bedtime – the flat was too small and the family too large for set sleep times. There wasn't a meal time either. Our conversation started again and Vlad could hear it through the frosted door.

'We are all thin in my family,' said Marcel, no hint of defence in his voice.

'You're all thin in your country!'

Vlad looked down at his legs poking out from beneath his nylon shorts before re-focusing on the TV, all the while trying to work out what was so very different about me. I was a giantess, that was for sure – taking him by surprise and filling his room, making him feel tiny on the bed. And now he listened, I even seemed to have a louder voice than everyone else.

He was still there watching TV when I readied to leave some two hours later. Against the screen he had a stern profile; a large nose and brown eyes set wide apart like a baby hawk.

'Hey, waz up doc?'

Vlad got to his feet and looked at me solemnly, bemused by my Bugs Bunny and the way I filled the doorframe.

'You know . . . just, I just thought I'd say good night.'

'Oh. Good night.'

'Oh look! *Twin Peaks*! We have that.'

'Yes?'

'Yes. So anyway good night! Nice to have met you.'

'Good night.'

And Vlad sat back down in front of the TV very aware that for the second time in one night and for the first time in his life he'd spoken in English to a proper foreigner. She was not a gypsy or Ukrainian or Hungarian. She was foreign and definitely a bit weird.

Five Days Later

'Eh Tessa! Very good! One coffee. Yes!'

Tuca had a small felt hat perched on his head and a face the colour of a raspberry. He introduced me to the sum total of his English as soon as he met me.

'Super! Chin chin!'

Marcel remained impassive as his father drew a knee up to his chest and began what looked like a Russian barn dance. He broke into song; a simple ditty in Romanian rhyming couplets:

> *That's how good people drink!*
> *From Saturday till Monday*
> *That's how beautiful people drink!*
> *From Saturday till Tuesday*

Vlad now soundlessly slid into the room along the wall and dropped his satchel to the floor. He was thrown by my being there; Marcel had not mentioned anything about the foreign girl coming around again.

I raised my brow in the direction of his father. I didn't know Tuca had a drink in him. It was 5pm and I was enjoying the spectacle.

> *That's how rich people drink!*
> *From Saturday till Wednesday*

I would've enjoyed it more if the expression on his small son's face hadn't made me feel a fool for laughing. Vlad, like his mother, rarely found cause to move his mouth. He would not smile, especially not now with his dad doing his thing and the blonde girl laughing.

Vlad couldn't remember a time when his dad's drinking hadn't messed things up. Apparently the problem started the year he was born. Tuca the electrician was moved to a bread factory. It backed on to an alcohol factory and the workers swapped bread for spirits and drank themselves happy.

'Eh Tess, sankyou!' Tuca reached to take my arm with his tawny worker's hand.

'Nu!'

Marcel stepped in wielding a bottle of *țuică*. I was a guest and must be offered a drink.

'That is how it is in our country.'

No matter if your father is an alcoholic.

*

Vlad's school had finished for the summer. He was still holding a coronet of flowers in his hand, a dainty spray of red roses and white daisies. Tuca plucked them from his son, exchanging his felt hat for flowers. Vlad ducked the hat, resisted the chance to dance, and remained shrunk against the wall. He felt acutely self-conscious, even more so when Marcel acknowledged his sibling's prize.

'For coming top of his class,' Marcel explained.

'Flowers for a boy! Can't they come up with something better than that?'

'I know. It's rubbish, isn't it.' Vlad looked at me and almost smiled.

The school brain box wore a Mickey Mouse T-shirt, under which he'd hidden his floral coronet all the way home. School Ten was not about to change its ways. Flowers would remain the gift for the gifted.

We sat at the table and were served by Elena. Tuca was removed from the room. Small pieces of fried meat glistened on our plates.

'I have an idea. Why doesn't Vlad come to our classes? Vlad, your English is so good. It's amazing!' I wanted to say that his English was better than his brother's but didn't. 'How old are you, Vlad?'

'Vlăduţ is twelve.' Marcel leant across the table, his body language almost paternal.

'Vlăduţ?'

'It means little Vlad. Uţ is, how you say? Diminutive.'

'*Vladootz*.'

Vlad focused on his plate and picked at a piece of meat. He was the centre of attention without saying anything; he could feel his cheeks burn.

'Vlad is too shy to come to classes, aren't you Vlăduţ?'

I didn't think Vlad looked shy. Quiet, yes – but not shy.

Vlad carried on staring at his plate. He knew as a rule he was only shy when he couldn't be bothered, which was quite a lot of the time, but he felt very shy in that moment with me, the noisy foreign girl, talking about him, filling the room with questions and excitement. So maybe Marcel was right – maybe he *was* shy.

Marcel was generally right, what with him being the oldest and the most important son. Vlad had arrived a whole decade later; an autumn leaf wanted (demanded) by the communists but not by Elena and Tuca, not even by Marcel and Dumitru. Elena had prayed for a girl; instead, she got another boy. He'd arrived in the dark decade when his father started drinking and Ceauşescu's toxic cocktail of crazy economics and personality cult did their worst. Soon there were no nappies and no powdered milk; Vlad was breast-fed until he was two – his first word was *ţâţă*. Elena lost three teeth that year; it was the year she stopped smiling.

'Where did you learn your English, Vlăduţ?' I was still speaking a little too loudly.

'From the cartoons. Looney Tunes . . . '

'Vlad was lucky,' said Marcel. 'The Revolution came in time to make learning English easy.'

I looked at Vlad; he looked thin, he did not look lucky.

Vlad didn't comment. He'd never given any thought to whether he was lucky or not. He'd been eight when the Revolution began. He vividly remembered sitting on the sofa-bed and watching the action unfold on TV until the screens went blank and panicky officials played patriotic music. Two days later and after two bottles of country wine his dad cut up their obligatory communist party membership cards, and his mum went back to the factory to make more Russian underpants because what else do you do on a Saturday? She was sent home again, where she sat on the sofa not entirely sure what to do with herself. Vlad was on Christmas holidays; he ran around the building site of a half-finished block with two friends and made the V-sign at a worker, then he came home and ate a warm slice of boiled maize. For a week he stayed awake as long as he could because he wanted to see the change when it came.

Vlad still didn't say anything but he lifted his eyes from his plate and gave me a very quick smile. I was, after all, part of the change.

'Hey Vlăduţ, why don't you come to our camin and help me with some Romanian? I'm rubbish. It's *soo* embarrassing!'

Marcel snorted over his pork. 'Vlăduţ is far too shy for that, aren't you Vlad?'

Vlad moved his hands as if to say *how would I know*, so bamboozled was he by all our talk. Due to meet his cousin outside, he shrugged his pointy shoulders, swung his legs to the floor and walked out of the room without a word. He left his coronet on the table.

Before I left I gave my address to Marcel.

'In case Vlăduţ wants some pocket money.'

In fact there was never any question in Vlad's mind; he would give the foreign girl the lesson she wanted in Romanian. Why not? He was surprised one person could fill his flat with so much noise, like steam rising off a big pot. Vlad decided I was like a storm. By landing in his home I had broken up the steady hum of his hot summer. He liked the winter best, the bitter cold and the deep-packed snow that pulled out every child with tea trays and toboggans until the path to the city centre was so slippery old women stayed inside and mothers came out to find their children (so many children) to remind them to eat. The summer, in comparison, was stifling.

That July, Vlad stood on a chair and found some blank paper in the walnut cabinet, borrowed his brother's best pen and let himself out of the flat.

Mama, gone out, back later. Vlad

Iaşi, Student Camin

'I want to be able to explain when something belongs to something else. You know, like, "*The girl's skirt . . .* " ' I was talking a lot – it's possible I'd not stopped talking since Vlad entered the room.

There was a small steel balcony attached to our room. I had stood on it, looking down at the concrete below, willing, waiting for Vlad's arrival. Jeff sat inside with Emma, one of the other volunteers. I had hoped he would leave but Emma managed to persuade him that he too wanted a lesson. He didn't. He just wanted to pat Emma's bare thigh.

'I think she means the possessive article,' Emma offered.

Vlad was perched on the end of the bed in plastic flip-flops and a vest, but now he moved to the wooden chair and leant over the desk with his brother's pen, glad to have something to concentrate on. He wrote in neat, foreign loops.

Roţile fotoliului

'What the hell's that?'

'The wheels of the armchair.' Vlad smiled, the blood now thumping a little less in his head.

'I don't understand. That doesn't make sense. Where's the word *the*? And how do you say *foto*? There aren't enough words.'

'Language does not work like that. If I translated the words directly in English they would read *wheels the armchair of the* . . . '

'It's beyond me.' Jeff lay back on the bed and cocked his arms behind his head.

'Me too!' I rolled my eyes.

Vlad laughed. We both did. Emma took notes.

I was enjoying myself so much I'd almost forgotten about my boil; that is, until I sat back down on the bed with an unguarded suddenness. The shooting pain forced an involuntary gasp. Vlad furrowed his brow; I smiled apologetically. This was a second and larger sore in the very centre of my left buttock. A possible hangover from my year in the children's hospital, I'd already used up my British antibiotics and the heat made things worse. Worry saw me confide in my English colleagues. A mistake. Jeff found the notion of a bottom with boils very funny. So funny he found it necessary to tell Vlad.

'Hey little man, don't go to Tessa's classes'

'Why not?'

'Because she's got a . . . ' He blew up his cheeks like a hamster and slapped his hands against his face. 'BOIL! Ha ha ha!'

35

'Ha ha ha. Thanks a lot, Jeff. Why did you go and say that? Just ignore him, Vlad.'

'On her bum!' Jeff was loving it.

Vlad shrugged. 'Oh this is no problem,' he said quietly. 'We have many of these in our country . . . how do you say? Boils?' He took his time with the new word. 'We call them *furuncule*.'

The sound of this Romanian word made me feel sick. Emma wrote it down. I ended the lesson. It was suddenly too much; my boils, the noise and little Vlad sitting in the room.

As he readied to leave I asked him if he would come to classes on Friday.

'Why not? My mum can sort out your boil if you like. My brother had one once.'

And with that he turned and left, leaving my $5 bill on the table.

Iaşi, University Campus

'Ooh,' they all poured over my expanding hand, totally unafraid.

'Yes yes,' they nodded.

It seemed everybody in my class knew someone who'd had a *furuncul*. I did not find this reassuring. I waved them back to their seats and that was when I saw Vlad. He was sitting at the very back. I forgot about my boils.

Early on Vlad had made up his mind to come to my lessons. He secretly knew his English was better than his brother's. He was unsure why exactly, but when he watched American TV the words stayed in his head like the lyrics in a song. But he didn't come alone. He invited his cousin Alin who was taller and talked more but whose English was not as good. His other cousin Mihaela also wanted to come. She loved to speak English but Vlad and Alin told her it was only for children over ten. Within a week Mihaela was also in my class.

Vlad was unsure what to expect. He had never been in a university building and wanted to look around but he didn't want to draw attention to himself. He was surprised when I started explaining the rules of a guessing game. He listened as I outlined the concept of hangman and wondered why his brother was always so stressed if they played games like this at university.

'The aim is to guess the word that's in my head.'

I avoided eye contact with Lili and Marcel; I concentrated on Vlad and Alin. I just couldn't do the proper stuff, not with the heat and the boys and the boils and the argument over multiculturalism from the day before. It was my fault. I was trying to explain the word *diverse*. It was going well (we talked about migration and why people moved to rich countries) until we came to Romanian diversity, which meant talking about the gypsies. They all hated the gypsies. I felt I had lost the argument. After all what did a blonde foreigner know about the Roma? Still smarting after class, I ostentatiously gave ten thousand lei to a gypsy girl in a floaty yellow skirt. With her bright ribbons and patchwork apron she was perched like a misplaced bird of paradise on the edge of the drab city street. One arm cupping a newborn to her breast, she tackled me with the other.

'For the love of God give me money!'

She held on to my shirt. She wouldn't let go. Everyone was watching. How could I refuse?

So hangman it was. It took the class a while to work out they were meant to enjoy the game. Desks hammered through the floor and a collective desperation to absorb any knowledge I might offer did not lend well to party games. Was this blonde girl not from Oxford? What did they do in the West that she should suggest playing children's games in a language class?

Alin saved me. He shouted out a letter. See! It helps you practise the alphabet! Then Vlad, even Marcel joined in. Vlad guessed the first word.

'Heavy metal,' he volunteered, his arm half-raised from the desk.

'Yes! Brilliant! Now you come up with one.'

He stood to take the chalk. His hand shook when he scored his spaces on the board.

'Only five letters, this'll be a short game.'

'BOILS! OK, OK – very funny . . . '

Vlad's eyes creased with delight. He sat back down feeling as though there was a lot of sun shining on his head. A bit too much? He'd never put his hand up in class before, nor had he stood at the chalk board. He turned around and saw his brother looking at him. Marcel stuck his tongue out and made up his mind that this would be his last lecture.

Chicerea

We were in a pale blue Dacia. A trill mix of gypsy folk music spewed out of the radio. La da da da da da da, la da dee da dee da! St Maria was dancing on a gold thread beneath the rear-view mirror. Vlad sat beside me wearing his foam headphones and Marcel smoked out of the window. We were on the road to Bessarabia in Uncle Bogdan's car. Bodgan swerved to miss a cart and over-corrected. The road was narrow, locals straggling home – one led a cow, another wheeled a barrow of cabbages. No one looked up when Bodgan sounded his horn.

Tuca had always made do with a pre-war bicycle but two years after the Revolution Uncle Bogdan got a car and a more important job in an even bigger flour factory. The tokens that were distributed to workers, the people's share of the nation's limited assets, had shored up in the hands of a few. Bogdan was one of the few. He had a bushy black beard and his flour factory made a profit, and he was always on hand to buy more tokens when people got desperate. Tuca kept his shares in an old briefcase – this prodigal son had hidden his nuts. Bogdan had grown a tree. When I asked Elena how her brother-in-law had managed it she put her index finger to her cheek. No further questions. But everybody in the family liked the fact there was an uncle with a car.

Now Uncle Bogdan was giving the foreign girl a lift to the country-side. La da dee da dee da! Vlad and Marcel did not like the countryside but they came too, with Alin and his little sister Mihaela.

We were on an excursion to Chicerea, a small village where Tuca had grown up that stretched like a ribbon along a road ten miles from the border with the Republic of Moldova. Tuca was the eldest child in a family of seven siblings; he had six younger sisters. As soon as he was old enough, he worked the surrounding fields with his father – tracking the plough, milling the corn, stooking the hay. And every year he drove the horse and cart filled with fruit and flour to market in Iaşi; that is, until the communists took his family's smallholding away and Tuca was forced to leave for National Service in Bucharest. In '69 when he finally returned home there was no land left to work and he was too old for school. So he put his country spirit on a shelf in his head and moved to the city where he became an electrician in a bread factory. But he never learnt to love the block just as his sons would never learn to love the countryside.

'There is no running water,' explained Marcel as we passed the city power station with its jumble of wires and cylindrical vats.

I didn't care. I wanted to get out of the hot concrete city. I thought the fresh air would help flush away my problem. When I thought of the countryside, I thought of my Scottish home; solid granite walls, black pools of fresh water, yielding mossy banks.

'In the countryside there is only sometimes TV. The current is spasmodic.'

Marcel dragged hungrily on his cigarette. This was not his idea of fun. When food was scarce in the 80s he'd been forced from school to plant corn and pick potatoes but by then it was already too late – the tide had turned. Marcel didn't like planting and picking. He liked electronics, cards and pirated music. He also liked it when there was hot water in the block so he could shower before he met Simona.

Simona had refused to come on our trip and cousin Mihaela was sitting on Marcel's knee. Every time she turned her head her pony-tail hit him in the face. Mihaela was turning her head a lot to look at her new blonde friend.

*

39

Elena was ready for us, standing at the top of the steps in front of the small blue cottage, pleased her little party had arrived safely. A scarf was knotted prettily at the nape of her neck and she wore a brown dress tied at the waist. Her feet were bare. A few hens scratched at the baked clay, a screaming goose and a rash of morning glories defied the heat and parched roses cast sharp angry shadows in the midday sun. Beneath its broad tin roof the little house was hiding from the glare. Uncle Bogdan led the way. The main room was dwarfed by a walnut cabinet showing off a piece of Palmolive soap and glasses etched with forest flowers. Elena reached for the glasses one by one, holding them by the stem and rubbing them until they shone; six glasses all in a row waiting for wine.

And as she worked she knew immediately, instinctively, her guest was not right. Was it that I refused a drink or that my rich pink flush had faded? The change in her demeanour was quick as you like. She laid down her cloth and led me to the window, taking my bandaged hand in hers. Her short expert fingers were soft and kind; they held me firmly and pressed against any attempt I made to wriggle free. Elena had a cure for everything and issued instructions. Vlad left the room, his bare feet inaudible on the wooden floor. I didn't tell her about the *furuncule* on my bottom.

Elena had seen boils before, many times, but never on a woman. What had the foreign girl been doing? Tuca once had a boil so large that it replaced his nose and one day burst into his supper. Dumitru had a boil in his groin when he was at high school. It gave him a fever and she could not find any paracetamol in Iaşi to take his temperature away. Elena believed boils came from dead animals infecting the water. Tuca's mother Anica thought they were evil spirits trying to escape. Marcel felt sure my case was an infection picked up in the orphanage, but he knew better than to comment.

In the rudimentary kitchen Anica set about her work.

'Vai de mine!' She had puckered her lips and her eyes boggled in a shrunken head when she heard. 'Yo yo yo yo.'

A pan of milk began to boil beneath a slick of rich cow's cream. Vlad watched his grandmother as she deftly sliced onion into the white crest of foam. A fetid milky mess was duly delivered and pressed onto my hand.

'This will pull the pus out of your boil,' Vlad diligently translated.

Tuca finally filled my glass with wine.

'Noroc!'

Vlad knocked on the door and entered with a small cup of ceai. Mihaela followed behind him. I'd been dozing in the belly of the house, tucked behind shutters and lace.

'Ceai?'

'Tea. Lime tea.'

'Ah thanks.' The yellow translucent liquid was sweet and tasted summery. I took a sip and lay back on a large pillow.

'We used lime tea to make ill soldiers sleepy in the war. Are you feeling better?'

'A bit, yes. Sorry, I'm not normally so pathetic.'

'It's OK.' He fingered his Walkman, unsure what to say.

'Is it Metallica?'

'No.' Vlad pulled a face. He had moved on from Metallica.

'Oh?'

'Dismember. They're a new Swedish band. I made a copy from my cousin.'

'Oh. Is it heavy metal?'

'No. Death metal.'

'Of course. Death metal.'

He replaced his foam headphones and left the room, his head full of metal.

Uncle Bogdan and Marcel were talking politics; Elena was no longer listening. Her son still hadn't forgiven her. She twice voted for President Iliescu and that, according to Marcel, meant she had no right to complain about price rises and the pyramid selling that ran away with her money or factory closures that stole jobs. She had been a typical Moldavian baba. How could she be so stupid? Early on Elena's parents had got their five hectares of land back – it had been a very big deal. But she would not make the same mistake again. Nor would her wayward husband, who danced a jig on the way home from casting his first vote.

When I entered the kitchen the men stopped talking. They would not discuss politics in front of a stranger. Not yet, not even in front of one who couldn't understand. I smiled and pulled a face. Elena looked helplessly from her unlikely guest to Vlad as I crossed my knees and pulled another face.

Outside, beyond the courtyard, was a small wooden shack sheltering a hole in the ground the shape of a large pear drop. I nearly cried, squatting over the human excrement, my sore bottom extending upwards in the dark where the flies were dancing.

Vlad waited patiently outside. Together we went to fetch water so I could wash my hands. He jiggled and wiggled the bucket on a string at the bottom of the well like it was a fish on the end of a rod.

'Don't you like the countryside any more?' The contents of his catch slopped over.

'I prefer it in Scotland.'

'Ah yes, much is broken in my country. But I am very proud to be Romanian. We come from the Dacians, you know?' He squinted against the sun.

'Yes.' I meant no, but I was studying history so felt I should say yes.

It was early on Sunday morning and Mihaela was stroking my hair. It was our second and last day in the countryside.

'Ce fain,' she sighed, her ten-year-old face alight with love. She would tell me years later how, that summer, I was her star.

'Tessa, when will you come to our flat?'

I did not want to visit Uncle Bogdan's block.

'My mum is a very good cook. She works in a pizza restaurant.

Once she was selected to go to the Social Democratic Republic of East Germany for a cooking course.'

Vlad was listening to our conversation. He was pretending to read a book about Greek mythology but in fact he was listening.

'Maybe Tessa doesn't have time,' he said under his breath, his cousin embarrassing him.

'Tessa, Tessa . . . '

Mihaela leant further in. It was like being back in the children's hospital. Mihaela got so close I thought she might lick me.

'Tessa, can I come with you to the polyclinic tomorrow?'

'What?'

'I can show you the way.'

'No Mihaela. No!' I wanted to sit in the cool dark room with dust and rugs and Vlad with his old Greek book. I wanted Mihaela to go away. I was still sick from the boils. Tomorrow I would return to Iaşi and go to the polyclinic for some medicine without Mihaela.

'Will you come to church later, Tessa? You stand in our church. It won't hurt your bottom.'

'I don't believe in God.'

'Vai!' Mihaela stopped stroking my hair just like that. All of a sudden her small fingers were pinched together and her arm went up and down, head to chest; right to left, breast to heart. 'Vai . . . ' She shook her head and repeated head to chest to breast. Her hand rested on her heart. Mihaela believed only bad communists didn't have faith in God. Perfect foreigners, surely, had a perfect faith?

Vlad smiled. From the corner of the room St George and St Nicolas stared benignly down from wooden frames. St George was ready for action in a red mini-skirt, his sharpened lance pointing skywards. St Nicolas looked old and fed up. He didn't appear to have any presents. According to Mihaela his other job was to save girls from unseemly adventures. Better surely to be a *big woman*?

'A what?'

'An old virgin.' Here Vlad helped translate.

'Oh.'

43

'Yes but he makes sure they all get nice men in the end.'

'What? Even the ones that don't go to church?'

Iaşi, University Campus

Vlad waited by the door after class, watching me as I nodded and smiled and made promises to students who requested me in town, at their flat, to drink a fizzy orange and talk some more. Everybody was trying for a little piece of me, he noted, and because Vlad didn't like to hang with the hoard he felt embarrassed that he too was waiting. But then the foreign girl had asked him to, so that was different – wasn't it?

Yes, he would pass my thanks on to his mother and, yes, he knew of the polyclinic. He would not have offered (too forward) but, as I asked, he could show me how to get there.

Vlad and I picked our way between the broken bottles and lumps of miscellaneous concrete towards the polyclinic. He talked (when pressed) about the medical options for boils. 'They will either cut them or inject you.'

Vlad was not entirely reassuring about my pending appointment; his only brush with the Romanian Health Service had left its mark. He thought he was four but maybe he was five when he broke his collarbone – his brother pushed him down the stairs and it had not been a good time of year for bribes. In the country the hens weren't laying and Tuca had drunk the last of the summer wine. Money wasn't much use back then. Vlad was seen by a student (he must have been a student) who pressed his arm against his chest in plaster. Three months later his collarbone had to be re-set and his arm was again pressed against his chest (not a student this time – his grand-mother had sacrificed a chicken). It took months and months to heal and Vlad would keep growing, all of him that is, except the bit of chest constricted by his bandaged arm and hand. Elena cried when they took the plaster off for a final time.

'So I have a crooked chest with a hole in it.' Vlad was surprised to hear himself tell this story. He was embarrassed by his lopsided body.

'I don't suppose you would come into the clinic and help translate?'

'Hmm . . . OK.'

I stopped to buy us runny pink ice cream in cones on the way. It felt like the least I could do.

They injected me. I lay down and a large syringe full of antibiotics was plunged into my good cheek. I asked Vlad to stand outside after he translated the planned procedure. I consoled myself that this was the country of *furuncule* – they ought to know what they were doing. A dog slept in the corner and somewhere in the room there was a large dark green rubber plant. I stood up when it was over and vomited pink ice cream.

On the way back to my camin I decided it would be fun to go to a film with the class.

'One in English with subtitles.'

'They're nearly all in English now. There is a blockbuster movie showing at the moment.'

'Great. Let's go to that.'

'It's called *Pelican Brief.*' Vlad looked up with a smile. 'D'you think you'll be able to sit down for that long?'

I gave him a gentle punch. We walked on for a few moments in comfortable silence.

'You know, Vlad, in the West life isn't like the movies.'

'Yeah, I know. And England is different from America, right?

'Right. And by the way I live in Scotland. It's very important you understand the difference in case you come over for a visit some time.' I looked down at him, his straight back and proud straight gaze. *In case you come over for a visit* – that was what I'd said and I knew as soon as the words were out I had meant them. Vlad in Scotland. Now there was a thought.

Vlad said nothing. He continued to pick his way between the blocks of flats he'd not yet learnt were ugly.

As planned we all went to the cinema in the centre of the old city. Vlad sat next to me, Mihaela on my other side. I leant on one cheek and wondered if Julia Roberts ever got boils. Afterwards we drank Coca Cola looking out at the statue of Alexandru Ioan Cuza, a Moldavian hero under whom the modern nation state of Romania united in the nineteenth century. After the ravages of the Great War when the Central Powers chased Romania into Iași, its poor northerly corner, the country expanded outwards well beyond its original frontiers – but the success story didn't last. I heard how chunks were bitten off in the Second World War. None of it was Romania's fault, Lili assured me. It was the Hungarians. The Bulgarians. The Germans. And it was the Russians. Marcel's father had voted for reunification after the Revolution, but nobody else seemed to care.

'The Republic of Moldova is even poorer than us,' said Marcel. 'Dad's got his head in the clouds.'

'They have Russian accents,' Alex added gravely. He was wearing an *I Love NY* T-shirt tucked into shorts. He stretched out his elongated legs; they lay in front of him like strings of well-cooked spaghetti. This was his favourite part of the city; faded and elegant with its boulevards and mosaic paving stones and neo-classical architecture. He brought Lili here on Sundays. They visited the Metropolitan Cathedral and ate small cheesy snacks and held hands. Lili and Alex knew their city well and they were keen to share all they knew.

'I very much like Traian Grand Hotel. It is for very important dignitaries.' Lili kept her hand on one of Alex's spaghetti legs. The other she fluttered in the direction of the hotel.

I didn't tell her I'd stayed in Hotel Traian the year before. I felt it might burst her bubble, what with me not being an important dignitary – just a volunteer from an orphanage celebrating her birthday. It was indeed a majestic building.

'You know, Tess, it was designed by the same man who built the Eiffel Tower. Every room is lux.'

'Actually Gustave Eiffel only designed the iron structure.' Vlad was surprised by the sound of his voice, which cut across Lili's. He'd been listening to Guns N' Roses but with half an ear on the clamour around the English (Scottish?) girl, and he didn't like inaccuracy. Vlad had seen a history documentary and they clearly said that Eiffel was just involved in the iron structure. There was even a shot of Iaşi in the programme.

I was pleased Vlad had stopped Irina. And anyway, the rooms had not been *lux* – not at all.

'Probably a good thing that's all he did here, Vlad. The Eiffel Tower is very ugly. You wouldn't want that horror in Iaşi.' I reassured him with a smile.

'We have enough horror of our own, yes?' Vlad looked across at me, an eyebrow cocked.

I shrugged. Was this not the city I had chosen to return to? And there was something faintly continental about the evening with its pigeons and couples promenading in the sunshine. It was almost romantic.

'They say Iaşi is like Rome, because we are surrounded by seven mountains,' Lili began again, her breath moist across my shoulder. She started to recite the names. 'Cetăţuia, Galata, Copou-Aurora, Bucium-Păun, Repedea, Breazu . . . Alex, what is the seventh? We are Rome's eastern twin.'

'Sorogari.'

'Sorogari, yes that's it! And our language is the nearest to Latin so really we are *soo* like Italy. Romanian comes from vulgar Latin, you know.' Vlad returned to Guns N' Roses.

'Do you like our city, Tessa?'

'Yes, Lili. I like your city.'

47

CHAPTER THREE

Iaşi,Student Camin, One Month Later

'You're crazy. Why would you want to do that?' Emma pushed a lock of glossy hair over her shoulder and refolded her hands.' It was not yet 8am.

'Let me get this straight. You want to send Vlad to boarding school in Britain? Some poor little Romanian kid! You're going to uproot him and stick him in a boarding school? You must be off your rocker!' Claire was unusually animated. Her cheeks were a livid pink and she'd forgotten to pick the onion out of her breakfast tomatoes. Claire was a vegetarian socialist and the most intense of our British quartet. Maybe I should have tried out my idea on Marcel first.

'I'm not suggesting sending him to prison – only boarding school. It's an opportunity, don't you see?'

'Boarding school! What planet are you on? He'll be bullied to death. You're weird, Tessa. Really weird.'

'It's not like that at boarding school nowadays. It's different. You get your own room and posters and stuff. They'd look after him.'

The coffee arrived, thick and black, and the brief silence was hostile. Claire was still wobbling her head when Jeff sat down at the table.

'Boarding school,' she began again. 'Boarding school!' Claire had been to a new-build comprehensive where the pupils sat in circles and called the teachers by their first names.There was a lot of talk about the earth's resources running out. Claire did not believe in boarding school, especially not for little Romanian boys – definitely not for little Romanian boys.

My idea hung, delicate and precious, beneath this premature scrutiny. I should have waited – of course they wouldn't understand. How could they? I didn't even fully understand. Alone at night, unable to sleep, hot with boil fever, I'd nurtured the idea and it had not felt weird. It felt fresh and powerful – elemental, even – but not weird. Vlad was twelve. He would come to Britain and see how we lived and learn about another world. What was the problem with that? I was in his country; he would come to mine. And public school was the best way of formalising, *maximising* his experience. After all, it hadn't done me any harm – had it? They might even sponsor him. They would have to sponsor him. Then he would return to his grey, hot and cold home with an education, a vision and a future and I would've helped. Vlăduţ in Britain, standing on his spindly legs reaching into something beyond his block and the pictures on his Goldstar TV. My cheeks stung with the thought of it all.

In private I'd been mulling the idea over for several nights, ever since my conversation with Vlad outside the polyclinic. That was when I entered a room without a door. What emerged was vivid, its emotional grip unshakeable. But that morning was the first time I'd discussed my plan openly and I was hurt by the rancour it provoked. Was it the selection of Vlad they objected to? Or a general hostility towards private education? A bit of both, I decided. Not really so different from the Siret volunteers and their disapproval when Westerners adopted orphans.

'It's not right,' they'd protest. 'Ripping a child from his homeland.'

'It's not fair,' went the moan when the most physically able, indulged orphan was airlifted into another world – its skin white as mist, its ten fingers and toes intact.

I never won the argument. Didn't they realise life was unfair? Wasn't Romania a case in point?

One year on, I was again a lone voice among volunteers. Only this time I was the problem. Little Vlad in a boarding school in Britain was entirely my idea, my late night dream.

'Why Vlad, Tess? Why not any of the others?'

I shrugged at Jeff, momentarily floored. 'He's . . . he's really good at English. He'd cope well.' This was true but it was not a satisfactory answer. I couldn't give them that. I couldn't even explain it to myself.

Iaşi, City Centre

Marcel took learning very seriously. He did not know exactly why. Not yet. Later he'd discover he possessed a tireless ambition, and claim that the best thing about communism was the education – then he'd mend his sentence to say that the only good thing about communism was the education.

That morning he'd been bent over his graph paper, pushing a mechanical problem this way and that. He rose with his worker-mother and drank a small coffee to the sound of wood pigeons in the lime trees. He took his cigarette on the concrete step outside as the light came up and then he set about his studies. We met after my classes, to which he no longer came.

'Hey Tess, you don't look so well.' He nipped and cracked a sunflower seed and stared at me.

I smiled defiantly. I could feel sweat on my face that wouldn't wipe away and a *furuncul* was beginning to grow out from under my arm. I swatted the air to make room for what came next.

'The thing is, Marcel, I've had an idea about Vlăduţ . . . ' I kept it focused, a verbal torrent, fine-tuned after its early morning assault.

Like a deft bird he continued to pick and snap at his seed meal, his head cocked, his ears open. I occasionally paused for breath – to underline and punctuate.

'So what d'you reckon? Nice idea or what?' I beamed at him.

'Tess, I don't know what to say. You really think this could happen?'

'Oh definitely!'

'Vai . . . ' Then he paused. He crossed his chest, his face arranged in disbelief. 'Do you really think is possible?' The surprise now hammering his English.

'Oh yes! Absolutely! You've no idea, Marcel. Britain went mad over your orphans. Romania was huge news. Still is. Europe's Africa and all that. Everybody wants to help.'

His smooth brow knitted together above his nose. 'But Vlad is not an orphan.'

'Oh, that doesn't matter! The top line is a big school will agree to sponsor a little Romanian boy – nobody cares about the details so much!' I had leapt ahead. I was writing the letters, sealing the deal, telling the world Vlăduț was coming to Scotland!

'This is very kind offer. Very kind. I don't know what to say.'

'Good good! I am so glad you agree. Oh, and Marcel – it's not kindness by the way.' I was waving at the waitress, wanting something other than sugary cola.

'This seems kind to me.'

'I'm doing it because I want to. Now, how do I ask for a Diet Coke?'

'Diet Coke? I am afraid we do not have such a thing.'

Marcel spoke to Vlad.

'I do not think it will be possible, but would you like to go?'

Vlad looked at his brother. He was meant to be outside playing football with Alin, and Marcel kept on repeating that the foreign girl's plan probably wouldn't be possible, so he just said yes. Yes, he would like to go to a Scottish school you slept in, with the misty mountains and his blonde friend and the men who wear skirts, but it probably wouldn't be possible. And he had never been further than his granny's house in the country with the big cherry tree in the garden, which he once fell out of, so he didn't really know how far away *far away* was, so he just said yes. And no, he did not think he would miss home. Then he went to find his flip-flops and Alin.

'Do you think you're maternal?'

'Good God, no! Not at all.'

Claire and I were on a tram heading to the hospital where my boils had an appointment. Claire had finally decided she liked me. I was a character, she'd decided. Now she was looking to excuse my misjudged decision to send a little boy to boarding school. But I couldn't sell myself as maternal. I wasn't.

'But you worked in the orphanage last year!'

'That was different.' And I squirmed on my plastic seat. I didn't want to talk about the orphanage with Claire. She might ask me why I hadn't gone back and I didn't have an answer for her. Occasionally vivid images of Mariana and Vasilica, hair cropped short, rocking and chanting on a hospital bench still took me by surprise.

> *Christ has risen*
> *Christ has risen*
> *Hallelujah Christ has risen*
> *Haaallleeelujah*

And guilt – sometimes a longing, too – would briefly bubble to the surface. But still I did nothing about it. After all, my new project was Iaşi and classes. And Vlad. You only had so many bullets in life, I consoled myself.

Spitalul Şfântul Spiridon. That was the name of Iaşi's main hospital – so-called after St Spiridon, Mihaela informed me, her young face puckered with a devout intensity. I followed Claire's doughty bottom up three flights of stairs and felt glad of her company.

'What are you expecting them to do to you?' she whispered.

'They're going to lance me.'

'Oh. Will that help?'

'Dunno.'

'I think you're very brave.'

'What choice do I have?'

'You could go home.'

It had never occurred to me to go home.

The doctor smelt of garlic – an overpowering aroma that sat in the room. He stood in black leather shoes and a white coat with a splodge on it. His assistant wore a mini-dress beneath her apron. She smiled and patted a plastic chair. I signed I could not sit.

'Furuncule,' I explained. The assistant stepped on a stool in her purple heels and unwrapped my armpit. I'd been hiding the lump with swab and tape. Now naked, it hung like an engorged testicle.

Claire hovered in the doorway, her camera around her neck. The doctor gripped my shoulder with his pudgy square fingers and sunk a needle into my flesh. I closed my eyes as the assistant brought a metal bowl and the doctor selected a small knife and deftly sliced the boil from one end to the other. We were all lightly sprinkled with its putrid contents. The girl grabbed a mop and started making good and the doctor wiped his glasses and sewed me back together. An image of St Spiridon with his silver whiskers all sparkly in the sunlight eyed us from the corner of the room.

He wanted to look at my bottom. Had I not said I was unable to sit down? I shook my head feverishly. *Nu!* And I backed out of the door, away from this doctor with his knife and needle, bumping into Claire and the hard nose of her camera. *Nu!*

Iaşi, Toma Apartment

Elena stood and stared at her eldest son. Her instinct was to say no. How could he think it a good idea to send away her little boy who was meant to have been a girl? Her Vlăduţ. A surprise package who'd arrived on St Nicolas's day – her very own present from God. And to the West, that dangerous paradise that had flooded her country with gaudy trinkets and cosmetics and tobacco and splashes of unkempt colour that no one could afford but everyone wanted.

'You want to send our boy to England? Where they look after a dog before another man? With all the drugs and crime and look how it has been no good for our country. What will he learn? We will lose him.'

'I think it would be good for him. This is the future, Mama. Tessa is going to try and get him in a boarding school.'

Elena carried on standing. She was too tired to sit, and now this. She tried to imagine Vlad travelling on a highway like the ones she'd seen in *Dallas*, in a big silver car, living in Southfork with drink decanters and gravel driveways and smart ladies in shoulder pads.

'Boarding school will be strict, Mama.'

Elena took a little comfort in the idea of a boarding school even though she had no real idea of what it might be like. In Romania their gymnasts sometimes went to boarding school and they did very well and worked very hard. Maybe Vlad would be OK.

'Of course he will be OK. And anyway it might not happen. Tessa's going to try.'

And there it was: a hint of doubt. Of course it would not happen. The tall blonde girl would leave and that would be that.

Elena sat down, massaging her foot as she unstrapped her shoe, noting as she did a small hole in the sole of her leather sandal.

Siret

It was very hot. The windows were closed tight shut and my legs were stuck to the mock leather seat. I sat opposite a young man who was working his way so methodically through a word-search magazine he'd not noticed my tears, also hot, streaming down my cheeks, pooling on the seat between my bare thighs.

What had come over me? Had I not promised myself I wouldn't go back? That I would leave Siret alone? But then, quite suddenly, it was all too much (especially after Claire's probing) – I could no longer suppress an overwhelming urge to go and see.

I made the necessary arrangements the very next day before I could change my mind and caught a train to Suceava early on Saturday morning.

I knocked on Irina's door.

'Hi Tay-sa, come! Come quickly and wash your hair.'

'What? Hello . . . '

'We have hot water in the block, come! Come and use my shampoo.'

I'd already washed my hair in Iaşi but I dutifully washed it again.

We (Irina, Valentin, their one son Nicu and me) spent the day at Siret River sunbathing. Irina stretched out on the grassy bank in a turquoise bathing costume with lots of clean hair. She had a slender figure with pert breasts. I had boils. Valentin was lying next to me. This was not what I had imagined. After a couple of awkward hours I kissed them goodbye and slipped away.

I chose not to remember what happened next. It was easier that way; soon the memory became foggy, almost forgotten.

For sure, I walked down the road flanked with chestnut trees, keen to pop in on old Ana first. I knocked and rattled the glass and eventually a sharp woman came to the door. It was Ana's daughter, returned at last from Germany. She told me Ana was dead. She'd died that winter alone in her bed above the ceramic stove. I expressed my sadness and walked on.

The hospital was exactly the same; the colour, the grime, the noise, most of all the smell. It was the weekend so there were no volunteers. I passed the porter and moved towards the vast wooden door, my heart thumping in my head.

You weren't allowed to bring presents (the bullies stole them), and I had nothing to offer (or so I believed). What was I doing there amid the tragedy no longer entwined in my life? A tragedy that seemed all the more appalling for my distance from it. I didn't get as far as Salon Sixteen. I stopped on the ground floor, putting my head around the door of another room, and there she was: Dana, dirty wheedling Dana, almost womanly now with hips and a little belly, still bending over the cots. Beside her, sitting in an arc of light before the window, was a shifty carer. There was no sign of darling Mariţa.

Dana stopped mid-task and made her way towards me. 'Tay-sa!' She flung her arms up and out and crashed across the room. I smiled and stepped back, wary of her, of me, of my infection.

I didn't turn and run. No. But I didn't stay long. I couldn't – I thought I might faint. Nothing had changed. Was it in fact worse than before?

As I left I bumped into Mariana – sweet, dark, naughty Mariana. She poked me in the eye, just like that. I began to cry but not because my eye hurt. I said goodbye between the tears as soon as I'd said hello. I was out of the gates before I looked back, Mariana still standing in the dirt track before the hospital, also crying.

I waited a long time in Suceava station until I gave up and found a hotel for the night. My penance perhaps? At least, the beginning of it. And the next day on that hot train back to Iaşi I vowed to dwell no further on Siret, on what I'd seen, what I'd left behind. I'd tell no one about my visit. I looked through the window at the parched plains, peppered with shacks and industrial accidents, staring out at the enormous expanse of this majestic, pulverised country.

Was it then my thoughts again returned to Vlad? Yes, I think it probably was. I would, I decided, definitely find him a school – a very good school.

Iaşi, Toma Apartment

'You might not go tomorrow if it carries on like this. It can block the train tracks.' Marcel looked out of the window at the water thrashing onto the cracked soil beneath their apartment and running in potato-coloured rivulets across the pathway. I joined him at the window.

Elena crossed herself and worried about her mother in a house with a tin roof and a sloping courtyard. Tuca's parents had lost their home in a flood in '71 – half the village had succumbed after twelve days of rain poured down on baked clay. The Romanian Communist Party had built them new houses five miles further south, and Tuca had helped. The painted villa on the road to Bess-arabia was made with clay and straw and many helping hands. It also stood at the bottom of a hill. Elena cursed the torrential downpours and then the heat and drought that caused them. Nothing had grown that year; the tomatoes were stunted, with shrivelled brown bottoms, and her mother's cabbages were crinkly and had no hearts. Instead she was making sarmale with salted vine leaves.

I watched her hand push and pummel the mix of rice and meat into small flecked sausage shapes planted in the centre of individual wet leaves. With an expert touch she rolled and packed each edible bundle and added them to a conical green stack. This is how she cooked; quickly, calmly and without words. She added more rice when money was short and left out the meat when she had none. She knew how to make a schnitzel from chicken battered so thin you could see through it, she cooked a bean borsch that left you farting like a tractor and she could make this foreign girl coo with her plump sarmale that had a mere spattering of pink minced pork.

I spooned soured cream onto my green pile and speared a tomato. Vlăduţ managed just two parcels of rice and vine.

'You don't eat much, Vlad. You'll have to eat more if you come to Britain. You're very thin.'

'I eat when I am hungry,' he said, his eyes resting on my plate. 'Do you like to go home tomorrow?'

'Yes, I think so. I've been here ages. Mum's going to cook me my favourite roast beef dinner. And also I can see our doctor about my *furuncule*.'

'Ah yes!' Vlad smiled. 'Your present from Romania.'

On the recommendation of Lili, and once I could no longer bear the fevers, I swapped St Spiridon's hospital for a private doctor. The woman was old with white, curled hair. Disconcertingly, she arranged to meet me in her flat. She answered the door with a grey cat in her arms and small blankets wrapped around her calves in late July. But she had a kind face and I was desperate.

I returned the following day and picked up forty small glass files of a clear liquid wrapped in brown paper. For the possibility of boil freedom I paid a hefty fee.

'Inject their contents twice daily,' she explained, loudly counting her rolls of lei before I'd even left the flat.

'You really are insane, Tessa. You can't be serious about this. You're going to inject yourself with some unknown foreign liquid?'

'And what other option do I have?'

'You could go home.'

There was a pause when I decided to try my luck. 'Claire, you can practise on an orange and I've bought needles. I was wondering if you would help me inject myself . . . '

'Erm, what happens if I get it wrong? I just don't think I can face it. I'm sorry, Tessa. '

'No worries. I can't either.'

It was Vlad who first injected me, watched over by Mihaela and Alin. Three children scrunched around a needle hovering above my arm was not ideal, but Vlad had greeted the idea with a cool nonchalance. We'd been on one of our many walks after class when I found myself asking a twelve-year-old to do me a favour.

'Why not?' he said and meant it, so we stopped and sat down at a Coca Cola table.

Mihaela selected the glass file, I snapped off its top and siphoned the contents into a needle and Vlad gently pushed it into my upper arm.

'Was that OK?' He only looked up when all the liquid had disappeared, worry running across his brow, through his body.

'Yes, it didn't really hurt at all. Thanks Vlad.' I smiled, relieved.

Mihaela walked over and kissed the place where the needle had been. I knew I would be able to inject myself in future. I did, twice a day for twenty days, and still I couldn't sit properly and spent every night with my bottom stuck in a bucket of salt water cursing the heat, St Spiridon, the corrupt old woman, the children in the hospital and infectious Romania in no particular order.

And before long it was almost time to go home and I was in Vlad's flat with his mum and Marcel.

Vlad looked at the table of photos. He couldn't believe his eyes. How many had I taken? There were piles of black and white pictures. He sat beside Marcel and watched as I raked through them – almost violently, he decided – until I found the one I wanted.

'Here it is!'

Vlad stared at the whole class sitting in the courtyard outside the university block. He was pleased I'd asked him (and not his brother) to write the names of everyone on the back. He obliged, only including the first name where he was unsure. When he came to himself sitting bare-kneed and cross-legged in the front row Vlad simply wrote *me*. And he made a mental note not to wear those shorts again.

In one photo I was presenting Vlad with his English Language certificate. Mihaela took the picture and the camera had wobbled slightly. Vlad picked it up and decided he looked very small; his head was half-bowed and he noticed my hair was still wet from the shower. The bandage on my hand was clearly visible.

'I like this one,' Marcel offered, taking it from his brother.

'You can have it. I can get more developed back in Britain.'

'Are you sure?'

I nodded, looking at the picture over his shoulder. It was a formal occasion and Vlad and I were both slightly embarrassed. The rest of the class had turned to look at us on their benches and they were all clapping. Did they know he was the favourite?

'I will be in contact, I promise, when I find a place for Vlad in a good school.'

'Don't worry. It's been a fun summer – hasn't it Vlad?'

Vlad shrugged. He always had a little flat feeling but now he felt distinctly disappointed. Disappointed the summer was over and disappointed I was going home. He knew he shouldn't care so much, how everyone smothered me because I was British, but he couldn't help himself. He liked that I was weird and noisy and I had bought him a lot of ice cream. Not what he'd imagined when his brother came home one hot day and announced he'd like to bring a foreign girl to the table. I had become his friend and now I was leaving.

'So we'll see each other again. OK Vlad? I'll make it happen, you'll see!' I cuffed him gently over the head. Vlad ducked and smiled with his lips pressed together and I stood up with a bottle of *țuică* from Tuca (for my father), a bag of chicken schnitzels from Elena (for the journey), and their address (pressed into my palm) from Marcel.

'You will get wet. It's still pouring!'

'That's OK, I'm from Scotland!' I ducked out of the flat with a funny feeling in my throat and ran down the stairs, out into the rain.

Elena watched my progress through the puddles from her kitchen window. She shook her head – there she goes leaping out in the rain with a nasty current in the air, wearing just a T-shirt. No wonder she got sick. What did they teach their children in these countries?

'Upon my life. God save them all.'

CHAPTER FOUR

Scotland, Rannoch, September '94

'Darling, you are remarkable! How did you manage? So brave, isn't she brave Donald?'

'What? Don't know what all the fuss is about. A few hives, I've seen worse on my cows.' Dad stood in the doorway – a giant of a man – huge broad shoulders in dung-coloured tweed, a twinkle in his eye and calf skitter down the leg of one trouser.

'Well, I would've been terrified. We must get you to Dr Dreghorn. I'm so glad you're OK.' Mum was standing beside her husband, gamine and alert. They were tall, privileged people. Their daughter had come home. They were happy and proud.

Dr Dreghorn was the local GP in Rannoch. He was well-paid by the state and had a modern surgery with a view of the loch. I would have to show him my bottom and he would refer me to a specialist. It was a pity he played bridge with Mum and Dad.

'Do tell us all about your travels, Tess.' Mum eased a three-tiered home-made chocolate cake out of its tin and filled a silver pot with scalding tea. 'We've been longing to hear, haven't we Donald? Are you glad you went back to Romania again? We were worried you might have got there and felt like a change of scene. I hear Alice is working in Kingston this summer.'

Was it then I told them about my plans for Vlad? Or did I wait ten minutes?

'You are a funny girl. You want to bring a child over to Britain? Is he an orphan? I thought you were teaching English to older students, darling.'

'No Mum, they're not all orphans over there you know. He is just an ordinary boy. Except he's not. Well, I don't think he is.'

'Not what?'

'Not ordinary.'

'What do you mean?'

'I don't know. I can't explain. I just know he's special.'

'Top-up?' Mum refilled my cup, catching the Assam leaves in a silver strainer. 'How old did you say he was?

'He's twelve.'

Mum was a primary school teacher. She valued charity and family and triumph in the face of adversity. Her conservatism was respectful and old-fashioned. She tried to picture Vlad. In her head, he was small with very short hair. Maybe it was shaved? He had an eager face like a pup and she was helping her daughter help him. *He's Tessa's friend from Romania. He's experiencing the British way of life. He's from such a poor country, you know.*

Dad was scratching his head through a thatch of curly hair. He wanted me to pull it. He loved having his hair pulled. I obliged. There I was, his adult daughter, pulling his hair and talking through my plans.

'It'll be a like a cultural exchange. He would only need to stay with you for half-term. He won't be any bother.'

'Bloody hell, Tess! Why would we want a Romanian boy for the summer? We've only just got rid of you.' Father traded insults as curious compliments; his contradictory belly-aching a match for Mother's exquisite Englishness.

'Purlease, Dad! I know you won't regret it. Purlease.'

'Oh go on then. If you get a school on board, your mum and I will see you good. We'll take care of the lad.'

'Thanks Dad!'

Did I mention I was his only daughter?

Iaşi, Toma Apartment, November '94

Vlad was watching the Discovery Channel. He was not in the bedroom because Marcel was in there with Simona listening to music – or so Vlad thought. His mum was sweeping beneath his feet with a straw brush; an American voice-over filled the flat with the story of the microchip. Vlad got up and changed the channel.

It was a repeat episode of *The Streets of San Francisco*. A very young Michael Douglas was pink-faced and confronting a long, blonde girl. That other blonde girl had never got in contact like she said she would, he thought. Vlad decided he knew I wouldn't but, thinking about it more, it made him feel hollow. He focused on Michael Douglas's puffy hair.

'Did Tessa ever write to you?' Mihaela once quizzed him.

'No. Did she write to you?' Vlad was annoyed with himself for even asking this question. As a rule he did not speak to Mihaela. She was a girl and a swot.

'No. I have written to her twice, though. I shall write again next week.'

Over the television Vlad heard the telephone ring in the hall. His father answered.

'Alo.'

'Hello. Scuzaţi-mă, Marcel?'

'Alo!'

'Marcel!'

'Nu, sunt Tuca. Tuca aici! Cine-i? Eh?'

'What. Marcel please! Marcel?'

'Este o străină la telefon. Ai o străină la telefon!' Tuca began to shout down the receiver at me to Marcel in the other room.

Elena stopped sweeping. Vlad carried on watching the TV. Michael Douglas was steering through an underpass in a brown Ford Galaxie. The blonde girl had disappeared.

Marcel emerged from his bedroom and took the receiver.

'Alo!' he sounded slightly out of breath. 'Alo Tessa!'

It had been Mum's idea to approach Strathallan first. Strathallan was the Scottish boarding school I attended for three years. My brother went there for six but Granny thought a girl's education less important.

'They know you, darling, and they were so impressed when you went to work in the orphanage.'

Dad helped me write the letter. He sat beside the Rayburn blowing smoke rings and adding panache to my sentences.

'I hope your lad can live up to this.'

'So do I . . . '

'Hi Marcel – thank goodness it's you. I think your dad thought I was mad just then! Sorry it's taken so long. How are you? Guess what? I've got good news!' My words tumbled out in a breathy clump. 'A school's prepared to take Vlad for a term. You need to contact his school so they can give us the go ahead . . . Marcel?'

There was a silence at the other end of the phone.

'Marcel! Marcel are you there?'

'Yes, Tess. I am here. This is . . . wow! We thought you had forgotten us.'

Marcel sounded very far away. The phone started to bip.

'How could I forget? Don't be silly. Listen, it's all good just like I said. Hey, I will call you again from Scotland on my parents' phone. Tell Vlad won't you? Won't you?'

I hung up before I was cut off. I didn't get a chance to mention there would be exams involved. The college telephone had eaten five pounds.

It was the Christmas holidays when I called again.

'Hi Vlad!'

'Hello.'

'How *are* you?'

'Hmm. OK. At home.' Vlad did not often speak on the phone. It felt foreign in his hand, against his ear.

'Are you still up for coming over?'

'I'm sorry?'

'Coming here. There's a school that will take you for a term. They will pay your fees. All you have to do is pass some exams. You need to get a fax number from your school so that they can send you the exams and a teacher will have to sit with you.'

'Oh.'

'The exams will be easy. A synch. Honestly you know we're still learning to do long division at thirteen over here. You'll find it easy-peasy.'

Vlad was very quiet. He was relieved when Marcel prised the receiver from his hand.

'Hello Tess, Marcel here!' Marcel flicked open his notebook and licked his pen.

'Shut up, you damn fool!' Elena had not expected my call and did not need her husband to make a spectacle when she was trying to solve all the problems with her son.

But Tuca was high. *Waayee!* Was Vlad not going to school in the West? Ha! *Noroc!* Could life be better! Where had he put the *ţuică*? Had he finished it? Or given it away?

Where Elena saw problems, Tuca chose not to. That was how it was. Marcel was like his mother and would do all he could to help his brother to the West. But a fax machine and a willing teacher and the education authority and then a visa? There'd be travelling to Bucharest and buying favours and that meant money. A lot of money. Marcel didn't have any. Not one bean. Not enough to buy his Romanian Carpaţi cigarettes, which even some gypsies had stopped smoking. Elena didn't have any either. She'd spent her month's salary that she'd not yet earned on the electricity bill and buying a coat for Vlad, and he'd need new shoes, of course – and that meant yet more money.

Vlad, the cause of all the trouble, was sitting at the table. 'It doesn't matter,' he said. 'I don't have to go.'

He didn't like the sound of the foreign exams nor could he imagine asking his teachers to help with all his needs. Vlad liked to sit quietly at the back of the class. He didn't like to make a fuss. He'd sung the national anthem when told to, but never loudly; he'd worn his cravat and costume when he became a communist pioneer but not proudly, and when the change came he carried on getting on with it at the back of the class. He was bright but had made sure he didn't shine, and now this? What had happened?

The foreign girl had called, after all.

'Vlad didn't sound keen. He sounded a bit flat.'

I couldn't understand. Had I not just delivered the golden goose like I promised? All he had to do was lay the golden egg and – hey presto! Vlad would fly high.

I sat in front of the log fire in our sitting room in Scotland and almost called Claire. We'd stayed friends. I liked her honesty; she liked my energy. She still didn't approve of Plan Vlad. Had she seen vulnerability there that I had not?

'He'll be OK, darling. It's the shock of it all. The poor little chap has no idea what's about to happen. Now what do I have to do to get him this visa?'

'Mum, I think we should wait until he passes the exams.'

How to find a fax machine in Iaşi? How to find a fax machine in Iaşi with a connection via Bucharest to Britain? How to explain that Vlad was keen, I was keen, we were all incredibly keen and grateful for Strathallan's kind offer but finding a fax machine was proving a little harder than anticipated? No, Vlad's school didn't have one. So Marcel would have to ask a teacher to meet the exam papers at a different fax machine – once he'd found it.

Vlad was meant to be studying for his British exams, the ones that hadn't arrived yet. Vlad had never studied for anything and he didn't have any books in English, so Marcel asked his friend Alex with the handle-bar moustache if they could borrow some. Alex only had a book on quantum physics and *The Shining* by Stephen King. Vlad forgot he had scary exams to take, with lots of added pressure (everybody in their block and in his class knew), because he started reading Stephen King. *The Shining* was his first novel. He read late into the night, marking the words he didn't understand. Vlad was a little short of sleep when he finally got the news that a fax machine had been found (in Uncle Bogdan's flour factory) and that his English teacher, proud of her silent pupil (she had been unaware he could even speak English), had offered to pick them up and sit in the room while Vlad worked his way through Science, Maths, French and English exams from a Scottish boarding school.

8th February '95

Dear Vlad – Yippee! As you probably know by now, you passed the exams. Well done you! You have a place in Ruthven House, which is one of the cool houses, and you've a got a really decent house master.

This is just a short message to say congratulations! (I knew you would do it.) The school said they were very impressed, especially with your maths and English. I think it's because in your country they work harder at lessons than we do here. Oh yes and because you're a genius, obviously. ☺

We have to get some boring stuff organised now for your visa and things but it shouldn't be a problem. I will talk to Marcel. Send my love to Mihaela. I feel guilty as I haven't written to her.

Lots of love,

Your friend, TESS x

I sent the message on a Metallica postcard. It was scarlet with two blonde, long-haired men head-banging in the company of a blood-encrusted devil's head. Vlad decided not to put it on his wall; instead he kept the postcard in his drawer. Later his mum would put it in a cardboard box along with the faxed copies of his Strathallan exam papers.

He looked for the word 'Yippee' in his English dictionary: *An expression of extreme happiness.*

3rd March '95

Dear Tess – Thank you for your letter and all your help. I am glad I got the exams. I ironed my English by reading a good book. Mama is worrying about the visa but Marcel thinks it will be OK. I will have to get a passport, so that will mean some queues. You know Romania! Thank you for organising for me to maybe fly over with the Under-21 Scottish Rugby team. That sounds cool. Mama is worried about the aeroplane. She keeps talking to God about it.

I gotta go now as gotta do some work. Mihaela says hello. She was here and watched the Miss World (yuk) and said how the Miss UK was the best but she didn't win.

Yours truthfully,

VLĂDUȚ

25th March '95

Dear Marcel – I have had no success trying to fax you the copy of the fax Strathallan sent to the British embassy. Therefore I have sent it to you via the post in a separate envelope. I hope it arrives so you can use it to get Vlad's passport.

I will call you on 4th April, 7pm our time, in order to discover whether you've had success so we can book the flight. If you haven't got a passport please explain why not so we can get the school to send out any further documents etc. that might help. Yours sincerely and with love,

TESSA x

Marcel frowned. He did not have the passport and he didn't have permission from the Education Authority for Vlad to leave his school. The Board in Iași said they had lost all the documents – or they'd decided not to find them. And the foreign girl was telephoning that night.

'Because they don't want this success for a son of a worker. They have stolen his chance.'

Elena cursed to the *mother's church* when she heard the problem. Damn it. Marcel said he would queue again and take Tuca's I-D Bulletin with him and Elena gave him the last few thousand lei she kept between her towels.

'Then what will we pay for the passport with?'

'We'll work with today before tomorrow,' she said to her eldest son, who was restricted by his pessimism and honesty. They shared a little smile they both knew and understood.

Marcel took his studies for the next day's exam, a packet of soft cigarettes and Tuca's Bulletin and stood in line.

'Da?'

'I have come for Vlad Ion Toma's documentation. I was here yesterday. And the day before.'

'Yes. Here are your documents. You will have to take them to Bucharest for verification.' The assistant slid the brown package beneath the wire netting pulled taut between them.

'What?'

'You will have to go to Bucharest. We cannot help you here. You need a stamp from the State Department of Education. Next!'

Bucharest? How the hell was he going to get to Bucharest?

'Alo!'

'Hi Marcel. It's me, Tess.'

'Yes Tess.'

'How are you getting on?' I was keen that we should buy Vlad's ticket before it got too expensive. Alice said her brother was touring Romania with the Under-21s Scottish Rugby squad, and suggested Vlad should fly back to Scotland with him. Mum thought it was an awfully kind offer so I accepted on Vlad's behalf.

'Well Tess, it is a bit difficult here.'

'Can I do anything to help?'

'Nothing Tess. We're trying to resolve the matters. It will be just a few days, I hope.' Marcel was worried about his exam the next day and how to pay for the train to Bucharest and when to go to Bucharest and how to pay for the passport. He was too polite to say it but he wanted to get me off the telephone.

'It's OK, Tess. We will resolve the problems.'

'Can you give me a date?'

'No Tessa, I can't. I am sorry for this.'

He was very sorry. Most of all he was full of sorrow for his country and his poverty.

And I was sorry we still couldn't buy the flight – it was getting expensive. I would have to write Granny a really good letter to see if she would help a bit more with Vlad's expenses. It never occurred to me that Marcel had any costs. We were buying the flight and the visa and Strathallan were paying the fees. What other costs were there?

Tuca was behind the fridge. Tuca loved to be handy. He would take apart the fridge to find the fuse for the TV and go into the old cassette-a-phone to get the fuse for the fridge. When he ran out of parts he would visit colleagues. He never arrived empty-handed. Tuca would stand on their doorstep with a bottle of country wine, his felt hat on his head and a smile on his face.

'Wayee. Ce faci?' Slap, slap on the back. When he had no alcohol left to give, he would rewire their house for them, or help plough their field, or take their grain to the mill in a sack on his back. Or if they were city folk he'd mend their fridge by taking the fuse out of their TV. Tuca was always busy or drunk or asleep. He slept very soundly.

From behind the fridge he could hear Elena and Marcel. There were frantic whispers. They were trying to solve the British problem and didn't want Vlad to hear. Elena was crying. Money was the problem and he, Tuca, suddenly had the solution.

'ARCOM!' he shouted, and leapt like a sprite from behind the kitchen door.

'What! Be quiet you old fool! Shh . . . there's a baby downstairs.'

70

'ARCOM. I have the money. We will take it out of ARCOM.'

Marcel stared at his father while Elena sat down suddenly and heavily, relief pushing up through her feet. Thank the good Lord! She would not have to ask Uncle Bogdan. There was ARCOM – why on Earth hadn't they thought of it sooner?

In his Romanian construction account Tuca had $50 untouched since 1980. Tuca went to work in Syria in 1979 as an electrician in a cement factory. Ceauşescu had valued his relationship with the Arab countries. He would export anything he could to the Middle East to pay off the country's debt, including his socialist workers. Tuca left his family and flew for the first time. He landed in a heat he could not tolerate, in a country where the women hid and the men didn't drink. He lasted a year. He missed his family; most of all he missed his little wife. He got home and told them about a land of curiosity. He related tales of shopping centres and dirty streets, desert scapes and moaning mullahs. And he told them how empty Romania seemed. Tuca's Syrian wage went to the Romanian state, and Elena picked up his factory wage in his absence. The $50 pot was his saved daily allowance for food back in 1980. He'd never had a big appetite.

Tuca had been so pleased to see his wife when he got home that, ten months later, Vlad arrived. Now Marcel was going to buy a passport and travel to Bucharest for Vlad's documents with his father's Syrian nest-egg.

CHAPTER FIVE

Bucharest, Otopeni Airport, April '95

Alistair saw Vlad before Vlad saw Alistair. I had described him in minute detail and the airport was a small one.

Vlad was standing in front of his father when Alistair approached. Tuca was dressed in black trousers and a thick wool tie, and Vlad sensed it was not cool to be right next to him. He'd always been independent; at least, he thought so until Alistair bounded up, and then for a brief moment he wanted very much to stay beside his father, maybe even hold his hand. But he didn't. Instead he focused hard on the Eurotraveller British Airways ticket he was holding. He stared at the price: £395. That, Vlad worked out, was one million, two hundred and sixty thousand, seven hundred and sixty-five lei. He'd always been good at maths.

He felt very small beside Alistair. It was not so much that Alistair was tall, but he was a sportsman – a scrum-half who would almost, but not quite, be good enough to play for Scotland. He was broad not fleshy; densely packed limbs and bright skin and blue eyes in Otopeni airport, all focused on Vlad in his winter coat in April. He chatted away in a funny accent and didn't ask too many questions, so Vlad could sometimes just pull faces and that seemed to be enough to make Alistair and all his teammates laugh.

'Pity we didn't have you on tour with us, you could've been our mascot.'

'But I'm Romanian.'

'Oh yeah. Ha ha! Never mind!'

It was OK, being a little Romanian with big Scottish boys high on the success of beating a smaller Romanian team – and enjoying looking after their mascot who looked like he needed a good meal. He was going where? Strathallan!

'Oh man, my brother went there! You'll be fine.'

'What house? Ruthven? Yeah, that's cool. The girls are a bit rough at Strath. Suppose you're a bit young for girls. Ha ha!'

'It won't be rugby this term, it'll be cricket.'

'Want a Fanta, Vlad? Packet of crisps, mate?'

'We're landing in a minute. You all right?'

Vlad had been so all right he'd forgotten to listen to the safety instructions. He felt his tummy flip-flop. He'd forgotten he had to land and say goodbye to his new friends, then meet the foreign girl who no longer seemed so foreign.

I wasn't foreign in Scotland but when Vlad looked at me through tired, scared eyes he worried, just for a second, he was looking at a stranger. I had cut all my hair off and bleached it. I was trying out a new roll-neck and skinny jeans, and I was very aware that the Under-21s would be at Edinburgh airport. As it turned out Alistair was more interested in seeing Vlad into my mum's car than acknowledging me. Despite the hour they were relaxed with each other. Somehow that made it harder when it was just the two of us. Vlad was exhausted and looked smaller than I'd remembered, and I was a novice driver. The journey home to Rannoch was a particularly quiet one.

'The little mite's asleep.' Mum returned to the kitchen having stood on the landing outside Vlad's new room.

Vlad had managed to duck her homemade macaroni cheese and only just failed to escape a compulsory call home. She'd stood over him as he pushed the numbers to his far away flat and checked in with his mama. Elena answered the phone within half a ring. Thank the Mother of the Lord he had arrived safely.

Mum took a sip of her Pinot Grigio (always white, never Chardonnay) and sat back down at the table. 'What a day for the little man.'

'Mum, I think it is important we don't patronise him.'

'Sorry darling?'

'It's easy to forget that he's thirteen. When I was thirteen I was, well, a nightmare.'

'And you still are. Now where are my car keys?'

Vlad was not sound asleep. He was lying very still underneath a green Celtic FC duvet in my brother's bedroom trying hard to empty his head. He could hear noises coming from downstairs; Dad riddling the Rayburn, me begging for a dishwasher, Mum scolding a dog. (A dog in the house!) Here he was in the West in a proper boy's bedroom with posters on the wall and *Commando* comics on the floor and a computer in the corner. Vlad began thinking he might need the loo and wasn't sure he could remember where it was – it seemed like a very big house.

The next morning he sat on the bed while Mum helped him unpack and I stood in the doorway. As the youngest he rarely got new clothes, so he was surprised when his mother bought him leather shoes just before he left for Bucharest and wished she'd bought him a pair of trainers instead, with a logo and a pair of jeans like the ones he saw in the American movies – a bit loose and not flecked. Vlad had a keen eye for what was right and he knew his leather shoes weren't. And he knew his winter coat wasn't either, nor were his trousers that were just a little bit too short, and now this Mrs Dunlop was unpacking his pants that had come from his mum's old factory.

'Mrs Dunlop it's OK. Really, I can manage.'

'Do call me Anthea!'

Anthea was feeling extremely relieved that Vlad had been offered a free school uniform by Strathallan. How jolly thoughtful of them. She laid out his possessions in a neat pile on the bed and found, at the bottom of his suitcase, three tiny painted plates wrapped in a polyester tracksuit, one of which had not survived the journey. There was also a crucifix made of straw and a bundle of one and five dollar bills – the remains of Tuca's ARCOM account.

74

'Ah, we'll get these changed for you in Pitlochry and you can buy a souvenir when you go home.' She took the Toma family's entire life savings and stashed them in a pot, deciding to supplement the dollars with her own money so he could get something nice.

'Now Vlad, what would you like to do today?'

Vlad looked at her blankly. He wasn't exactly sure what the question meant. I should have stepped in here but I didn't. I was struggling to remember why I thought bringing Vlad to Britain was such a good idea. The irreducible force a year earlier that had left me wakeful at night, propelling me to brush aside doubters and forge ahead with my unlikely plan, had disappeared.

Vlad, meanwhile, had arrived. He was sitting in my brother's bedroom in a finger of sunlight, dust moats dancing above his head – and it was all my fault. What had I been thinking? Had he changed or was he always like this? Unresponsive and very, very thin. Not the sort of child who openly enjoyed himself and where was the fun in that? For him or for me? He was at a difficult age; I hoped he wouldn't be bullied in the showers at school. Did he know we showered every day in Britain? Should I tell him? Oh shit.

'I've had a thought! Chokkie's tricks!' Mum suddenly left the room in search of her mongrel charge.

Chokkie waddled in. Vlad had already talked to him over breakfast where he gave him a rasher of bacon.

'Don't feed the dogs at the table!' Dad shouted. Vlad jumped. Dad shouted a lot but Vlad didn't know that yet. Nor did he know the many contradictory rules that governed our house dogs.

Chokkie duly performed on command. He danced on his hind legs. He pretended to die for his country and live for the Queen. He shut the door and jumped on a box. Chokkie would do anything for food. Vlad sat on the bed and watched. He had to admit the dog was impressive. So that was why this family put up with the nasty smell in their kitchen.

'Do you have dogs, Vlad?' Mum asked.

'In our country dogs have fleas. They live outside.'

'Oh. I see. Yes, I expect you'll see many differences when you're over here.'

Vlad patted Chokkie's head and didn't say anything. It had never occurred to him that a dog should come into the house.

'Why don't we take them all on a walk?' I suggested. 'I'll get the collies.' Vlad followed me as I let Dad's five sheep dogs out of the kitchen, the kennel and the car.

Up the hill we went together. Vlad blitzed by canine attention as he struggled in the spring bracken, feeling like a wave was crashing over him, submerged in the greenness of it all and the dogs that didn't smell outside, and came when their names were called, and the foreign girl who wasn't as friendly as she'd been in Iaşi.

We set off for Strathallan two days later. Vlad got in the car feeling full. He'd been feeling full ever since he arrived. He was constantly being called to the table, or called to help lay the table and then to sit at it and eat two courses from plates as big as the moon. It began with breakfast; a very important meal, said Mrs Dunlop, but one which Vlad noticed I never joined him for.

'Half a pig's arse and six dozen eggs, now that's a good breakfast!' boomed Mr Dunlop, who was so enormous that he couldn't fit his legs under the table; he sat side-on and poured salt over his bacon and squashed slabs of stilton cheese between slices of white bread before cramming it all into his mouth. Vlad found it very hard not to stare at his giant host who talked in a loud voice over the radio.

'Get stuck in, son, you're wee for a lad. Romania will never make a full back of you!'

Dad was a wartime baby. He went to a preparatory school a thousand miles away from home aged six where he learnt to be tough and nearly died of measles. He thought men should be big and strong and interested in outdoor work and rugby. Vlad didn't meet any of these criteria. He'd been brought up on minimal food in a city block.

He might be from a poor country but Vlad was not a peasant and had no intention of being bullied into becoming one. Not by anyone, not even a Scottish colossus who let his dogs lick his bare feet and was obsessed with sheep and rugby.

'So Vlad, how do you rate Romania's chances?' Dad had been keenly following Scotland's build up to the Rugby World Cup.

'I don't know, Mr Dunlop. I prefer football.'

'What! A bloody poof's game. Rugby is the game for real men.'

Vlad said nothing. He wasn't entirely sure what a poof was.

It was with some relief, therefore, that Vlad got into the car to go to boarding school. Surely at boarding school he could eat what he liked and wouldn't have to clear the table. Or lay it.

The school was an hour and a half's drive. Vlad had strapped himself in over one of my brother's rugby shirts, his hands neatly folded in his lap. We were going to collect his uniform in Perth on the way to Strathallan and I suggested we might also buy some tuck.

'Tuck?'

'It's extra food for break time and stuff. All the kids have it.'

Vlad couldn't imagine ever wanting to eat again so said nothing.

Once we left the glen and hit the main road south he peered intently and silently through the car window. The Grampian mountain range straddled the skyline, its bulk cushioned with rich pine-filled forests. The River Tay slid alongside the dual carriageway, dark, pure and unpolluted, and the silver birch had just broken out into a mint green halo. Rubber on tarmac thwacked beneath us, firm and reassuring. No holes, no horse-drawn carts – just shiny signs and shiny cars and sunshine.

If Mum had been in the car she would have said, 'What a blissful day darlings! Aren't we the lucky ones?'

She wasn't, so I said it instead. Vlad didn't reply. But some-where near Dunkeld he suddenly banged his fist off the plastic dashboard.

'You are so lucky! You have so much in your country – even

77

your roads . . . ' And then he stopped mid-sentence, shocked by his outburst and silenced by the perfect picture and the injustice of it all.

'Yes, I suppose we do. I'm sorry.'

'Why are we stopping?' asked Vlad.

'For tuck, remember? I told you all the other boys will have tuck. It's for eating in between meals and after games and stuff.'

'Games?'

'Sport. Vlad, just believe me. You need tuck!'

'I don't think I do. I don't need *tuck*.' He said the last word in a peculiar voice.

Vlad followed behind as I marched on with a silver trolley. Why was Tessa obsessed with food? Why was her whole family obsessed with food?

He was still behind me when I burled through the automatic doors. To the Big Mother above this is why they were so obsessed with food! A whole factory of food. Food, food, food – and fizzy drinks! Winking under fluorescent lights. Vlad didn't know where to look because wherever he did there were packets of food and fruit he'd not seen before, and English words on signs he couldn't fully understand. *Ready Meals. Dairy Products. Spreads and Snacks.*

'Wagon Wheels or Twix? Peanut butter or Nutella? Which crisps do you want?'

The choices. The money. The expense. Vlad didn't want any of it. He wanted to run very fast away from the food. He told me to stop but I wouldn't, not even when he put out his hand to push back the peanut butter. I was enjoying the freedom of the moment buying all the junk food that my mother had never allowed me in my tuck box. I threw in a bottle of Lynx shower gel.

'I tell you what, Vlad, you'll be so glad you've got this. Really, you will. You're going to have the coolest tuck box in the dorm!'

Vlad didn't reply. He'd just found the aisle for house animals.

*

I'd sent Vlad a school prospectus back in January. He distinctly remembered its delicious smell. It was not a smell he'd come across before so he spent a long time inhaling the crisp aroma. He also looked at the pictures with Alin. They defaced the girls and boys in kilts and decided Scotland had a worse national costume than Moldavia with its embroidered tunics and sheepskin waistcoats. Anyway, Vlad hadn't worn a traditional costume since fourth grade.

'You won't have to wear a kilt at Strathallan. It's just for church on a Sunday but, because you're not a Scot, you'll wear a suit.'

'But I don't have a suit.' Vlad also wanted to add that he didn't go to church.

'We are going to pick up your uniform now.'

'More shopping?' He couldn't believe I'd just spent £36 on tuck.

'No, the school are providing you with a uniform.'

As it happened Vlad enjoyed trying on his new clothes. He decided it was like being in a film. A woman in a pink jersey with a strange accent was so bossy he just did what he was told. There was a bottle blue blazer (slightly too big), a mustard yellow and black and blue stripy tie, a tie with purple motifs on it for a Sunday, white shirts with stiff collars and grey flannels for the weekdays, shorts for tennis and long white trousers and a white jersey for cricket.

'But I don't know about this cricket.'

'It disanae maitter ye'll learn. It's fae ye go tae schul fur son.'

He was even given socks and special shoes for sport, and a pair of leather brogues so he wouldn't have to wear the pair his mum had bought.

Strathallan School, April '95

Like so many private schools Strathallan began life as a large stately home, with imposing gates, spacious grounds and multiple outhouses including a porter's lodge. During my time there the geography teacher Mr Barnes lived in the lodge. He was now the head of Ruthven house. I told this to Vlad as we swung through the gates and took on several speed bumps with gusto.

'So he will be your housemaster. Oh my God! Look, look! There's the valley . . . down the valley, that's where it all happens.'

'What? What happens?' Vlad's voice was a rasp.

In fact very little happened down the valley. As sixth formers it was where we smoked cigarettes, drank home-made alcohol and fumbled in each other's pants. Pathetic, really – and certainly not appropriate information for a thirteen-year-old.

'Nothing – just, you know . . . '

But Vlad was no longer listening. He had to work very hard just to remember to breathe. How could this be a school? When Vlad thought of a school he thought of one purpose-built block with rows; rows of rooms and rows of chairs and rows of desks and rows of pupils. Not this. He couldn't bear to look out of the window at the emerald green of the grass glaring back at him, the chapel with a polished bell and the glossy clusters of boys and girls, well put together with floppy hair. And an enormous castle! There were turrets and gables and chunks of death grey stone.

'That's the main building, Vlad. It's got the library and some dormitories and if you get into trouble you have to go there to see the headmaster. I'm sure you won't have to see the headmaster.' I wrenched the handbrake on with a degree of satisfaction. We had made it in one piece. I looked across at Vlad. His face was a waxy yellow and he was sitting very still.

The year before we had been together in Vlad's country. Aged twelve he'd been in charge and I was impressed. Now he was foreign and I was in charge and I wanted to impress but it wasn't the same this way around, one year on. Neither of us said anything, but we knew it wasn't. Nonetheless at that moment, stationary in Mum's VW Golf, Vlad longed for me to stay right there. He wished that we might stay sitting there forever, until Mr Barnes began to stroll towards us; a well-groomed, muscular man, his gelled hair a little thinner than I remembered.

'We're going to have to get out now and say hello.' I put my hand on Vlad's knee and gave it a squeeze. 'You'll be fine, you'll see. It'll take a day or two, that's all.'

Vlad was shown around by two boys from Ruthven house, Ed and Robin. They were polite and impressive – strapping, even. Vlad looked very small tripping along beside them, his blazer loose across his shoulders and an errant lace flapping on the parquet flooring.

He'll be all right, I thought. He's so small and foreign he'll be all right. They'll look after him.

Vlad had watched me unpack his case and transfer his uniform into an assigned cupboard. He did not offer to help. He watched as I placed the contents of his controversial tuck into the drawer under his bed, put his pencils and pens in a row on his desk and left our telephone number on his bedside table. He declined my offer of a ten pound note.

'Vlad, you will need some money.'

'What for? More tuck?'

'Well maybe, yes. And for the phone.' I left the money on his pillow.

It was then Ed and Robin came up and introduced themselves. They'd been sent by Mr Barnes. They shook Vlad's hand and said he was lucky because he'd got a wicked new bed. I was surplus to requirements.

'Bye Vlad, call if you have a problem. It'll be half-term before you know it.' I held him by the shoulder, overwhelmed by the familiar smell of fresh pine and disinfectant.

Vlad didn't say goodbye – he just stared ahead. He was holding tight to the edge in a land of giants; he was looking out across a different world where he had temporarily checked-in. Ed and Robin were surely too big to be thirteen? They had to bend their heads to find him.

'You just here for the term then?'

'Yes.'

'Oh right, cool. I wonder if you'll be in the same sets as me. It's a bit of a dump here but you'll get used to it. That's the dining hall over there – the food's rubbish. Man, am I going to miss my mum's cooking!'

'Are you down for cricket or sailing, Vlad?'

'I don't know . . . ' (Sailing? Tessa had not mentioned sailing.)

'Probably cricket then. Where are you from again, Vlad?'

'Romania.'

'Romania. Oh right . . . where's that then?'

Vlad had always known that you shouldn't say too much. If you said too much you might say the wrong thing. Vlad said just enough. He thought people who talked a lot were either brave or foolish.

At Strathallan he said just enough and occasionally a little bit more. Like on the first night when he discovered that Chris, the boy in the bed next to his, had a Motorhead poster. Or the time when Robin needed help with his French prep.

'You're good. Thanks Vlad. D'you go to France a lot?'

'No. I don't like their music. Their time is over. We should not have to learn French.' Vlad was the only boy in the class who hadn't been to France. He was one of two who could speak French.

'Yeah right!' Robin started pretend wretching. 'You're right, they're real tools. Do you have any French swear words to surprise Mr Clayton with?'

Vlad wrote a neat and comprehensive list of French obscenities down the side of Robin's manila folder. Instinctively he knew how to survive.

Vlad hadn't been away from home before, with the exception of summer weeks at his granny's house when he slept in a scratchy hemp bed with his cousins and ate warm ducks' eggs for breakfast. He had, however, often been home alone. For a whole year Vlad had sat in his flat and waited for his mother to come through the door. He would hear her key in the lock at 2.15pm every day, unless she had joined a queue. (She'd never pass a queue without standing in it.) Vlad was four when Elena sat him down and explained that he was too big for the factory crèche and too small for school and there was no room for him in the grădiniţa. With contraception banned, Romania's future socialist workers were arriving at such a rate that there was nowhere to put them. They had to share beds and names and clothes and food. There were three Vlads in the local grădiniţa and one Vlad waiting at home alone.

'What did you do all day?' I couldn't believe my ears. 'Your mother left you at home aged four for a year!'

Vlad hadn't considered his time alone particularly exceptional. He sat at the table and taught himself to read from his mum's medicinal plant book and his brother's comic, and one day he even read the phone book and counted the Tomas. When there wasn't a power cut TV broadcasts were daily. He would watch state parades and mimic the saucy blue few who marched beside Ceauşescu. If he was very lucky a random cartoon, Mickey Mouse or Tom and Jerry, might slip under the state net and he had his first taste of English. Dumitru's yellow plastic cowboy was now his and he turned it into a friend and called it Bobby. Sometimes he talked to Bobby but not often – even then Vlad went whole days without speaking. When his mum came home he would be sitting waiting for her, in her immaculate empty flat where it was impossible to make a mess.

Ed and Robin and Chris were being fitted out for preparatory school when Vlad had finally been granted a place at School Ten. They learnt to cope alone by sticking together, and grew up away from home needing each other, while Vlad grew up at home needing no one. But he did need time. Vlad had always had plenty of time and now, at Strathallan, he had none.

'What's that bell for?'

'Prep.'

Prep was homework supervised at school by a prefect in a noisy room. Even when Vlad finished his homework quickly – which, by week two, was often – he was not allowed to leave the room.

'What's that bell for?'

'Chapel.'

'Chapel?'

'Yeah we have to go every morning, before classes. Just so the Head can make some poncy speech. Mate I can't believe your mum let you bring that much gum into school. Don't let the pigs catch you with it!'

'Where are we going?'

'Art. It's still life. Load of bollocks. Dare you to steal a piece of the fruit without McCleod seeing you.'

Vlad came away with a pear and the respect of his peers. 'In my country we had to steal to survive!' He stood outside the art block, grinning, eating his prize.

It was only on the cricket pitch that Vlad had time out, which he didn't realise he missed until he found it fleetingly, standing in the gentle spring rain on grass so soft it felt like a sponge. He was the only boy who liked fielding. He was not a cricketer. He had come to it too late and he didn't like the weird rules that no one could explain or the weird names that made no sense or the hard red ball that stubbed his fingers and missed his bat. No, he was happy to field on the periphery and pray the ball didn't bounce his way. Cricket really was a very pointless game, but it gave Vlad time to be still.

Rannoch

'Do you think I should ring him?'

'Good God no Mum, he'll be fine. Call him the week before half-term.'

I knew Mum had discussed Vlad with Dad in my absence the day I drove him to school. I didn't like the thought of what they might have said. Although I had my doubts about the sense of him at Strathallan, I felt protective of the idea and of Vlad. They were mine to criticise. But I was leaving for Oxford the next day and that changed things.

In fact they hadn't said much, as there wasn't much to say. Vlad wasn't an open book – he wasn't needy, or a performer, or much of a talker. He was, as far as they were concerned, something of a let-down. Mum was a teacher, a very good teacher, but in order to shine she had to have a cause or a problem or even a little streak to love. With Vlad all she got was silent, self-containment. There was no way in.

Dad had not paid for Vlad's flight; Mum and Granny had. Nonetheless he was feeling rueful. 'The little bugger is going to have to be a bit more helpful at half-term, Tessa.'

Dad meant that Vlad didn't anticipate what needed to be done. He didn't realise he was meant to *do* anything. In his flat his mother did everything. Children, boys especially, were precious objects of hope and wonder, not little serving people. Vlad had just come from the other side of Europe and he was only thirteen years old, but he had arrived as the chosen one and the stakes were high. Dad hoped for a better performance at half-term and Mum felt she must try harder. Somehow Vlad's silence had become her failure.

I, meanwhile, returned to university. I was enjoying my second year. I bought lots of lycra, started rowing, pushed weights and rubbed cocoa butter into my body. By the summer term I had made the university squad, we trained alongside the men and, by week two, I had kissed stroke (a technical term for the person who sits in the first seat). He had large, tan hands and a girlfriend. It didn't matter. I was keener on number six, a Canadian called Jon with glossy curls and bee-stung lips. I invested in waterproof mascara and turned up at the boat house ten minutes early every morning, just in case.

Back in the confines of St Hilda's there was Hina. She rarely left her room, smoked copious cigarettes, segued effortlessly between Chaucer and Channel 4 and always had a slightly surprised look on her face.

'So, did the Romanian boy arrive?'

'Yeah, he's fine. Mum says the school are pleased.'

In fact I hadn't spoken to Mum since my return from Scotland. Chastened, I sent Vlad a postcard of the River Orwell, inquired after his welfare and told him he was lucky he didn't have millions of stupid essays to write.

Strathallan School

It was Silent Reading. This was the only time Strathallan allocated to reading, except Vlad was told he had to write a letter home, which he thought slightly defeated the purpose of a reading hour. He knew he should be writing to Alistair because Alistair had written to him, and it was a very kind letter but Vlad had never written to anyone before (except me, once), so instead he re-read Alistair's. There was one paragraph in particular that puzzled him:

> *Having been to Romania I would say that there is a huge difference between my country and yours. I am sure you would agree. Both countries have good points and bad points. So Vlad, you should always be proud of your country. We are lucky to have seen both worlds.*

Vlad had always been very proud to be Romanian (until recently national pride had been obligatory), but now outside his country he wondered exactly which bits of Romania he should be proud of – other than the football team, of course. The team had got through to the quarter finals of the World Cup and only just lost out on penalties to Sweden. But that was the year before and the day after the Swedish defeat had been a very black day in Vlad's head. Things had only improved in the evening when he went to give me (the foreign girl) her Romanian lesson and I told him how bad the English were at football.

Vlad thought about me and how I seemed different in my own country. Older? Maybe. Or just in more of a rush? I was less fun anyway, more like someone in charge. He looked at my picture postcard with a river twinkling on the front. He re-scanned my scrawl: *you are so lucky you don't have to write a million stupid essays.* There it was – that word 'lucky' again. Vlad knew that everybody back home thought he was lucky, too, and he couldn't understand why he felt less lucky in Strathallan than he had in Romania. Lucky Vlad felt weirdly unlucky. He did, however, have to admit I'd been right about the tuck.

I was not coming home for half-term. I stayed south and sent Vlad another card.

> Dear Vlad – How's life? The work? The boys? The girls?! Sport? Blah blah blah. Essays here are still a nightmare but my rowing eight is going well and next week I'm holding a barbeque, which should be a pretty drunken affair.
>
> Anyway I won't keep you from the pleasures of Strath any longer! Enjoy half-term, sorry I won't be there – I gather you ran a mini-marathon. How very brave. I've never run that far!
>
> Love, TESS xxx

The card had a puppy on the front. I bought it in a hurry in WH Smith. Project Vlad had been relegated to a footnote in occasional telephone conversations home. I was distracted. Jon the Canadian had become my main preoccupation – rather, what I should do with him had. Never relaxed around sex I had to make a big deal of not having it. My up-bringing was a hotchpotch of opinionated atheism (Dad) and Victorian moral 'values' (Mum and Dad), so lying on my back with a Canadian hulk I couldn't shake off their peculiar mores.

A couple of recurring childhood memories got in the way. There was Mum clearing out the grate with her back to me.

'Darling, do you promise you will never sleep with anyone until you're married?'

Aged eight and determined to avoid sharing a room with either brother I solemnly replied, 'Yes.'

Or Dad, bawling in indignation at the thought of something that hadn't happened.

'If any daughter of mine crosses this threshold pregnant, I will disown her!' Then, to add parity to his rant, 'Or any son of mine comes home with his ear pierced, by Christ that'll be the end!'

Keen to keep both Jon and my father on side (albeit different ones), Claire met me for an emergency meeting on pleasuring men minus penetration. We sat in a café in Jericho, she picked up a long thin glass and with some deft movements gesticulated how and what should be done. A corduroy don eyed us over his *Telegraph* and I took notes. I found the prospect rather repellent but before I could perform my new party trick Jon dumped me. I rang home broken-hearted.

'Oh Mum, I'm so depressed. It's too far to come all the way north. I can't face it. Couldn't you pick up Vlad at half-term?'

'Really darling! You are the bottom.'

Without me Vlad realised he'd be home alone in Rannoch. He was unsure about the prospect of Mrs Dunlop on his own. She always had lots of questions and he never managed to come up with an answer to prevent the next one, no matter how hard he tried.

'Are you enjoying yourself?' she inquired down the phone in her motherly way.

'Yes.'

'What kind of things do you get up to?'

'Just, erm, stuff . . . ' said Vlad, acutely aware there was a queue of big boys behind him.

'But you are enjoying it?'

'Yes.'

'So you're managing then?'

'Yes.'

'I will pick you up for half-term on Saturday. OK Vlad?'

'Yes . . . ' then, just in time, 'thank you Mrs Dunlop.'

I can't seem to make any headway with that little chap, she worried as she later pricked out lettuces in a sun-filled porch. No headway at all. She was determined not to leave the long weekend ahead to chance.

'The devil makes work for idle hands.'

Mother's half-term planning was meticulous. For the first day she had organised a bike ride around Loch Rannoch with two local girls his age, Danielle and Shona. She wanted him to see how beautiful it was. It would, she thought, put roses in his cheeks and give him an opportunity to enjoy the old Caledonian forest with its wonderful Scots Pines.

But, on that first morning when Vlad woke in my brother's room, rain was careening down the window pane. No cycling then, he thought, in no small part relieved.

'Cancelled because of the rain? This is Scotland, Vlad!' My mother was having none of it and proceeded to kit him out in a selection of wet weather togs including mackintosh trousers with an elastic waistband and a cagoule. Vlad struggled around the loch behind his two larger female companions. They giggled together and their wet T-shirts were, he decided, so much cooler than his clothes, which made him sweat and caught in the bike chain.

'Did you enjoy yourself, Vlad?' asked Mother that evening. 'What was the best bit?'

Vlad paused for a moment. 'My favourite moment was when Shona gave me an orange Chewit.'

Vlad was disappointed the Dunlops didn't watch much TV and the one they had was very small. It was discreetly tucked into a bookshelf in Mrs Dunlop's drawing room, although she didn't do any painting.

At home Vlad watched a lot of TV. All Romanians did. It was a national essential; cheap entertainment and a means of accessing a world otherwise inaccessible. Vlad heard British TV was high quality, and had been looking forward to seeing what that meant. But at Strath there was prep and chapel and cricket and community service, and at Mrs Dunlop's there was helping in the garden, going on walks (to nowhere in particular), working on the farm with Mr Dunlop and clearing the kitchen (always inexplicably cluttered). There really was no time for TV and even if there had been Vlad didn't like to switch it on when it was so evidently meant to be off.

One wet afternoon, however, he relented. He closed the curtains and huddled into the sofa to watch what appeared to be an Australian soap opera. He'd just flicked to a quiz show called *Blockbusters* presented by a man who possibly had a speech impediment when Mrs Dunlop entered the room.

'My dear boy, what are you doing sitting in the dark? Would you like to come and have a knock at tennis? The sun's just put his hat on.'

Vlad knew that this was not a question. He obligingly left the sofa, traced his missing trainer to Chokkie's mouth, and spent the rest of the afternoon ingloriously leaping around a pink clay court belonging to a man who made a brief appearance with a walking stick on the doorstep of his enormous house.

'Don't worry, Vlad. Everyone thinks they have a hole in their racket when they start. You'll soon get the hang of it! There we go! Whoopsee – that's your third one in the undergrowth!'

Later the same day, squashed and sodden under an enormous scarlet rhododendron bush searching for Mrs Dunlop's ball, Vlad vowed he would never play tennis again.

Iaşi, Toma Apartment, May '95

Elena was at the door, unlatching it ahead of Marcel, so keenly had she waited for him all afternoon. Dumitru's wedding was in less than a week but since her return from work she'd been unable to make any headway through her list of tasks.

'Marcel, I need your help. I have a letter from the foreign girl. Look! Is everything OK with Vlad?'

Her son had not taken off his coat, and there was no time to unlace his boots. His mother was thrusting a feather-light creamy envelope into his hand.

'What does it say? Is Vlad OK?' Her voice shook slightly, oh that Vlad might return soon so she may sleep soundly again.

Marcel lifted the page to the light and stared at it quizzically for what felt like an eternity.

'What? What is it?'

'It is not from Tessa. I think it's from her mother.'

Marcel moved to take a seat at the table and, having located his notebook and dictionary, spent the next half an hour teasing the meaning from behind my mother's scraggy hand.

19th April '95

Dear Mrs Toma – I write to tell you how much we enjoyed having Vlad with us for a few days before he went to the new school. He had a very big sleep to recover from two very tiring days and then he was fine. Very composed and always so polite.

Last week I spoke to Vlad on the telephone. He assured me that he is very well and that he understands everything. I also spoke to Mrs Barnes the housemaster's wife and she told me Vlad is fitting in with everyone very well. She said he is remarkable!

Please find enclosed a photo of Vlad in his school uniform. I took it in our garden before he left.

Vlad tells me he is playing cricket – a very English game! I am pleased because I am English. Vlad assures me his brother will translate this letter. I hope he can read it!

I have three lovely plates, a straw cross, and a big bag of Romanian biscuits – I think they are from you. Thank you very much.

Please get your son to write to me if you are worried about anything – I think Vlad's term at Strathallan will be a great success. We all look forward to seeing him at half-term.

Yours sincerely,

ANTHEA DUNLOP

Elena sat poised against the window while her son falteringly broke down the sentences as he understood them, stopping occasionally to double-check a meaning in his dictionary. And all the while she held tight the photo of Vlad, looking at it for the hundredth time, but now in the context of the unfolding narrative. (A garden with a mountain in it!) Her boy, her remarkable little boy bundled up in foreign clothes with anxiety peeping out from beyond the picture, the bulky landscape swamping his tiny frame.

'Mama, stop crying. You will spoil the picture. Vlad is fine. Understand? Just fine!'

And Marcel stood abruptly from his stool, caught off-guard by his mother's emotion and coughing to disguise the swell in his own throat.

Rannoch, Half-Term

'Aye, she's a good beast this one, a fine breeder.' Mr Dunlop slapped the butter-coloured cow hard on her sizeable rump and began talking to her in an altogether different tone. 'You're a good lass, you'll do us another year. No no! Don't do you get shirty with me.'

Vlad watched as his host opened the gate and ushered through his cattle. They filed out, one by one, then – in a sudden rush – onto the road.

'Now Vlad I want you to walk behind them. Understand? Any cars that come up, just keep walking! Make 'em wait. Look ahead and keep going. Any stragglers give them a little tap – like so!'

Mr Dunlop wielded his crummock and brought it down on the rear of another butter-coloured cow. After a series of guttural hisses and glottal stops and much arm movement he forced his beasts into a gentle trot. With a sudden and surprising break of speed for a man so large, he then took off up the bank, out of sight in front of his herd. Vlad was on his own.

He tripped along the road in what was almost a jog to keep up with his bovine charges, relieved things seemed to be going smoothly. He began to relax into his work, mesmerised by the swing of cows' udders and the steaming velocity of their piss when it hit tarmac. Even the cowpats, splatting down as they walked had, Vlad decided, a curious appeal. It was not so bad being a farm hand, after all; that is, until the cars came.

'I say, young man! Aren't you going to let us pass? We have a train to catch!'

To Vlad's horror the large shiny black nose of a BMW came into vision and drew up alongside him. Then there was the impudent blast of a horn.

Keep walking was what Mr Dunlop had said. Keep walking! The car inched forward and Vlad trotted on.

'Young man!'

The driver revved his engine, and Vlad thought (but did not dare look) that there may now be more than one car in the queue. He thrust his hands deep into his pockets, stared down at the road and walked on. His nerve may have held – Mr Dunlop was more intimidating than a man in a car – but without warning, spooked by the noise, a bullock started running in the wrong direction. The terrified animal split from the pack and careered back down the road, beyond the line of cars and beyond Vlad.

Vlad let out a stream of unusually vocal expletives in Romanian and set off at breakneck speed after the bullock, which was gathering pace in the wrong direction. Mr Dunlop was waiting at the gate of the new field for the cows that were no longer coming. And Mr Parson's BMW was in a cattle crush.

It was a man in a Land Rover, a tenant farmer from further down the glen, who eventually helped stall the bullock and steady the cows. 'Dinnae fash lad. Eh! Nae probs!'

On hearing the story Mr Dunlop was surprisingly sympathetic. And amused. 'Ach well, son. You did your best! And that's all that can be expected. He's a bloody awful little man anyway, that Mr Parsons – some English second homeowner who lives up the loch.'

'Better to be Romanian than English, right?' Vlad risked a joke for the first time.

'I wouldn't go that far!' Mr Dunlop smiled and lit a cigarette.

CHAPTER SIX

Oxford, July '95

I was pushing through the station concourse, late. Vlad was due to arrive any minute from Edinburgh where he'd been staying with my older brother.

With the summer term over Mum insisted it was now my turn and, of course, she was right. I'd avoided contact with Vlad when he was at Strath; he did not like the telephone and I knew a part of him felt let down I didn't appear at half-term. My absence had been about more than a fleeting broken heart. The mixture of my mother's efforts, my father's gruffness and Vlad's accidental display of nonchalance was an uncomfortable combination. I realised, too late, his study in self-containment was an acquired taste my parents didn't share. Vlad had arrived at my family home with the wrong survival instincts. And of course there was my own vain folly. Oh that Vlad might have shone and bathed me in reflective glory!

His train was on time and Vlad stood, waiting on the platform, his hands by his sides and his face inscrutable. I saw him first.

Overcome, moved briefly beyond words, I ran towards him and stopped suddenly. 'Blimey! You look great!'

And so he did. There, in front of me, was touchable, tangible change; an extraordinary conversion from winter white to something so ruddy and real it must, I decided, be the essence of rude health. Three meals a day, constant cricket and a timetable with no time to think had forced Vlad up and out like a plant in a sunny spot. The transformation was disconcerting.

I reached to ruffle his hair – he flinched – and tried to take his case. 'Good to see you. How are you? Hey, who gave you the hair cut?'

I already knew (Mum had crowed down the phone) that Vlad's two days with my older brother were, by all accounts, a *huge* success. It was Douglas who picked him up from school, made comic gestures behind Mr Barnes's back that got the other boys laughing and drove him down to Edinburgh in a borrowed, uninsured car. They went to the hairdresser and Douglas paid for him to have a wedge. He bought Vlad hair gel and helped him style his crop like the boys from Strath. They ate pie and chips, pushed silver into arcade games and watched Hibernian play Celtic.

Over shared bags of Walkers crisps and cans of Irn Bru time passed easily between the two of them. Vlad played on his accent because it made Doug laugh, who in turn was amused by this young boy so unlike his own noisy family. Had his sister taken leave of her senses? Douglas and I never did understand each other, or at least never took the time to. Vlad was just another sibling conundrum. Still I was grateful (humbled) by Doug's help on this occasion. It was a weekend that, in the light of what was to come, he never forgot. Nor did he allow me to.

Now in Oxford at the other end of the same day, Vlad started walking lopsidedly behind the sister of the brother he'd left behind in a different foreign city, and let my incessant chat wash over him. There were racks of bicycles with baskets and a ribbon of static cars, and evening sunlight with unexpected bite. He sensed I was eager to share, pointing and laughing loudly. Did I mean to hurry so? He watched as I strode ahead and then spun around suddenly on my heel to check he was still following. Such noisy confidence was, Vlad realised, a special public school privilege. One I had honed to perfection.

'Hey Vlad, it's so good to see you!'

Not a great communicator himself, Vlad hadn't given much thought to my silence during term time. Although on two occasions he'd stood in the back entrance of the main school building, surrounded by the watery smell of stone, his neck craned upwards, oblivious to the boys clattering past as he tried to locate me in one of the many school photographs. He thought he'd succeeded – dated 1989-90, was I the long-haired one in the third row, a huge unabashed grin stretched across my face? Now he saw me in the flesh again Vlad was no longer sure. He struggled to summon an image of me at Strath, plugged into the ugly blue uniform, standing obediently in line.

Is she relieved I'm going home?' Despite himself he hoped not. He still couldn't quite imagine going home; his block, his parents, his life – the familiarity that that now seemed so utterly other.

'So Vlad, my friend Jana is meeting us in a minute. She's got a car. And tomorrow Hina's going to take you on a bus tour around the city. It's a pretty cool place as you'll see – just because I'm working – but then she'll bring you to my restaurant and you can have lunch there. After that do you want to come out in the boat when we go rowing? Our coach says it won't be a problem.'

Vlad nodded.

'You don't mind sleeping on the floor, do you Vlad? It's just we've got no spare room in our house. I've got a camping mattress. You can sleep in the sitting room. Or on the sofa if you like?'

Vlad nodded again.

'So how did you like Strath in the end?'

'It was cool.'

'How did you find the work? Oh God, and end of term exams? Boarding schools love exams. Fuckers!'

'Yes.'

I wasn't exactly sure what 'yes' meant. I was taken aback by my language, by my noisy self-conscious effort. I turned and held his shoulder and said for the third time it was good to see him. And so it was.

'Vlad, is it? So how was it when you met Tessa? Let me guess, you didn't get a word in? None of us can!'

Jana tipped back her stool and laughed. It had been her idea to stop off at Ed's Diner. Vlad watched my Danish friend's shiny

96

reflection in the mirror behind her head. Mid-way through a cheese-burger he didn't immediately reply. He prodded his Coke float with a pink straw and tucked his foot behind the leg of the breakfast bar.

'I liked to meet Tessa. She was different.'

Jana was not satisfied with the answer. 'Were you worried about coming over here?'

'Not so much. No.' Vlad stared at the retro tat on the walls and the neon lights behind the counter; he felt this might be a film set and my white-haired friend an actress. She wore a puffa jacket and he liked her stubby plaits and the red VW Beatle we'd pulled up in.

'You're a cool customer! Hey Tessa, where did you find such a cool little guy?'

'I told you. Romania! It's where it all happens, isn't it Vlad?'

Vlad shrugged. He was uncertain of my sincerity and anyway was trying very hard not to think of Romania. He liked to live in the moment – he found it easier that way.

'My father met your king at a conference recently. King Mihai is it?'

'Yes. It is.' Vlad was surprised. This Danish girl was the first person who'd offered him something on his country that was not Count Dracula (who didn't exist) or the orphans (whom he'd never seen except on TV).

'It was in Italy they met. Dad now boasts he's shaken hands with a man who shook hands with both Hitler and Churchill.'

Vlad smiled. 'He is an old man now living in exile. But sad to say Mihai would be better than our current leader. Romania is not so lucky when it comes to leaders.'

This was the longest sentence Vlad managed during his Oxford stay. I wished it'd been me who'd mentioned King Mihai.

The bus rolled over Magdalen Bridge and the tour guide started on the student ritual of jumping into the river on May morning.

Vlad looked out from the open top onto the bridge over the soupy river with its wooden punts waiting on the water. Hina

97

was sitting beside him. Every so often she would gently add and occasionally correct the guide within their duo. With a pretty finger she pointed to Gothic and Regency, even Tudor. She talked of the creamy hues beneath the grey stone slabs, dated the quads and gabling and named the imposing buildings as they swung past.

'And there's Christ Church, they have a famous cathedral and kept the king when he couldn't keep his capital!' On occasion she would catch herself. 'Oh listen to me. I'm like an old woman. Are you bored to death yet, Vlad?'

'No. I'm not.' Vlad was taking it all in; the stories of the city that looked like it had been there so long it might stay forever. He liked my friend Hina. He even accepted the offer of her jacket, which had a rich floral scent that masked the musk of tobacco. He was cold on the bus and she'd been very insistent. As I had been, insisting he went on the city tour with this strange Hina. But Vlad decided he didn't mind the attention; too much to seem real so he just floated along the top and listened and said thank you.

'Thanks a million, Hina! Was it OK?' I spied them as soon as they came into the restaurant where I was working. 'How was it, Vlad? Did you like our city of dreaming spires? Fancy fried fajitas? My manager says he'll give us a discount.' I felt a fraction foolish in my harlequined shirt and *A Taste of the Deep South* cap.

Hina lit a cigarette and exhaled away from Vlad. 'I was more into it than him, wasn't I Vlad? Reckon the next stop's a busman's holiday! You up for it, Tess?'

I grinned at my friend and gave Vlad a fruit cocktail with an umbrella in it. He'd enjoyed the day. He found Hina endlessly fascinating; wise with funny here and now snippets (and a lot of giggles about Boris Becker), and a nose-ring that twinkled in the light. Vlad wondered if she was a gypsy but because she was at Oxford he decided she probably wasn't.

It was very early in the morning, and we had only just made the coach to the airport. It moved through a heavy mist that smothered the city. One man and his dog strode across Headington Park. I watched them make their way, preferring to sit and stare out of the window. Vlad sat beside me and said nothing, his head very upright on his neck. The silence felt personal.

Vlad hadn't said a word since rowing practice the day before. He'd gone in the coach's motor boat up and down the river at Henley-on-Thames, and I sat in the bow of our fibreglass eight and waved to him when we turned.

'Concentrate, Tessa. You're still rushing your catch. Just drop it in, that's it, quick hands.' Coach Kevin talked through a loudspeaker clamped to his mouth. He let Vlad take the tiller while he made jottings in a spiral notebook. Vlad perched (nervously) on the edge of the inflatable craft and felt the engine vibrate through to his hand. He'd never been in a boat before but didn't tell Kevin that.

'So you know Tessa, do you?'

'Yes, and Jana.'

'They're a pair. The cocktail shakers, I call them, always causing trouble in the bow of the boat.'

The oars thumped in the rollicks, up and down on the sun-spangled water, up and down and the cox was counting. Vlad, still holding the tiller, marvelling at the gloss and shine that seemed to fill the cracks of my curious student life, was suddenly and acutely aware he was a stranger in this weird world; a world he was about to step out of, back into his life that he had left behind.

By the time we arrived at Gatwick we were running late. The coach met traffic and before Vlad queued through security I decided Mihaela and Alin needed presents. I bought a red double-decker key ring and a pencil case with *I Love London* on it.

'But I didn't go to London,' Vlad objected.

'It doesn't matter. Say they're from me.'

Vlad obediently added them to a present collection that included a tartan headscarf for his mother and for his father a china highland cow. He'd really wanted to buy his mum a box of chocolates (the creamy, individually wrapped ones Mrs Dunlop sometimes ate after lunch). His mum loved sweet things but Mrs Dunlop said they wouldn't last.

Because of his age Vlad had automatically been registered with the British Airways Childminder Service.

'Hello Vlad, lovely to meet you.' An airhostess came between us very suddenly at the check-in desk, just when I was trying to work out what to say next. 'You're going to have a lovely flight. Do you want to come and sit in our play area?' She bent down to talk to him.

'He's really grown-up,' I insisted, but Vlad was already being led away by his made-up escort in shoes that clicked. I shouted out goodbye, shocked it had come to an end so soon, but he chose not to turn around.

I travelled back to Oxford on the bus with a funny feeling in my stomach. It poked me like an invisible finger every time I tried to think about something else. It was my fault. I'd deliberately not discussed with Vlad what would happen next. I'd not known what to say. His more assured manner, his fledgling adolescent frame, his unflinching gaze – it all bothered me.

Seventeen years on it's still difficult to explain why my every instinct told me Project Vlad must come to an end. I'd started something that I knew I couldn't finish. I didn't want Vlad to come back to Strath. It felt too weird.

The bus dropped me at the end of the Cowley Road where I stood for a full five minutes, waiting for a wave of nausea to pass.

Bucharest, Otopeni Airport, July '95

Vlad couldn't believe his eyes. His father was standing in Arrivals, and hovering beyond the sliding door just behind him was his grandfather. It had never occurred to Vlad that Gheorghe Toma could exist anywhere other than in his Moldavian cottage. And here he was strip-lit, stooped and smiling, waving at the return of his prodigal grandson.

'Ce faci Wayee?' Vlad's hair was being ruffled (again). He stood still, astonished, embarrassed by his granddad who was talking very loudly in a burbling, singsong peasant voice.

'Eh! How is the foreign land? Our foreign boy! Eh you've grown big! My lad you will replace the horses this harvest.'

Vlad was now staring hard at the tiled airport floor pretending he could hear neither his grandfather nor father, shifting his shoe back and forth on the slippery surface. All *eees* and *rrrs*, his paternal escorts wore their Moldavian badge with unaffected pride. Did they not know that everyone was watching? Vlad knew people in Bucharest were sly and greedy and standing in Bucharest airport he knew that these same people thought his Moldavian relations were coarse, red-faced country fools.

Shit! Vlad was not prepared for this. Re-entering Romania was immediately and suddenly hard. (Even the lights in the terminal gave out a dreary light.) How could it be so colourless with so much sunshine? It was harder than Vlad had imagined, but then he'd tried not to imagine. And he certainly hadn't imagined his father and grandfather in the terminal, then on the bus crossing Bucharest.

'Upon my word!' Gheorghe Toma was pressed up against the window holding on to the leather strap swinging from the ceiling. His huge moustache stubbornly curling up and over his ruddy cheeks, twirled to fine points at each end (never cut, never trimmed – always, mysteriously, the same length).

Gheorghe had never been to Bucharest. He'd fought the Russians almost as far as Stalingrad but had never visited his country's capital. He'd spent over a year in a Siberian POW camp but had never seen the flat plains of Wallachia, the pug-faced people of Bucharest or the messy unregulated nightmare that now spewed out of the city on the way to the airport. Already a bit confused in old age, he was struggling with this extraordinary excursion. Everywhere he looked there were so many people, like maggots crawling on a concrete carcass, tunnelling and sucking, trying to survive at any cost. He shook his head at the sight of it all.

'Why did you bring Granddad?' Vlad was shocked by the sound of his own voice.

'He had a free pass for the train.'

It was a very long journey home. Vlad felt slightly sick. He had no appetite for his father's picnic wrapped in paper; a lump of smoked pig, a wedge of bread and a bag of cherries. He had no interest in the country scene as it slid by, every stretch an extra-ordinary event for both father and grandfather.

'They're further ahead of us down here. Haymaking already!'

'It's been dry. Look at those vines, left to ruin! The shame of it. What's happening to our country?' Gheorghe finally removed the straw hat perched precariously on his head, and began to scratch his scalp long and hard. So hard, Vlad worried he might break his thin, old skin.

Pulling into Ploieşti caused considerable excitement. His grand-father stood up and tried to crane forward out of the small open slit of window. Ploieşti, with its oil fields, had been bombed badly in the war, he explained. It had been terrible, really terrible – the allies were smashing them to smithereens. Vlad looked out of the window and thought Ploieşti looked like every other Romanian railway station.

And then came the war stories all the way home (in the same loud raggy accent). Vlad listened. By the time they'd arrived in Iaşi he'd heard his favourite war story three times. His grandfather (a scout and a talented marksman) was cleaning his rifle when a Russian sniper shot at him from the trees, the bullet ricocheted off the barrel of his gun (inches from his face), saving Gheorghe's life and costing the sniper his – Gheorghe shot back and the Russian fell like a dead monkey from a branch.

By the end of the journey Vlad no longer had a favourite war story and Gheorghe had forgotten why he'd travelled all the way to Bucharest and back again.

'Ptah ptah! Don't be evil-eyed!' Vlad was being spat at (and admired) by his grandmother Anica. 'Ptah ptah.' She pursed her dry lips and smacked her pink tongue between her few remaining teeth. 'Ptah ptah! Don't be evil-eyed.'

Anica had come all the way into Iaşi to see her grandson return from his travels (and to collect her husband). Neighbour Sorin had offered her a ride to the city – an invitation she accepted, promptly placing her bony bottom in his cart. And here she was, twisting Vlad's cheek, declaring him fit to eat and spitting at him and cursing *the eyes* like all other superstitious babas – those who feared the delectable little person in front of them may draw the wrath of evil, ill-intended spirits.

Elena watched from the corner of the kitchen as Vlad silently tolerated his grandmother's affections. Her eyes were brimming, so she hung back and pushed a tell-tale thumb beneath her glasses. Her boy had returned, taller – a good size, too – and there was something else about him, something she couldn't put her finger on. So instead she busied herself at the sink and occasionally stirred a saucepan of chicken borsch.

Vlad was struck by the smell; the intense familiarity of that same smell, the tang of being clean with just a bit of bleach, of warm dusty air and the same hot, wet something boiling on the stove. It was, Vlad realised, the smell of home. He was right back where he'd started, standing in front of his grandmother who smelt slightly sour.

And there was Alin and Mihaela and Marcel and all the others, everybody wanting a little piece of his adventure. Vlad wasn't mean – at least, he didn't think he was – but he didn't want to share. He couldn't just turn on a tap and talk. Not like Tessa, he thought – Tessa talked all the time. It felt odd standing in the kitchen thinking about someone so impossibly far away, so he decided not to do it again.

'Yes. The food is good over there.'

Then suddenly and without warning he lifted up his T-shirt and exposed his tummy (tight as a drum) to the assembled audience. No one was more surprised than Vlad.

Dear Mrs Anthea Dunlop – We received your letters, the first sent on 29th April, and the second sent on 6th June. Thank you for these letters. We didn't receive any letter from Vlad and we don't know why. Maybe the SRI (Information Romania Service) is still studying it.

First off all I want you to forgive me because I write to you so late but I was very busied. (I don't know if 'busied' it is correct but I hope you will understand what I tried to say.) I send many apologies for this problem.

We are very happy to know that Vlad handles school and we are very proud of him. We aren't worried about him any more and we hardly wait to see him again. Please tell him that all family is very well and we miss him much.

Mr and Mrs Dunlop with this occasion we thank you, very, very, very much for anything you did for Vlad. If you'll be in Romania sometime don't hesitate to visit us. You will be most welcome.

Yours sincerely,

Toma Marcel

p.s. I wait news from Tessa. Send her my best wishes.

p.p.s. Sorry for the mistakes in this letter.

Mum was sitting at the kitchen table. Marcel's letter touched and surprised her. For a foreigner she decided it was beautifully written, in watery black ink on faded paper smothered in lots and lots of stamps and yet still it had arrived days after Vlad left. Marcel's looped hand was immaculate and the tone so formal it almost pained her. She really hadn't done *that* much, and Vlad was such a shy little chap she'd found it all rather difficult. So typical of Tessa to choose the only child she couldn't crack. Marcel sounded more like her sort. Still, on re-reading the letter Mrs Dunlop couldn't help feeling she'd missed a trick with Vlad.

'Oh Mum, don't dwell. It was fine. Honestly, Vlad seemed to have had a great time. When I saw him off at Gatwick he was just the ticket. Anyway, if it was anyone's fault it was mine.'

'What do you mean, darling?'

'Well, maybe it was the wrong thing to do. I should have told your more about his life. You know, nothing happens there. They don't have any money.'

'Oh I know Romania is poor. Don't patronise me.'

'No it's not that, Mum. It's … oh it doesn't matter. I can't explain. Let's not talk about it any more.'

The subject was dropped; that is, until Vlad's school report came.

Summer 1995

Vlad's achievements at Strath this term have been remarkable. In a short period of time he has set new academic standards, established close relations with his peers and surprised every member of staff he has encountered. Vlad's friendly yet wholly committed approach has been responsible for his success and it would be a great shame if he were not to return to Strathallan in the future. A view shared by everyone at the school. We wish him well until the next time.

D. J. BARNES, *Housemaster Ruthven House*

Mum stayed at the table until the old clock startled her. It was unlike her to lose track of time but Vlad's school report was little short of exceptional.

The headmaster's comment said it all: *It has been a privilege to have Vlad at Strathallan.*

Mum was shocked. She knew Vlad was bright – how else had the whole extraordinary project come to pass? But the superlatives, the consistency of his grades in all subjects – even those he'd never encountered (Spanish, German, fine art, craft, design and technology) – and, most perplexing of all, the invitation to return. It had been the standard middle-class, capital-guzzling struggle, paying for her own children through bouts of public schooling, and here was that same school extending a second fee-free invitation to a Romanian boy, whom she had always quietly considered rather unremarkable. Why had Vlad not shown his friendly, bright side to her, she wondered. Mum read the report again and beneath her astonished wonder felt just a smidgeon hurt. Her public response, however, was one of pride.

'It's quite remarkable, darling! What an incredible little boy.'

I didn't find the contents of the report startling. I had a clearer idea of the rigours of the communist education system yet to be analysed, re-jigged and modernised to fit into a more inclusive, flexible European model. And had I not handpicked Vlad?

What did surprise me, though, was his universal appeal. Even the music teacher, a loathsome curmudgeon in my time, had been woken from his pre-pension slumber: *Vlad has brought a breadth of vision and understanding to a rather blinkered group and I congratulate him on his willingness to share his feelings.*

Vlad had been taken aback by the music lessons. Listening to a spot of Chopin or Mozart and talking about how it affected him was not learning as far as he was concerned; however, it beat the tub-thumping that accompanied the music history of Romanian composers. Brought up forced to bawl about 'three colours' and the glorious land, Vlad detested compulsory group singsongs and was relieved Mr Black didn't go in for them. In return, he'd been happy to share his feelings.

Iaşi, September '95

Vlad was watching the telly when the phone rang. He was meant to be working on his Romanian grammar and had got as far as opening his brother's old text book – the one with a picture of Ceauşescu inside, filled with poems about workers and comrades and their socialist paradise. Vlad defaced Ceauşescu, giving him a blue moustache on his upper lip and spiky fangs, but he didn't touch the grammar.

He was surprised to hear my voice. It had been two months since his return home and he'd tried very hard to block the memories that pressed into his head all of a sudden in a coloured jumble. He found the more he pushed them down, the less likely they were to jangle him awake in the morning.

'Vlad, your report was really good! We haven't sent it because Mum's worried that it might go missing in the post. Do you want us to send it to you?'

'No. Don't worry.' Vlad was taken aback. He'd forgotten how I talked all in a rush.

'There's something else . . . ' Here I paused. 'The school would like you to come back. I wondered what you thought about that. Would you like to come back?'

Vlad didn't answer immediately. He couldn't imagine being back in Britain. On his return he'd felt so hopeless, so helplessly at sea in his own life that he was stumped by the idea of ever leaving again. He couldn't think about his time in Britain as real. Strath, Scotland, Mrs Dunlop, Tessa – these were psychedelic labels to a fantasy land that didn't belong to him; shorthand for an idea he now struggled to take seriously.

'I don't know. Sorry . . . '

'You did really well, Vlad. I mean, I never got a report like that.'

'Uh.'

The conversation ended inconclusively. Vlad didn't tell me what he told his friends and cousin Alin. Strath, he'd confided, was not like proper school. The classes were a breeze, all talk and basic with questions that only needed short answers written on prescribed dotted lines and science minus numbers, just a funky Bunsen burner and some plastic goggles. Third form at Strath was too easy to be real. His parents, when they heard, were appalled and reminded Vlad on several occasions that he must get his high school exams if he wanted to get into Romanian university – in their opinion the only way of avoiding factory life.

I put the phone down and shrugged. Dad was reading the *Herald* in his chair. The call had been uncomfortable and Vlad sounded detached, almost aloof; he certainly didn't sound like someone champing to come back and I, deliberately, hadn't pushed him. There were, of course, practicalities; the cost, red tape and responsibility.

And Dad, long suffering, ready to do the right thing but not keen.

And me, unable to recall why I ever thought boarding school in Britain was a good idea and aware Vlad wouldn't be a little boy for very much longer – if indeed he still was. Not to mention the small matter of my final year at Oxford.

It was Mum who held the door open. Vlad was, after all, a nut she had yet to crack.

Dear Mrs Dunlop – I am sorry there seems to be a delay in my letter. I do not have a good reason for this. It is, however, very hot here. The sun is baking his head off. I am writing to thank you for all your kindness and to say that I appreciate all you have done for me. There is nothing happening here and I sometimes think about Scotland and you all. How is Chokkie? Mama does not believe my story about Chokkie.

I feel sad sometimes if I think too much about things. It is depressing here.

Regards to Tessa and Mr Dunlop.

Yours sincerely and thanking you,

TOMA VLAD

This was the only letter Mum received from Vlad – his mother and brother had insisted – but one was enough.

Dear Vlad – I think about you <u>so</u> much and marvel at the way you managed life in Scotland, life at Strathallan, life with foreign peers . . . the way you adjusted to our strange habits/ways of life and seemed to enjoy the different food and how you totally mastered the language and seemed to cope so calmly. VERY well done indeed – and thank you for your letter; it was so good to hear from you although we thought you were missing everything a little bit and probably feeling VERY hot.

I have a few photos to send you. Will they arrive safely if I post them? Did you get the photocopy of your report? If so I can send the real report?

Tess rowed and rowed and worked in a café and then came to Italy with us to stay with friends. Chokkie married a Daschund called Daisy. We hope she will have pups. The duckling is now a large black drake with a white bib. My chicks are big and grey and speckled and mostly cocks. We have eaten three – jolly good they were, too!

I hope you are helping your mum in the kitchen and about the house?!

Strathallan will miss you so much, Vlad. Your friendliness and the brilliant, indeed, incredible way with which you coped with so many subjects. Donald, Tess and I feel very proud of you – well done indeed. Let us know if you would like to continue your studies in Scotland so that one day you can go back and re-organise and run your country – if that is your wish Mr Toma!

DO please write again.

Lots of love,

ANTHEA x

P.S. Have you written a thank you letter to the headmaster and Mr Barnes?

Vlad had not written to Mr Barnes or the headmaster, nor did he have any intention of doing so. He was sure that he'd not go back to Strathallan. He decided that Britain was so ahead in the world (it certainly looked ahead) children could escape proper lessons, but he was not British. He'd missed one term already and Vlad was not the sort of pupil who enjoyed diligently catching up. It didn't occur to him that he could swap the Romanian system for the British system in perpetuity. He was not a dreamer or an optimist and he didn't like to be a bother. There was only one person who could've persuaded him to take the risk, and that was me.

A herd of elephants was on the front of the postcard and the caption on the reverse read *Elephants at Hanapangala, Sri Lanka.*

Dear Vlad – I am sorry it has taken me so long to write – I was busy and lazy, neither of which is a sufficient excuse. And now thirteen hours of flying later I find myself in Sri Lanka. The Sri Lankans are unassuming and cheerful and very poor – they cycle about barefoot and are very small. I bang my head on their buses and can't fit my knees under the table. Still, it is all good fun.

It was great to have you in our country. On my return to GB I shall do what I can to help you to maybe return in two years. Until my next letter all love,

TESS xxxxx

The postcard made Vlad feel stuck and sad. He knew it meant I was very OK in my bizarre international student life. (What was she doing in Sri Lanka?)

I shall do what I can to maybe help you return in two years.

It was clear from that one slack sentence I didn't really want Vlad to come back and that meant Vlad didn't want to go back either. Really, he didn't. But knowing that didn't make being a teenager in Iaşi any easier.

CHAPTER SEVEN

London, September '98

Mark was over forty although his age was not immediately discernible, hidden as it was beneath jeans that bagged around his crotch and a sherbet pink T-shirt. Dark-rimmed specs finished off a face peppered with an almost beard. He was a TV executive and I was sitting in his office in Leicester Square listening to him tell me I'd make a good presenter.

Earlier that day I'd been unemployed and waiting for the telephone to ring. Now I was in front of a TV God hoping he hadn't noticed my dark roots. But Mark wasn't looking at my hair. Indeed, he wasn't even considering my raw 'presenting' potential. He was working up to asking me a favour. Mark, like so many TV execs, hoped he might just be able to get something for nothing.

'I think the boys could do with a female presence on screen. Let's face it . . . ' Here he stopped and allowed himself a dry little laugh. 'Most of our viewers are men!'

I blushed through my rouged cheeks. It was too good to be true, an almost job offer to present alongside Britain's most famous comedic duo: Frank Skinner and David Baddiel. The programme's football theme was, I decided, only a minor setback. After all, I had once seen Celtic play at Parkhead.

'There's just one thing you could do for us, Tessa. Do you like Tess or Tessa?

'Oh anything goes!'

'I see from your CV you speak fluent Romanian?'

'Oh well, yes. Uh.'

'You *do* speak Romanian?'

Just like that Mark blindsided me. Four little words and I was flummoxed. I didn't speak Romanian. I hadn't spoken Romanian for over four years and even then it was just a few phrases. I lied on my CV. Didn't everyone?

'It's just we're looking for a Romanian footballer who played against England during the 1970 World Cup. His name is Mihai Mocanu. We need him for our Phoenix from the Flames feature.'

'What?'

'We want to get him over here to relive his career. Especially the bit when he was tackling our boys. I thought you'd watched the programme?'

'Oh yes I love it!'

There I was, enthusing about the prospect of finding a (possibly dead) Romanian footballer in a country with no infrastructure, and in a language I didn't speak. I was going to use my fantasy Romanian to find a player for Fantasy Football. Mark hadn't mentioned money but he did pat me on the knee before I stood up to leave.

'Thanks Tess, and next time we can talk more about your starring role alongside David and Frank. Eh?'

I had to find that footballer.

It was not the first time Romania had featured in my fledgling TV career. Clare was the production manager of the cult Friday night flagship show on Channel 4, *TFI Friday*, and she was looking for runners. Some years earlier Clare had been the producer on the *Challenge Anneka* series that had gone to Romania and spruced up the very hospital I once worked in. The programme rated well in Britain.

'You worked in that hospital for a year?' Clare said, scanning my CV. 'Wow, tough stuff.'

And so I landed my first proper job with a TV production company. Everybody had blonde hair and pink nails and orange faces, except for the presenter who had orange hair and a pink face.

My job involved approaching people on the street and asking

them to be fat lookalikes, buying tampons for the blonde women and meeting bands. I didn't know who any of the musicians were or what they looked like – I was brought up on Radio 4 and the *Scottish Farmer*. When I went to greet INXS at the train station I bought *Q* magazine beforehand so I could identify Michael Hutchence and give him a special welcome and his own dressing room. We talked about sandwich filling options.

A few months later he was dead and I was unemployed.

Iaşi, September '98

Vlad was feeling stupid, with a dry mouth and a fuzzy brain – even his hands felt stiff. He was watching MTV on his mother's sofa-bed. The VJ was an English girl called Davina. She was screaming and waving her arms and totally out of it, he thought, holding his own head.

He was waiting for Alin, who reckoned he knew some Russian girl whose Dad was in town doing business with Uncle Bogdan. The girl had loads of grass – at least, that's what Alin thought and Vlad agreed it was definitely worth the wait.

Anyway there was nothing else to do. Yesterday he'd been in hysterics on the river bank, sucking up the vapours from a vat of Quick-Fix glue. Alin had opted out but Vlad and Andrei went home mashed.

It was during the next day's long, sickly stretch in front of MTV that the telephone rang.

'Alo.'

'Hello, hmm . . . hello? Este Vlad acolo?'

'Alo?'

'Hello! It's Tessa, looking for Vlad or Marcel.'

'This is Vlad.'

'Hi. Is it? Gosh! You sound different. Hi! How are you?' I had clean forgotten about Vlad's way (and now with such a voice!) of reducing me to a blathering wreck without ever really saying anything.

'Uh.' Little Vlad with a deep voice had not been expecting my

113

call. In fact, he had long ago assumed he would never hear from me again.

'So how is everyone? Marcel? Alin?'

'They're OK. Alin, I am waiting for him and a Russian girl.' Vlad wished he didn't feel so caked.

'Russian girl?' When the words came out, they quivered.

'Yes.'

There was a Russian doll in my head.

'How old are you Vlad?'

'Sixteen.'

'Oh.'

His voice was older (more tired?) than sixteen – little Vlad. I tried to remember why I'd called. I forced myself to re-focus. But when I explained what I wanted, Vlad sounded unsure. Mihai who? What? He was a Romanian teenager, not a TV researcher. I found myself promising the production company would fax him £50. He said it wouldn't be necessary. He sounded embarrassed. Vlad found it hard to imagine doing anything that could possibly be worth so much money.

'Thanks Vlad, I'll call you in a week. Or maybe in a couple of days.'

I really wanted to find the football player – Mark had called me twice already. I put the phone down and tried to visualise Vlad at sixteen with a broken voice and a Russian doll but I couldn't.

Vlad let himself out of the flat, his head throbbing, and smoked his last cigarette in the cold. Alin didn't show up.

The extent of Vlad's football knowledge revolved around the Romanian National team's progress in his lifetime – the highpoints of which were few and far between, but they did exist. Vlad had never heard of Mihai Mocanu – nor indeed had Alin or Elena (Marcel was finally earning money with his meticulous engineering degree miles away in Bucharest). It was Tuca who confirmed the British girl wasn't barking up the wrong tree.

'Yes yes, Mihai Mocanu! He was a fine player, a defender from Constanța. Now Vlad . . . ' The room held its breath as Tuca leapt from the table and kicked forward his foot and began to dribble around the leg of a stool with an imaginary ball in the tiny kitchen.

Three colours I know in the worrrld
Reminders of a brave people

'Is he still alive?'

Since old times, with old renown
Victorious in baaaaatttttle!

It was clear Tuca had no idea what happened after national glory in the story of Mihai Mocanu. Vlad left the kitchen and wondered (and worried) what came next when you were trying to find someone you didn't know, for someone you didn't think you'd ever hear from again. Our telephone conversation still rang in his ears; the more he revisited it, the more surreal it felt. Vlad hoped the problem (he had given Mihai Mocanu problem status) might just go away.

London

There was a long pause on the phone while a girl went to find Mark.

'Hi Tessa, have you got hold of him?' He sounded distracted.

'Not exactly. But I've found someone who can find him.'

'I thought *you* could.'

'Yes but calling Romania is very expensive. It's much easier to find him within the country.'

'Right, fine. Good. Let me know when you find him.'

'OK, it's just I was hoping you could wire my helper some money. Only £50. Romania's so poor and he's doing us a big favour.'

Mark clicked his lips at the other end. I told him the name of the Western Union portal and he put down the phone. He didn't mention the on-screen idea – maybe he was busy.

Vlad was helping himself to a generous serving of egg plant salad when his mother came into the kitchen and told him the foreign girl had called, again. Exactly forty-eight hours after the first call. Elena thought it unlikely her young son would find a former national hero, let alone persuade him to co-operate, but she felt she should help him try. It was Elena who eventually suggested Vlad call National Enquiries.

Vlad spent two afternoons testing the communication networks of his own country. He'd never called anyone outside Iaşi and then it was only to set up drinking sessions with Andrei and Dragoş after his meagre pocket money had been distributed. His search for Mihai Mocanu was a protracted, sobering experience.

'No one listed under Mocanu Mihai.'

'No, this is the Professional Football League. Nothing to do with veteran football players.'

'Is Mihai Mocanu still alive? What? Who the hell are you?'

By day two Vlad had learnt to control his Moldavian accent, pulling his jaw forward and flattening his vowels into an indistinguishable verbal soup. It was the fifth person he'd spoken to in the Romanian Football Federation (Vlad hadn't been aware they employed so many people) who eventually saw fit to give up Mocanu's whereabouts.

'He is working in a training camp in the mountains as a football coach. No, I don't know where.'

Vlad finally found Mihai Mocanu and had a testing couple of minutes explaining to a national hero (albeit one he hadn't heard of) that his presence was required in England on a TV programme. No, Vlad did not know which one. No, Vlad did not know when. Who was Vlad? Why was Vlad bothering him? Goodbye.

'Aw brilliant! You've found him! Vlad you're a star. Well done! What did he say?'

'He didn't sound like he believed me.'

'Hmm . . . yeah. Don't worry. I'll ring and talk English at him – that should help. By the way your money is being wired to the main post office in Iaşi.'

Mihai Mocanu received one more call, this time from a foreign woman (me) who said *mulţumesc* and *Anglia* a lot in between bouts of English. He heard no more on the subject. The TV company went off the idea and the item was dumped. They paid Vlad on my third reminder.

It was his fourth (and definitely final) visit to the central post office where the cashier had started to look at him with suspicion when the money finally arrived – thousands and thousands of lei in crisp, colourful notes. Vlad couldn't believe his eyes. He went home with full pockets and gave most of it to his mother who stashed the cash neatly between her tea towels. The money lasted and lasted; Elena paid the electricity bill and the phone bill and bought minced beef and coffee and a small slab of chocolate. Vlad bought *Gallery of Suicide*, Cannibal Corpse's latest album, a whole packet of cigarettes, real vodka and his first Philip K. Dick novel – and there was still a little bump between the towels.

I didn't become a telly star. Instead (before the item was ditched) I was permitted the privilege of an introduction to Skinner and Baddiel. A slight man, Frank stood briefly and shook my hand. He said thank you. David said nothing; he stayed slumped on the sofa. I never heard from Mark again.

Iaşi, December '98

Before Vlad opened the envelope he knew immediately who it was from. On reassuringly high quality card was a Royal Academy of Arts Nativity scene in purples, mute reds and yellows. Sent in plenty of time for the festive season the greeting inside read: *With best wishes for Christmas and the New Year.* Around the printed message in inky disarray Mrs Dunlop had scrawled her own Christmas message.

Dear Vlad – This brings lots of good wishes to you from all the Dunlops. The boys are well, Tessa is working for some TV set-up and Mr Dunlop has had very sore legs. The doctor gave him warfarin but he is refusing to take it. 'Keep that bloody rat poison away from me!'

Muppet (cat) died in his basket aged twenty, Meg (goat) died in her house aged seventeen and the Goldfish are well – aged twenty-five! Chokkie is still going strong. Tessa says she spoke to you recently. I am still sad and puzzled as to why you didn't come back to Strath?! Send us a line.

With love from us all,

Mrs D

Vlad read the note and felt bad he'd not written. The idea of Mrs Dunlop was less overwhelming now; his vague memory of her was as a curious cartoon character with funny ways and ageing animals. Vlad still didn't write but he gave his mother the Christmas card. Elena popped it behind an enormous faded poster of two white kittens with impossibly blue eyes and tried to imagine Mrs Dunlop in Scotland with lots of time to write letters in a big house with bouncy sofas and bright lights. Elena didn't write or send cards, although occasionally her sisters gave her a posy of flowers or a makeshift brooch on 8th March for Woman's Day.

It was February when she took down the card and put it in Vlad's box beside his Strathallan exam papers, a photocopy of his school report, three other Christmas cards and four letters – all from Mrs Dunlop. She looked at the contents and wondered what it was that had come to pass one summer in Scotland to leave her son so altered, so detached and stubbornly silent. Her little Vlad.

CHAPTER EIGHT

London, November '99

I played with the strand of hair in front of my face and smiled from behind it at the man sitting opposite. He had auburn hair (combed back to hide the creep) and his eyes followed my every move.

'So what about the shifts, Nigel?'

'Ah yes, business before pleasure!'

It was late and the last train left for Peterborough in under an hour. My contract in the Midlands as a radio presenter was not being renewed – I needed this job. Most of all I wanted to return to London. I'd left eighteen months earlier, shortly after my dalliance with Fantasy Football.

Nigel fingered his wine glass. 'A young girl like you? Every weekend! How would you manage?'

'Oh, I would!' I laughed meekly and thought about pushing the head of my clean spoon into his open palm. I needed this job and I didn't want to miss my train but most of all I didn't want to touch his skin.

'I am very reliable and I've got a good voice for a Saturday night.'

'Yes, yes your voice is . . . very deep!' Nigel was looking at my mouth. 'OK, I tell you what – three months. I'll give it a whirl for three months, every weekend and Thursdays and Fridays.'

'Thanks Nigel! Wicked! Thanks so much!' No spoon needed.

'Now, what about another bottle of Burgundy?'

'I'd love to, but sadly I've got a train to catch. Of course, once I'm working in London, well, it'll be totally different then.' And with that I stood up. He did too and I briefly placed my hands on his shoulders. 'I won't let you down, Nigel!'

The sharpness of London's night air was instant relief. I'd pulled it off. I'd landed a job as a continuity announcer in the capital. It started in two weeks. In the meantime, I was on holiday.

As it happened no one wanted to go on holiday in November.

'Darling, if only you'd get a normal job then you could holiday with the rest of us.' Even Mum was otherwise occupied with a school play and Claire had just started at a new NGO.

So I would travel alone and I was secretly pleased. After all, who else would want to tread an emotional path back to Romania? Some six years late, I planned my return. I would go back to Siret and make amends. At least, that was the idea.

Yes! Doina remembered me. And Irina, too. Yes Tay-sa! Of course I must come and stay. Tay-sa, *păpușă blonda* Tay-sa! Mariţa didn't have a phone; I'd surprise her when I got there. My ticket was booked and suddenly I couldn't wait.

I laid my clothes out on the bed in my lodgings, stopping every so often to rewind the *Colloquial Romanian* cassette and re-catch the foreign phrases.

Romania has approximately 23 million inhabitants. Bucharest is the capital and has a population of around two million.

A parka with a furry hood, a pair of shiny black commando pants with zips, Cat boots and, in anticipation of my new job, a Ted Baker cashmere cardigan.

Romanian is shaped like an amphitheatre; in the middle are the Carpathian mountains, then a region of hills, followed by the plains of Moldavia . . .

And the trainers I'd bought nearly two years earlier, the ones I meant to send to Vlad to say thank you but never did, I laid them beside my warm, self-conscious clothes – just in case I made it to Iaşi.

Siret, November '99

I was sitting on a brown sofa in front of a large television eating peanuts with flaking salty skins.

'Say something, Tay-sa. Say something!' Irina was plying me with beer and olives and more peanuts, all from her new shop where she'd just come from counting money.

'What can I say, Irina?'

'How do you find us here in Siret? Has it changed?'

After so long I couldn't describe how I found it, not even in English. The memory of that year when I was eighteen, all raw and open, ready for this country and the adventures it offered up. And then the brief disastrous return trip with Irina and her swimming costume. And then, six years later?

'Beautiful! Everything is beautiful!'

I had forgotten how small Siret was, a lonely border town at the world's end. The volunteers had long since left. I stared down from the window at the quiet street and the word that sprung to mind was 'sleepy', but I didn't tell Irina that.

She'd been overjoyed when the Revolution came because lots of foreign charity workers arrived to help and spend money in the bar she'd set up with her husband. Now they had a shop as well.

'We must to think differently when the volunteers left our town and there was no one to drink expensive beer any more,' Irina explained, tugging on her cigarette.

They lived in the same block but since my last visit she'd made over the flat. It had lost its Spartan look, and there was laminate flooring throughout. Irina (probably still the prettiest woman in town) knew little of what was going on in the hospital so we sat smiling at each other, and I tried to think of something to say about change in Romania.

When I went back to Romania as a teenager, I chose Iaşi instead of Siret. Sitting there in Irina's flat I remembered why. Nothing's ever the same the second time around. Still, I was grateful Valentin had come to pick me up from the station.

Mariţa had got much fatter. She was so enormous she filled her tiny two-room apartment, which was already cluttered and shabby and impossibly small for her extended family. Marița never had any money but she cooked a feast I felt obliged to eat. She was about to lose her job. Pulling her mouth down at the sides, she explained the hospital was due to close. 'Part of Romania's progress,' she said and rolled her eyes. Not to be defeated, she had adopted adolescent gypsy twin orphans, brought them home and called them her own.

I lay on the bed that filled the room and let Lilica stroke my hair while Marița insisted on feeding me more egg and polenta. She showed me the cracks where Lilica and her twin brother had banged their heads over and over on her thin apartment wall and the stained mattress where they'd pissed in the night.

'But not any more,' beamed Marița, and her husband Mihai put his head around the door and gave me a big friendly grin, just like all those years before.

We stumbled along in my cack-handed Romanian. Marița signed at the bathroom with its rubber pipe and plastic bowl and the bath that no one sat in. She had saved and saved to make over her flat and kept her money between the sheets, then one day she got home and the place was burnt to a crisp, all her money gone up in smoke.

'The lead was faulty on the TV,' she explained. 'It was made in China.'

Marița promised to take me to see my two favourite girls, Vasilica and Mariana, the next day; that is, if they hadn't already left town. They were deemed unfit to live alone when the hospital closed, which was due to happen imminently. They'd have to move to another institution.

As she talked, my stomach tightened.

'Will the girls remember me?'

'Yes, yes they will remember you.'

But to my shame I found neither girl that cold November. I didn't go to the hospital. It was to be another nine years before I finally went back to Siret and tried to visit them all over again and then Vasilica, still in an institution, would look across at me and shout: 'Hey blonda, what took you so long?'

I got distracted, that's what.

Iaşi, November '99

Vlad was in his bedroom listening to music.

> *When empires fall*
> *And nightmares crawl*

On a small square of paper he'd jotted the name of the band, the track and then the time-code.

> *From the cradle to enslave*
> *This is the end of everything*

Vlad lay back on the bed and placed a hand under his shirt, tracing a finger up and down the raised scar that ran across his abdomen. It still pained him to go to the loo and on that autumn day he realised he still hadn't fully forgiven his foolish father.

For two days he'd complained of stomach cramps and Elena noticed her stringy son ate even less than usual. She forced him to the doctor who diagnosed gastroenteritis and Vlad, bent double, was sent home. Two days later and Elena and Vlad were waiting in the hall of St Spiridon hospital. He had acute appendicitis.

Tuca was somewhere, although Elena was not sure where, trying to find the right doctor to give money to. He'd arrived late, called as he was from the factory, and with no cash to hand and never able to concentrate long enough to hurry.

But Vlad's appendix couldn't wait. He was finally bundled on a trolley while someone pushed a needle into his spine moments before a doctor ran into the room and, cursing under his breath, started to cut into Vlad's stomach. The anaesthetic had no chance and Vlad screamed and jerked on his trolley, the doctor cursed louder and the nurse repeatedly stabbed Vlad's arm with a drip that wouldn't hold. Pink and bloody, Vlad's appendix was discarded overhead. Weird and woozy, he recalled his father coming through the door, shaking hands with the doctor in his now soiled white coat and discreetly handing over a bundle of money. Double the going rate, but then Tuca had always been generous.

Too bloody late, thought Vlad. I've already been butchered. Elena was crying in the corner.

> *That I might keep*
> *Thee with me in Hades*
> *Succulent, Succubus*
> *Succour me*

A girl from Iaşi, blonde with a prominent bosom, was reading fast from autocue. Vlad had left his music and joined his father in the main room. The news cut to President Constantinescu explaining his intentions at Helsinki; he was repeating the words *membership* and *European Union*. Sometimes he said *Tonyblair*, as if one word. *Tonyblair* was supporting Romania's entry – yes he was – and his well-meaning beard bobbed up and down.

Tuca got up and left the room, muttering about good for nothings, and Vlad shut his eyes. In an uncharacteristic moment of youthful optimism three years earlier he had gone around the city sticking up Emil's head in large shiny photographic form.

Vote for Change!

And the esoteric Emil with his soft shoes and geology degree had, like a lamb to the slaughter, duly become president, replacing his grinning ex-communist counterpart. The in-fighting and corruption had continued and Vlad felt the fool for believing so much was possible from one old man who was made of straw like all the rest of them. When, a year later, Constantinescu had stood waving beside Bill Clinton in Bucharest he switched off the TV. Next it was *Tonyblair* talking to their parliament. All change for supine

124

Romania with its venal leaders. The war in Kosovo had made them strategically significant. Beyond that did anybody really care?

Vlad stood up and joined his father in the kitchen.

'Shouldn't you be at school?'

'What business is it of yours?'

Tuca sighed and decided his son was at a very difficult age.

Siret, Doina's apartment

They had the same huge bungee leather sofa. I slid down into it and listened to Doina sing. Up, up and away went her voice and her eyes misted over.

> *The gypsies are passing, passing*
> *Partying and singing*
> *The gypsies are passing*
> *Never stopping*
> *Each other always loving*

Her daughter Olivia held my hand tight, her slim wrist decorated with small orthodox figureheads threaded on dark string. She was thrilled to see me.

'Tess! Tess!' Her huge Disney eyes shone like lamps and she pressed for more.

I was happy to answer each and every question. I was taken by this startling girl on the cusp of womanhood but still eager like a child. Could this be Olivia who once skipped by my side, the daughter of the hospital pharmacist with the same coltish mane and long pin legs?

'Tess, why you take so long to come back to Romania? Dave and Sylvia, they come back every year.'

'Oh, I did come back. I came here one weekend but you weren't home. Anyway, I was working in Iași.' I told Olivia, my new, nearly adult friend, about the hot summer of '94 and Vlad. I even mentioned my *furuncule*.

'Vai,' said Olivia, 'lucky boy to go to Britain.'

125

But by now I was only half in the conversation, skimming along the top, answering her questions. No, he hadn't been back. Yes, I knew where he lived. The rest of me was uncontrollably adrift, wondering and staring. I could no longer resist. If this was a grown-up Olivia, a fresh cutie-pie, was it OK then to imagine what a grown-up Vlad might be like? That's where I was, doing the maths – twelve plus five or six? – when Olivia sprang from the sofa, wresting her hand from mine.

'Mamă, mamă! Why don't we go to Iaşi tomorrow and take Tessa? She can see Vlad and we can spend a day there. Please mamă!'

And that was how Olivia came to plan our excursion, with Doina and her father Radu and the complicit foreign girl, to a city some three hours drive away where her mother had once been a student. A big city, said Olivia, which had shops and arcades and even a cinema (several, in fact). How generous, and Romanian, to plan a trip around the guest.

I would visit the hospital next time. I pushed the worm of guilt away, right to the back of my mind. Doina let me use her phone; I punched in Vlad's number without which there would have been no reason to bring the trainers all this way.

'Alo.'

'Hello Vlad?'

'Yes.'

'It's me! It's Tessa!'

'Tessa?' Vlad paused, stunned. The TV was a little loud and, well over a year since my last call, he wasn't ready. And his father put him off, now standing in the doorway having followed from the kitchen to find out who was on the phone.

'I'm here in Romania.'

'Uh? Romania. Really?'

'Yes. I'm . . . well, it's just we were thinking of driving to Iaşi tomorrow. Me and some Siret friends. I thought we could meet up. Would your mum mind?'

'I–I did not think I would hear from you again . . . '

'Would it be OK? It's just they're going to give me a lift.'

'What? Tomorrow?' Vlad let himself lean on the arm of the sofa, digesting *tomorrow* and *Tessa*. His abdomen throbbed with the suddenness of it all.

I explained where we would meet and Alin – yes of course Alin, too – on the steps of Hotel Traian.

'Nice and central. We can feed the pigeons!'

'What?' his voice croaked.

'OK! So you'll be there with Alin? You know the hotel that's meant to be in Paris!'

By the time Vlad put down the receiver he'd almost adjusted to the idea of *Tessa* and *tomorrow*. He massaged the back of his neck between fingers and thumb and as realisation seeped into his limbs he allowed himself, for that moment and that moment only, to look forward to the following day. Knowingly he stood up and walked past his inquisitive father. Giving nothing away he pulled on his coat and let himself out into the cool November day.

Olivia looked up at me. She'd listened to every word and her eyes were even bigger and shinier than before.

'No Olivia, it's not like that. He's younger than you for goodness' sake – and tiny! His family come up to here.'

How we giggled as I placed my hand below my breast and shook my head.

Iaşi,

'No, I think they're a bit too much!'

Olivia ducked back behind the drape, soon peeking over again and re-emerging, this time in matching blue polka-dot bra and panties.

'Definitely better than the red!'

The Moldova department store did nothing that wasn't showy; gaudy plastic flowers, ochre nail polish, a flammable lingerie collection. Standing in front of me, all elbow and leg in her dots and string, Olivia looked obscenely innocent.

And so we bought the knickers and bra and she re-held my hand. Did we skip out of the department store? Maybe.

'Vai Tessa! How fine is Iaşi?!'

Iaşi was hunkering down for the winter, its flashes of central European magnificence well hidden behind a wintry mist and tangles of piping and electric cables haphazardly linking concrete stacks. There was visible change; stabs of colour, the ubiquitous red of McDonald's, the yellow of a European bank (was that a hole-in-the-wall?) and a shimmering hotel, *Dallas* style. Casinos and gambling halls dominated and even the Dacia taxis had been remodelled. But there was no new vision, or at least so it seemed. The city was beholden to a few stubborn shoots of individual profit.

We regrouped outside the Moldova; Doina with a wooden chopping board, Olivia holding her g-string to the sky and me staring hard at the ground. Her mother laughed out loud.

'Tess, under Ceauşescu we didn't even have a stick of deodorant to be a woman with. So, how you say – panties? They are OK!'

The journey slicing across the top of Romania had felt all of its three hours, minus main roads and slowed as it was behind carts and a broken bridge. Radu didn't mind – nothing gave him more pleasure than driving his BMW. He'd travelled all the way to Germany to collect it as soon as there were sufficient dollars stashed in his safe. Who would have guessed ferrying charity workers in a Dacia to and from Suceava station could prove so lucrative?

'A salary in this country is not how people can make money. Money is made from business.' He rubbed his thumb against the tips of his fingers. 'Business!'

Doina ran her hand through the back of his thick thatch of hair, her husband who had worked hard to make his money – those were happy heady days!

It was Olivia in the back of the car who pushed me on my plans for Vlad, her hand in my lap. She wondered what I would do when I left them in Iaşi and where I would stay and how it would be. She was brimming with curiosity and her questions made me burn inside. I didn't know where I'd stay. With Vlad, surely? But I hadn't thought to ask him. I didn't really know him to ask him.

'I'm not sure what we'll do. Maybe we'll go to a casino!'

'Vai! Ce fain!'

Vlad was not fastidious; however, within his limited means he cared about his appearance and that day he made a special effort. His mother relieved him of his favourite black jeans, dabbed their spits and spots with methylated spirits and pressed them on the floor. Vlad polished his steel toe-cap boots. Then there was his brown jersey – how he longed for a black one. He pulled on his jacket, which was just a little short in the arm and, after wetting down his cropped hair over the kitchen sink, acknowledged his mother and took the communal stair two steps at a time.

Alin was at band practice with his Psychedelic Wolves – they had agreed to meet in the city centre. Which is where I found them, as planned on the steps of the Hotel Traian, near the paving mosaics mobbed with hungry sparrows – two boys dressed in black quietly waiting.

If I'm honest I'd felt apprehensive all morning; squirreling secret glances in my pocket mirror, re-applying bronzer, even breathing into a cupped hand. I hadn't seen Vlad for some five years and, yes, I wanted to make a good impression. (When he was twelve I had wanted to make a good impression.) But nothing could have prepared me for what came next.

It happened so fast. When I first saw him there was a brief moment, the smallest of lag times, and then it hit me. A sudden change, a physical surge so real it hurt all over. I stood still in stunned shock before I ran from my place on the pavement. I broke away from Olivia, Doina, Radu; I arrived at the steps and climbed to reach up, impulsively touching his face without words.

And I held this young man, astonished by him; his height, the sharp angles of his shoulder blades, the warm, distinct smell of tobacco on his skin. I inhaled, held on and very briefly closed my eyes. And then the moment was over and I turned, as I knew I must, to Alin.

I kissed him hello and then hugged Olivia because I really needed her to leave. Soon I was hugging her parents. I was going around in a frantic circle hugging arms and backs and pumping and squeezing and lips on cheeks and hands and words.

'Bye. Goodbye. Thank you . . . '

Please go now! I urgently wanted to be free of my kindly Siret companions. But Doina was not ready to go. Doina was, for the moment at least, keen to stay right there in front of us all at the bottom of the steps. She talked to Vlad in Romanian, which I did not understand, and she scrutinised him in her expensive fur with her silky bob.

'Go now!' I begged in silent breaths. 'Please just go.'

Vlad answered Doina's questions. He was composed, maybe a little offish, his long black legs straddling the two top steps. He spoke only when spoken to. Yes, he was still at school. Yes, they hoped to go to university the following year. Yes, he lived in Iaşi.

I watched on and swallowed – my throat dry, my hands hot. Had I always known? Or was I simply deluded? A lonely, deluded foreigner hungry for fresh adventure. I was definitely hungry; I'd been unable to eat all morning. I closed my eyes and waited.

At last, they left – all three moving up the side street away from the hotel, away from the central square, towards their silver BMW and Siret and away from me. Numbly I waved and waved although they couldn't see me, waving as I was to smother my desire, regain composure – still waving to work out 'what next?' as I stood in a peculiar limbo between two teenage boys.

'Siret was great! Just great. You know, the same but different and they are such a lovely family. They brought me all the way here today, wouldn't accept money for petrol or anything. Oh see! The evening sun has come out for us.'

God knows I prattled on; this and that, anything to resist staring and silence. I looked from Vlad to the solitary shaft of sunlight to Alin and always back to Vlad, then quickly to the light again and its long shadow. Together in our trio we walked, eventually stopping at a smoke-filled bar.

'Is this OK?'

'Yes fine! God, it's so good to be back. Does your mum know I'm here? Is she OK if I stay? Where's Mihaela?'

On I talked in a noisy stream; unformed thoughts and casting about for safe ground between me and two much younger men. And all the while I knew exactly how Vlad sat and where he looked. His eyes the sticky brown of packed dates, his occasional smile with a half-bowed mouth and his thin, soft cheeks that had never been shaved. There was one stray hair on his chin that I longed to touch. Instead I patted Alin on his meaty shoulder.

Vlad was seventeen, which also meant he was nearly eighteen – a point he quietly made despite his reluctance to offer conversation, preferring, as he did, to listen.

'When did you start smoking?'

'How do you know I do?'

'You smell of cigarettes. Everybody does over here. Everyone seems to smoke.'

'So the gum didn't work?'

'No.' I smiled, apologetically, colour rising in my cheeks.

'Do you mind if I have one?' His pocket-patting search had already begun.

'Go ahead.'

'Alin smokes, too.'

I didn't care if Alin smoked.

Vlad inhaled deeply, the delicious crisp first hit of nicotine helping ease his uncertainty. The extraordinary unexpected event of my arrival and matter of where things now stood – above all, he wanted to stay cool. He drew again on his cigarette. I noticed his hands; shapely, strong boy's hands holding his deadly prop, blue smoke curling upwards before his sharp profile. He sat back slightly in his chair, relieved, at last able to almost enjoy the moment and the beer in his belly and the energising, lip-sticked girl who'd briefly put her hand on his knee.

Elena was working in a full flat with Mihaela waiting and chatting in the kitchen. Vlad's brother Dumitru and his wife Monica were in the next room keeping charge over Laura, their little daughter. That was how it was when Vlad and Alin and I entered some two hours later. They were carrying my bags, and I was making the noise.

Maybe Elena was the last to greet me. Mihaela led the way, a perky fifteen-year-old enjoying the commotion. She had introductions to make. Dumitru had been doing his National Service all those years ago, with a fake AK47 that made his hands hot, trotting around in boots that rubbed, following orders from pig-brained seniors. Monica, his high school sweetheart, had kept him going, delivering home cooking to the barracks with the sexiest little bottom. Thus occupied I never met Dumitru during the summer of 1994. They'd got married the following spring when Vlad was in Scotland, and in case he wondered what he'd missed there was a framed photograph on the wall with Monica all trussed up like an iced cake too good to eat and a boyish Dumitru standing solemnly, with cherub cheeks and an arm formally wrapped around his new wife's waist.

I reached Elena last, beery, acutely conscious of my broken Romanian and the stack of food I must tackle on the same lace-covered table. In front of me was the mother of a grown-up Vlad, who'd retreated silently to a corner. Elena mattered. She hadn't aged and I noticed her more fully now, the remarkable smoothness of her skin and a bewitching still gaze that quietly took me in. So the foreign girl had come back, thinner this time, with the same active red mouth and minus those nasty boils. Elena gently kissed both my cheeks and returned to the kitchen to find the *țuică*.

'Where's Marcel?'

It was Vlad who answered (Dumitru spoke only Romanian). Marcel was a success story in Bucharest with a wife and a swanky job in an international company (Lili had been right – English was essential). Moving beside Vlad I saw another photo; this time the favourite son with his angelic face and a pretty wife in white net. They were both holding giant candles, like snowy maypoles, wrapped in ribbons and sprigs of green.

'Marcel will soon be full of money. He is off to Prague this summer to put up mobile phone masts.'

I felt relieved that Marcel was absent. He had too much of his mother about him, and may have seen something I wasn't ready to admit but *how* I felt it. Christ, did Vlad feel it too? Standing there with one hand on his hip, turning to crack a joke with Alin in Romanian. I bit into a gherkin and started pulling out presents. The trainers were the right size. Vlad didn't enjoy opening his ostentatious present in front of so many and obliged only because I insisted, keen he should see I had remembered him.

'Adidash,' said Elena, approving.

'Actually, they're Reebok.'

Vlad looked up from his new trainers and smiled. 'Thanks Tess.'

'No – thank you! I bought them yonks ago and some perfume for your Russian girlfriend but I finished that, I'm afraid . . . '

'Russian girlfriend? What Russian girlfriend? Vlad never had a Russian girlfriend!' Mihaela started laughing at her cousin, translating for Dumitru and Monica.

'Vlad! A girlfriend!'

What a hullabaloo with us all in the room. Tuca had just arrived, yet to receive his whisky. Only Vlad was silent, wishing Mihaela had stayed at home.

I accepted another glass of *ţuică*. I thought it might just settle my stomach, steady my nerve. In fact it widened the grin I flashed around the room. Only sometimes did Vlad smile back, the gathering all too much for his seventeen-year-old sensibilities. The noise, the lack of dignity, everyone's straining effort to impress offended his morose outlook, as did his sudden pressing urge to get things right in his own shitty little flat.

That evening Elena noticed her son drank more than her husband.

Chicerea

Vlad wasn't sure about visiting his grandparents on the road to Bessarabia. His head throbbed (he hadn't slept well on the pull-out bed) and we'd have to take the bus. But I was persistent, keen to light old memories, desperate to break free of the flat and Elena was going anyway, as she did most weekends to help her ageing in-laws.

'Come on, it'll be fun!'

An hour later all three of us were in the minibus, hanging from the rail, Vlad balanced with Elena's bag of carefully sourced foods from the city market: a good salami, baking powder, two packets of coffee, a bag of sugar, detergent.

Vlad made a special effort to explain that his grandparents had changed; his grandmother was very deaf, everything had to be repeated twice and Gheorghe had lost his mind, sitting all day in the same chair, singing workers' songs or just talking to himself, occasionally getting excited and emphatic about an event long since passed.

'It is hard work for Grandma, especially now the weather is getting colder.'

The blue house I remembered felt smaller, with much of it shut off for winter. Anica and Gheorghe had moved into the central room where they huddled around a ceramic stove, Anica constantly feeding this vast cenotaph of heat as if it were a suckling child.

Maybe Anica remembered me. She kissed my hand and stroked my cheek before shuffling up the iron bed to make way for her guests. Elena was already busy, unpacking the provisions, bringing in a pan to heat the coffee. The afternoon passed easily. Gheorghe with his faded gaze talked lots of foreign nonsense and Elena let

Anica prattle about the neighbours and the new priest. I enjoyed the unlikely scene; this was the inner family, after all. Only Vlad was anxious to leave, embarrassed by the domestic intimacy, the throbbing pain in his head tight and precise in both temples. Eventually he stood, keen to take a cigarette outside. We left the house together.

The noise was sickening, the violent rip of hot moving rubber and an unforgettable, tortured scream that punctured the hushed up day. We both saw it happen. Vlad had been unlatching the gate, but immediately he was the solitary observer and I, part of the action, careering out after the car, my fist in the air, livid, screaming a volley of obscenities at the retreating vehicle.

'You bastards! Stop now you bastards and see what you've done!'

The squealing animal, blind-sided with pain, shuffled pathetically to the side of the road. I crouched down, unsure what to do next, stroking the pup as it quaked and recoiled under my touch.

Elena came to the gate to see about the commotion. She was relieved to discover it was just a wild dog, and surprised in equal measure that the foreign girl was now stumbling up the steps with the animal in her arms, tears flooding down her face.

'Christ, Vlad, it will be covered in fleas. Tell her to put it down!'

Vlad said nothing; instead he rubbed his face, desperate for a cigarette, aware he was somehow, suddenly, caught in the middle of something.

'They didn't stop! I can't believe they didn't stop. I mean that's illegal, surely? We'll have to do something. Poor little thing, it's broken its leg.'

'Vlad, tell her to put it down! See! It can stand, it hasn't broken its spine – it'll be fine. Leave it be. It's dirty.'

'Oh Vlad it's too big to kill with a stone – I can't face it. Do you have a gun? We'll have to put it out of its misery. We can't just leave it.'

A gun? Is she mad! There was no gun or stone, nor a willing

135

volunteer, and Elena shook her head at my hysteria. Now Anica came to the step in her bright shawl.

'Pah, these dogs get hit every day on that crazy road. Die like flies, they do. Last year we lost a child. Bloody Russians driving like madmen!'

Vlad stood still as I burled through the options, translating select chunks.

'She wants to use the phone to call a taxi, take it to a vet.' He gestured with his head towards the animal.

'What? A taxi! You think there's money coming from the sky. I couldn't afford to mend my own mother's arm. A taxi. It's a wild creature!'

'I can't believe your mum wants us to leave it, Vlad!'

'You must understand. This happens all the time, Tessa. You know we are . . . we are de-sensitised. They are killing dogs in Bucharest.'

Elena started to cry as I forced Vlad to call a taxi. Her mind was fuzzy with all the fuss and to think so much was to be spent on a dog. To the Big Mother above, had the blonde taken leave of her senses?'

It cost an extra ten dollars to persuade the taxi driver to let me in his car with a pup. Much later we'd laugh about our canine adventure but not that day – it was too raw. I desperately wanted to call my mother. I knew what she'd say.

'Darling, you absolutely did the right thing – and while it's at the vet's why don't you make sure it has all its vaccinations?'

But most of all, once the panic cleared, I longed for Vlad to forgive my outburst. I tried to explain it was different for me; I had the money for the operation. I began to tell him the story of the Good Samaritan. I needed him to understand.

'It's OK, Tessa. You don't need to quote the bible. I get it.'

And with the puppy now drugged and shaved on my knee, sitting in another taxi post-operation, I knew he got it and that was when I reached out with my free hand and held his, all the way back to his grandparents' house.

Vlad was alone making coffee in the kitchen. I stood in the doorway unannounced and watched.

'Morning! Sugar?'

'No. No sugar.'

He opened another tin and helped himself into one of the small cups and there we were drinking black coffee in the tiny space, propped against the side-board, back in Iaşi. It was my last day and Alin would already be waiting in the centre of town. I smiled hard as if to indelibly mark the gap between us so that something should remain, even when I was gone.

Vlad smiled back, constantly surprised that it might be the case I was once again in his life. Surprised, and a little more than that.

'What's so funny, Tess?'

'I spent £100 on a dog and it's going to spend its life chained up in your grandma's garden.'

'Don't worry. They'll let if off occasionally.'

'Do you think your mum's forgiven me?'

'There's nothing to forgive.'

I hadn't slept that night; I'd been exhausted but not sleepy. My mind wouldn't rest as I lay wakeful in Vlad's room (with the same sticker on the door). How could it be I felt so strongly about a boy curled up on a camp-bed in the next room? He was, after all, just a kid; not quite eighteen, and there I was plunged in doubt, even self-loathing, that I might somehow be a Nigel – pink, desperate, older and deeply inappropriate.

But daylight had eventually arrived; I'd survived the night with my own guilty longing, craving sweet Vlad beside me that I might hold him tight. (What the hell, Tessa?) Thank God instead to be safe with him in the kitchen.

I smiled, and looked to the floor before I checked him looking back at me. Vlad stayed where he was – he said nothing. What could he say? We were in north Romania and Vlad was skipping high school. We were very late for Alin. I searched his exquisite face so extraordinarily thin, and noticed there was a tiny smudge of decay on his two front teeth. I wanted to tell him he must look after his teeth. They were very important, was what I urgently wanted to say. Instead, I said: 'You know the stupid thing is I don't even really like dogs.'

Vlad led the way down the dark stairwell carrying my bag and wishing it wasn't all such a palaver – so many people, such commotion, and we were late.

He wasn't feeling himself. It really had been a very stressful weekend and then came the hurried, undignified departure at the station. His cousins insisted on crowding into my first class carriage to have a look. He felt sidelined, standing across the sliding door unsure what to say and then the whistle blew and the train lurched forward. It was time to go and he hated himself for caring that he never got a final hug. I had not said goodbye to him at the end (somehow Mihaela was always between us) and he felt hurt, angry that something so small could make him feel so bad.

Damn the girl who everybody wanted and who made him feel fussed and unsure, who'd arrived so suddenly, made a storm and left just like that.

Damn her and her patronising, confusing letter. He'd found it on his desk when he returned from the station. It lay expectant, a piece of graph paper carefully folded four times.

5am

My dear Vlad – I can't sleep (I think it's because I know I've got to go by train tonight), so I thought I would drop you a line. Besides the downfall of writing letters to people in foreign countries is the time it takes for them to arrive. I like the fact you will read this tonight after I've gone.

I can't tell you how much I've 100% loved my stay. You can hope, but you definitely can't know what, or how, things will turn out when a self-invited foreigner plonks herself into the lap

138

of a family for the weekend, a family where she once knew a bright proud Romanian boy.

And the proud bright Romanian boy is still proud and bright – he's just not 12 any more, which I find a bit disconcerting.

I'm sure your exams are going to be OK. Being a bit fatalistic helps. What will be, will be – and I've got a strong gut feeling you're a survivor. (Seeing you again I am starting to believe more in my gut feelings.)

I am sorry about the dog. Thank your dad for making her a nice kennel.

I've just heard him leave for work so I think it's time to sign off. You're not a kid any more, Vlad, which means if we're going to have a friendship worth keeping it's got to be two-way. (I might not be Romanian but I'm proud too, you know!) However, if and for whatever uniquely Vlad reason the idea of a blonde foreigner in your life is too hard to handle I guess I'll understand. Either way I'll always be there for you. I'm sorry for my silence, too – somehow I thought maybe I'd mucked everything up by bringing you to Scotland so young but, seeing you now, I don't think I did.

I wish there weren't so many years and miles between us.

With lots of love from a big fan,

TESS xxx

What the hell? Vlad ran a hand through his cropped hair, letting it rest on his nape, longing for a cigarette, dreading school the next day.

You're not a kid any more. So many years between us.

Vlad winced. What was I trying to say?

You're not a kid any more.

So why treat him like one then?

In fact I'd written five letters in the middle of the night. The remaining four I destroyed. They'd been much shorter and all began, 'Dear Vlad – I think I have fallen in love with you.'

Help.

*

Clatter-boom, clatter-boom – the night train, steel on steel all the way to Bucharest. Clatter-boom was my companion and a man in a tight-curled lambskin hat who shook his head at the sobbing woman spread across the seat in front of him.

'A flower to the ear,' he'd muttered knowingly when I arrived with my three young friends, crowding into the carriage, and I'd started to cry (again).

'A flower to the ear?'

'It's an expression,' explained Mihaela.

'An expression for what?'

'It means, everything is easy. You know, you've got it sorted!'

Was it then the train leapt forward? When Mihaela was holding me close, looking for the flowers in my ear?

'Bye bye . . . love you! Love you all!' I rushed and leant out of the window with all the flowers of the world pouring from my ear and, full tilt, stretched as my three jogged along the platform.

'Bye Vlad and be sure to write. Te pup! Va pup Alin, Mihaela!'

'Shut the window!' snapped the old man in the lamb's hat.

'Byeeeeee.'

'Current!'

'Byeeeeee.'

And I stayed where I was, out of the window with the freezing night whipping my face and the silhouettes of Iaşi's crazy industrial past glowering back at me. I hung there long after I'd lost sight of Vlad and his cousins, when there were only miles and miles of broken buildings etched against the black. The hat man shook his animal head.

'Shut the window, blonda!'

And I cried all the way to Bucharest, crying for the boy I had left and the longing that hurt me.

It was 6.30am, and I'd made it through security in good time. The shops were disappointing, the coffee revolting and I was, after all, still in his country, not yet airborne. Surely it would be OK if I called him? There were lei to spare for the payphone. God, why the need for an excuse?

Please, please let Vlad answer. Please! I'll tell him I arrived safely. Surely he would like to know that?

Vlad was wearing a white cotton vest, thick and matching his Y-fronts. He was in the bathroom splashing water on his face, feeling groggy, and that was when the phone rang.

'Alo,' his voice not yet warm.

'Oh, have I woken you up?'

'No. I was awake. Getting ready for school.'

'I just rang . . . I just rang to say I had arrived. At the airport.'

And Vlad stood holding the telephone, a chill running over his bare skin, relieved his parents had left for work, knowing that in some way this call was significant.

'Good, did you get a cab?'

'Yes.'

Pause.

'And I called to say I miss you.'

Bip-bip-bip

'I . . . I miss you, too.'

Bip

He missed me. I loved him, and he missed me.

CHAPTER NINE

Chicerea, December '99

Vlad looked away, pulling on the wire in his hand, cutting through his palm, the pain near reassuring as his father continued shouting an agitated string of commands. The knife! Get a sharper knife! Dumitru hold it by the mouth! Roll the God-forsaken beast on its back! And the sow screamed like only a pig could, its rump in the snow and pale eyes with fine fair lashes turned skywards. Pell-mell it had crashed about the enclosure until, cornered – its hind legs lassoed, with Vlad and Dumitru, father and mad grandfather pinning it down – Tuca cut its throat. There was a noise no human could know until they heard it, and so much blood, its yellow piss staining the snow and hitting Vlad's boot. Elena crossed her chest – for the love of God and Christmas!

Like an imp, childish and full of glee, Tuca hopped around the burning pyre, readying himself for the first, fine cracked skin from the pig's chest, charred and crispy, sprinkled in salt – this was a feast, no? And somehow it was wrong not to take that first scraping of swine in their fingers outside, where the sun had dipped and the cold was intense and the pig fat and skin were warm and beyond words. Vlad was glad to be alive.

'Crăciun fericit!'

And so it was a good Christmas. Smoked sausage, fingers of fat and hunks of porky meat; even the gristle, ear, trotters (set in jelly, bound in a bladder) were too good to waste. It was pig for breakfast, lunch and dinner. With his parents in the countryside for the week Vlad opted to return to the city with a bag of meat, to work for his exams (at least, that was the intention).

It was back at the flat over a late morning snack – pig's liver – and with an inhibiting hangover that he realised there was something missing. It was not a big deal and he'd only just noticed as he sat opposite the near bare kitchen wall, but Mrs Dunlop hadn't sent her annual Christmas card, the one with the ages of all the animals and the Dunlop clan's progress through life. Elena had received a packet from me – a long excessive letter of thanks, which Vlad only half-translated, and a collar and lead for the dog – but my mother had not written and, thinking about it, Vlad was glad. He hadn't let himself dwell on my visit or my absence, even when he received a second ambiguous letter. Nevertheless, deep down he knew that if a card had arrived from Mrs Dunlop it would've seemed even weirder than previously.

Rannoch

Mum was filling a water container in the dog kennel for the vast white turkey Dad had bought at the mart. Once again she felt relieved that it was such a plain bird. Really, it was very difficult to feel sympathy for a creature so ugly, its fleshy body supporting a scraggy wattle and red pinhead. There was surely no room for a brain in that tiny skull? The sooner Donald wrung its neck the better. She clicked shut the kennel door, wondering how on earth she would fit the monster into her oven, and that was when the telephone rang. Helter-skelter, she ran back to the house.

'Hello!'

'Hi Mum. It's me. Sorry about last week. Sorry I haven't called sooner . . . '

'Oh don't worry, darling. It's just exhausting keeping up with you.'

Actually Mum hadn't thought it was OK but decided the best way of dealing with our last conversation was to ignore it, and in that way we could all have a jolly time over Christmas, seeing in the new millennium.

But I didn't want to ignore *it*. I wanted to share *it*.

'It won't go away, Mum. I know you don't believe me but I can't ignore my feelings. Why are you sighing?'

'Darling . . . ' She let out another long breath. 'It's just you chop and change like the wind. One minute you bring an Asian boxer home for Christmas, the next he's off the cards. Then there was the Jewish saxophone player – he lasted all of three weeks. Not forgetting the South African rugby player and that strange rower.'

'That's not fair, Mum. Anyway Vlad is . . . different.'

'You say that about all of them. And to be fair they all are *very* different. It's hard to keep up.'

'So what are you saying? You don't believe that I've fallen in love with Vlad?'

'It's not that I don't believe you, darling. It's just that, well, he is *very* young and *very* far away and I'm sure there's someone nice just around the corner. You need a good man to take you in hand.'

'What? Oh God forget I ever mentioned it!'

To give Mum her due, she had been trying to do just that – which is why Vlad, for the first time in five years, did not receive a Christmas card.

London

Dear Tessa – You've just left and I miss you so much.

Thanks for the postcard you've sent from Iaşi. I was surprised and impressed about it.

What do you think about Vlad? Has he changed or is he still a boy (that boy you knew then)? When I saw him I thought he was a good-looking!

I want you to tell me about the time you spent in Iaşi after we left. Did you go to the casino? What about your new job announcing? Do you like it there? I really want you to write me back. I learn, learn . . . for university.

Anyway not much room left, I'll write another letter soon.

Millions hugs and kisses and a very happy Christmas and 2000.

OLIVIA, DOINA, RADU

144

Olivia had covered the page in love hearts and enclosed a postcard of a white highland terrier. In yellow Romanian italics the caption read: *I can't forget you, don't you forget me.*

I found the letter on the doormat of my new London lodgings shortly before Christmas. The envelope was covered in clusters of stamps and I knew immediately it was from Romania.

For just a second I let myself believe it was from Vlad. That it was in Olivia's hand turned her sweet prose into a bitter disappointment.

I took it down to my basement room and cried a little for what it wasn't. Only after my tears did I see beyond the sender to disembowel the contents. I read and re-read the letter, snagging each time on the same sentence. *When I saw him I thought he was a good-looking!* Initially I was flattered that Olivia should be moved to write so generously about Vlad with his pronounced nose and angular body. Until then it hadn't occurred to me that anyone else might find him attractive. But the arrival of her letter changed that; a simple compliment from the other side of Europe upset my equilibrium and took away any certainty. For successive nights afterwards, when sleep eventually plunged me under, I would wake suddenly, panicked that my Vlad, my dear, silent Vlad was prey for all bony black-eyed Romanian girls.

Agitated, sometimes even breathless, I'd stumble from my bed to try and find words for a letter – *the* letter. Hours I spent crying, writing, rewriting thoughts I never dared send. Words on paper, rectangular over-used signposts, hateful symbols that mocked my anguish, transcribing it into mawkish, generic platitudes. They embarrassed me, that I might be so ordinary. And anyway it was hopeless – I could never declare my love from so many miles away. The letter might not arrive. I might go mad waiting. He might choose not to reply.

Maybe I revolted him. Maybe he resented me. Why did I neglect him for five years? He was a different person then. He was a child but had altered to fit the model of a man. He was a manboy, a sweet innocent hybrid. My Vlad. My destiny.

No, I simply couldn't send a letter I wrote in the middle of the night; I didn't trust my tired mind. Always I crumpled up my efforts. I would wait for sober morning light with its small reassuring routines.

It may seem odd that I was so affected by one letter from a young eighteen-year-old but it was all I had to go on. If Olivia piqued my possessive passion she was also the first person who set out clearly what I thought I already knew; arriving from thousands of miles away there it was, in smudgy ink, the proof Vlad had *something*.

I could tell my friends Claire, Hina, Annabel how altered I felt – I could show them photos of a very thin Romanian teenager and they would smile sympathetically – but they couldn't begin to believe it. That left Olivia, or rather her letter, as my accomplice. My proof! It wasn't just me being weird, casting about and building castles in the sky as I pronounced on a double bill of *The Golden Girls* at 11pm in London's West End.

'And next on Expedient TV is a real treat, we are heading over to Miami Florida for double trouble . . . '

'Slow it down a bit, Tessa, and you could sound more upbeat. We want to keep people watching.'

Nigel swivelled around in his chair, tapping the remote control to switch off the recording. His nails were cut very straight and I wondered if he paid to have them polished.

I stayed focused on his creamy hands with their splayed idle fingers. This was my second de-briefing in a week. In other words, Nigel wanted a date in his diary and I wanted more shifts in mine. Nigel got his date so that I could get my way and make him believe he might get his.

Still, I didn't touch him other than through his shoulder pads – another reassuring pat and a vague promise at the end of the night once I'd listened to the story of his first divorce, his lewd pink tongue moving and working for him and then telling the tale of his second wife (poor unfortunate creature). I listened – that's what he

146

liked – and nodded sympathetically. And occasionally, where there was an opening, when his fat mouth fell slack, I sought to convince him my voice was the right voice. No, not too posh! Really Nigel! Not out of touch! And again I sat and smiled and hated him and longed for Vlad over the table in front of me and God, sweet Jesus, just to stop thinking about a seventeen-year-old as Nigel thought of me – wanting, pressing, wheedling for what was fresh and young and out of reach.

Iaşi, January 2000

Elena absentmindedly tapped the snow from her boots before entering the block. She had not yet managed to shake the worry about her son. That morning she'd definitely heard him talking under his bedcover and yet nobody was there. She could safely say this as she'd been standing in the doorway and Vlad had continued to talk to an invisible something.

She flicked open the metal box – the one with *TOMA* on the front – and slipped the envelope into her pocket. It was from the foreign girl. It was the third letter in as many months. The first had been addressed to her, the most recent ones to Vlad. He'd only just made it to school that morning after his two-way conversation with no one, but Elena knew today, like yesterday, he wouldn't learn much. Vlad, her brightest son, with his grandfather's height and father's self-destruction: that stubborn refusal to see beyond his wretched impression of the world. *Vai* Vlad! What has happened to my Vlad?

Elena wouldn't say anything; it simply wasn't her way. She laid the foreign letter on his bed and straightened the eiderdown before retreating to the TV still reporting strikes, lots of them. What a mess, thought Elena, as she at last heard Vlad's key in the latch, relieved he'd made it home.

10th January 2000
Dear Vlad – I wonder how you are. I think about you and your

family often and still remember so fondly my weekend in Iaşi. I am OK. I'm still doing continuity announcing (my boss is gross) but luckily I've just clinched my first shifts on a call-in radio station, which has been my dream for ages – I'll let you know what it's like talking in the middle of the night.

I was so inspired by my stay with you that I've started having Romanian lessons with a woman at the World Service. She left Romania just after the Revolution so I reckon she must have had contacts! Acum pot să scriu un pic!

I wonder how the studying is going for your exams. I woke up in the middle of the night last night having a vivid dream that my Oxford finals were days away. I had a horrible, sick, uncontrollable feeling in the pit of my stomach. The fact I still dream about eight three-hour exams four years on means sitting here now I can sympathise with what you're going through. Horrible! Still, they'll be over before you know it. In the meantime I am thinking of you.

I know you won't have time to write but send an email if you can. I dream of returning to your country – please tell me when. I think of you often.

Your friend etc.

Tess xxx

P.S. How is the dog?
P.P.S. Happy New Year!

Vlad lay back on his bed and tried to picture me, his blonde friend who'd held his hand, but he was having difficulty. The memories were threadbare, overworked in his muddled mind. Recently the recollections had become increasingly faint, almost dreamlike. The reality was slipping (had it been real?) and my letter made it worse. Vlad did have a *horrible, sick, uncontrollable feeling* but it wasn't the exams that worried him; it was his inability to hold it, or anything, together. He let my letter drop to the floor, curled into his duvet and vowed to never take another hallucinogenic again.

It was Elena who picked it up and popped it in the cardboard box beside Vlad's Strathallan correspondence and my mother's many Christmas cards.

London, April 2000

Goddamn working in the middle of the night. My new radio show began at two in the morning and ended at six. My agent dubbed it 'the early morning breakfast show', which I thought showed spirit on her part. For mine, staying sane amid a sea of like-minded insomniacs and drifters who phoned in was the most I could hope for. The rest of the day and night unravelled somewhat unpredictably, which was fine so long as no one saw me.

My lodgings at the bottom of a Victorian town house in Clapham belonged to two civil servants, Jean and Tim. Unfortunately, talking to strangers all night and too much electric light did for me by daybreak when I'd keep bumping into them as they readied to leave for work and I came back from mine. The conversation was always stilted. Was it my bike or me they objected to? Sometimes I was crying, which made it worse. Jean felt awkward. I could tell by the way she hovered, shifting her weight from one foot to the other. She even asked me if I wanted to join them at their country dancing class on Thursday evening, an invitation I politely declined.

At least when I woke in the middle of the day they were gone and the house empty. I could feast on their food and walk the four floors mug in hand, often stopping to talk to the majestic portraits lining the stairs – what plain ancestors they had! But no matter how peckish or in need of tea my first move was always the same. Smeared in sleep, not yet dressed, every day I took the basement stairs two at a time to see what, if anything, the postman had brought.

It was there, on the non-slip doormat beneath Jean's English Heritage subscription, I found Olivia's letter and some months later a second letter from Romania in a loopy hopeful hand. From Mihaela.

2nd April 2000

Dear Tessa – I am writing to wish you a very happy Easter and send to you the best of my wishes.

I am missing you very much and want you to know that I had a very good time while you were here. Next time I hope that you will stay with me and for a long time.

Everyone is making a lot of traditional food and they are working very hard to prepare their houses and their meal for Easter. They are very happy and waiting with a lot of joy for the rising of Jesus from the dead. They will go to the churches with their red eggs and their Easter cakes.

Outside it's warm and nice and very pleasant – God's weather and a perfect time for Easter.

I send you all of my best wishes and love from the Lord. And I thank you once again for the time we spent together.

Please forgive me for not writing sooner and for any spelling mistakes.

With lots of love,

MIHAELA

I didn't tell Jean and Tim about Romania or Vlad. They would've worried about their telephone bill and anyway Vlad didn't write so I didn't ring. He didn't send me an email either. He didn't have a computer but he'd given me an address so every night at work I logged on, hopeful, nurturing a delicious sense of anticipation (just in case).

But every night was the same. No email from Vlad – nothing. Just the usual mutterings from late night nutters, administrative clutter from office bureaucrats and more Easter cheer, this time from Siret.

Dragă Tessa,
Christ has risen!
Love from Olivia and family
Many kisses xxxxxxx

I emailed back:

That is true, he has risen indeed!
Love Tessa xxx

Who was I to burst their bubble? And I wondered, not for the first time, how so many Romanians stayed faithful with so little to go on. Vlad, I knew to be an atheist. Initially this cheered me, that we might share a similar cynical worldview. But now, after many silent months, I fervently wished he might find faith, anything, something that he might see the sign and write. Please Lord! I needed a miracle.

My fifth letter to Vlad I wrote in a café by Waterloo Bridge as the sun came up. It was rush hour and I felt woozy despite the caffeine.

20th May 2000

Dear Vlad – Are you still alive? I miss hearing from you. Actually that's not strictly true as I haven't heard from you so it's not possible to miss it. Ha. I guess you must be in the middle of your exams by now or maybe they're finished or haven't started. To be honest I obviously have no idea when Romania has its exams. Anyway I hope they go OK.

I have just finished on the radio and all the commuters are coming into the coffee shop where I am for their coffee and sugar croissants – they look pink and disappointed. I'm disappointed I've not heard from you.

I hear a lot from my regular callers – they keep me sane with their insanity. I have Gary in Westcliffe-on-Sea (or mud, as he jokes). He receives disability allowance (free money) and his favourite sport is the breast stroke (ha ha Gary) – I like him the best and try to help him win the competitions. Selina from Bromley is a woman but she sounds like a man because she's had a sex change and the hardest thing to get right is the voice. She's been practising her exercises on air. She's skint, too, because her operations were so expensive and one they didn't get right so she has pubes growing inside her new fanny . . . eeewww! Oh yes and there's Jonathan who rings every night and reckons he's a virgin but I don't believe him.

Everybody in the night has problems including insomnia and me for company. Going to cycle home now to bed. Looks like it's going to be a scorcher, which means I will sleep like shit.

Do you want me to send you some free music – there's loads at the station although I don't think much is heavy stuff. No blood on the covers.

This is my last letter until I hear from you as I feel like an idiot writing by myself all the time.

Love (a bit grudgingly),

Your friend,

TESSA xxx

Iaşi, June 2000

'Yes yes yes . . . arghhh . . . yes!'

And the table crashed over; there was the snap of broken glass – a window maybe? Or the frosted pane in the door? Who gives a fuck? Vlad dug his face hard into the shoulder of Dragoş – could the sun shine any brighter? He lifted his head for air, into a wall of noise and swung his hands high up above his head, jumping beyond the other heads and hands.

> *Awaken thee Romania!*
> *We've fucked the English!*
> *Ah ha we've smashed the English!*
> *Our enemy has died*
> *Awaken thee ROMAAANIA!*

How they weaved their magic across the pitch and up and down, and the predicted soggy draw was not fair – Christ it was unfair – but supporting Romania was so impossibly tough. That's what they were saying then somehow a clumsy, ugly English boy delivered a foul as God wanted and surely must have demanded to give Romania a penalty in the last minute. Hello Italy! Goodbye England! Hello last sixteen and summer and life and *yes* fucking *yes. ROMAAANIA!*

It was later that same night and Alin was making an unfamiliar growling sound in his throat and down into the microphone, which he was holding very tight, his leathered limbs jerking in sudden spasms to the noise, only sometimes interrupted by a wail of feedback. Vlad thought the room was too small – it was certainly too hot and he was drunk. They were all pissed up on Romania's victory and post-exam euphoria. The Psychedelic Wolves were gigging, or at least that's what Alin called it, and Vlad noticed they had a new singing (dancing?) girl. Anyway she was shaking up and down at the front of the room, her body in something tight and black with sequins in her hair and one glove on the hand that was beating the air, thrashing at it with a delicate white wrist. 'Yeeeaaahhh and so Satan's worshippppppp . . . yeeeaaahhh . . . ahh . . . ahh . . . '

Her breath was sweet and warm and Vlad didn't remember much more – just that it must have been an easy fumble (clumsy as he was), and she had seemed briefly keen in the dark, against the wall, and he didn't need to apologise. There was no need to apologise.

Vlad didn't mention her to Alin the next day. It was, he knew, a lucky one-off. After all, he had no chest to push out and no set of car keys to leave, silver and shiny on the table. Even Alin had a pair of leather trousers. Vlad considered himself different (above?) the showy pricks with their mobile phones and waxy hair. Goddamn the slippery system that had made a few peasant parents the lucky ones so their sons could strut and swagger and drink fizzy orange to drive their cars back home at the end of the night. Unless *tata* was in the police, in which case they could drink whatever the hell they liked.

No, Vlad wouldn't see her again, but he'd liked the taste of her, her warm musky smell. There he was, a drunken defender setting up a surprise goal until she pulled away, moving on through the smoky party mood, leaving Vlad with his cup of beer and a hot, unfinished feeling in his pants.

London

Claire was leaning in towards the TV. 'Come on England! Oh come on!'

I was sitting on her sofa, sucking the back of my hand. Why was Claire supporting England? She hated football and its vulgar national badge, Kevin Keegan with his simple sentences, Shearer and Owen and the razzamatazz surrounding so few for so little, so over-hyped and under-skilled. *EnGERland.*

'You've got to support them, Tess!'

'Why? I'm Scottish.'

'But you live in England.'

'Inside I am Scottish. Anyway I want Romania to win.'

And so England lost when all they had to do was draw. Claire switched off the telly and made a pot of tea and I thought of Vlad, how happy he would be, all buoyed up on thin air and expectation and he'd never written so now I wished that England had won.

At least that would've pleased Ben. Ben was sleek, black, cool. He looked crisp in his chef whites spinning out one-liners and serving up lasagne at 1am.

'All wight! It's my favourite blonde.'

He liked my shiny hair pushed up off my shoulders in clips, and my arms defined from the cycling.

'Hi Ben, surprised you're here tonight! Thought you'd be out, drowning your sorrows.'

'And leave you all by yourself? Nah, couldn't do that.'

It was that same night, after he'd made good in the staff canteen, Ben set out to find me on the fourth floor in my studio. He gingerly pushed his head around the heavy door, beneath the red mic light, and waggled a polystyrene cup of coffee out in front. Here he was in my space and for one brief moment I didn't recognise him as I talked on to Selina, into the night.

I'd cocked the headphones off one ear and was nodding at Ben who handed over the coffee on the end of his very smooth forearm.

'Thanks Ben.'

He turned to blow me a kiss before closing the door and I wished he'd stayed. I had no callers left.

It was just a matter of time. I knew it, and Ben knew it.

'Once you've had sex, that's it. There is nothing to stop you having it again.' Mum sighed. She didn't think young girls should have sex, even though she knew (and liked) lots of young girls who did.

So I'd held on to this thing, this precious social membrane called virginity, until I'd almost finished at Oxford when I met an Afrikaner rugby player who took on a bet he could go where no man had gone before. Pier and I bought a green futon together in honour of the anticipated event and went out for a curry beforehand. He went on top smelling of spiced mushrooms. The next morning Pier tied a knot in the soiled pink condom and told me I should keep it for my scrapbook. I rolled over and wondered when he would ask me to marry him. I was dumped within two weeks.

Prophylactic anxiety remained a preoccupation well into my adult life. It prohibited pleasure and any relationship was short-lived (four weeks my record; the man in question blessed with an unusually low libido).

After our November together I often wondered about Vlad – surely he was a virgin? I flushed at my relief that this might be the case and imagined unwrapping him like a caterpillar prized early from its cocoon, then chastened myself for entertaining such thoughts.

Had I imagined it? Maybe.

'Man I don't see the point in badminton. It's such a nothing sport!'

Ben and I were watching the 2000 Sydney Olympics – pictures, no sound – the privileged few to see firsthand what happened in the name of nationhood on the other side of the world before ours woke up and we went to sleep. I played longer tracks and took fewer callers, looking for any excuse to stretch time and keep Ben amused and sitting there, watching me watching Britain chasing shuttlecocks in the semis.

'Don't be such a cliché, Ben. Sport's not all about Spurs and running fast.'

'Maaan, yous thinks I'm a cleeeeché?' (He extended his vowel sounds – mocking, playful, slightly pissed off.)

I stood up and handed over to him as he kissed at me in the corner of the studio. I chose the song (five minutes long).

Britain didn't make the badminton final and Ben came back to the basement five weeks after our first coffee. He wore a condom. I insisted and kept my head in the pillow when he stopped what he was doing to slide it on, the smell of latex briefly interrupting the fug of sex. When it was over Ben patted me on the bottom.

'Well, that's the first time I've shagged posh white totty.'

After our morning together I cut Ben off like a caller on the radio. In future I would pack my own supper to eat in the studio and he never again came by with coffee from the canteen. I felt sullied; I'd betrayed the Vlad I had not touched. I'd penetrated the thin perfect film between us. The frosted glaze now had a crack in it and I was screaming beneath the imperfect surface looking up at Vlad, whose face had a soft sure clarity for the first time in months.

Help.

London, September 2000

My radio show by now had its own late night pulse. Autumn was closing in and the nights blurred into weeks as my own little on-air soap opera crackled with real people who knew all about each other but had never met. We shared cures for sleeplessness, recipes, jokes, likes and dislikes. They knew about my childhood in Scotland, my basement room with mildew on the walls and my bicycle accident across Waterloo Bridge. But I never told them about my thoughts for Vlad. I didn't trust my feelings any more (he still hadn't written) and, besides, on-air it was better surely to be single?

I was well looked after by my listeners. We were, after all, kindred spirits; united by our wakeful state. Betty in Bermondsey, eighty-three, sent me homemade Turkish Delight, an anonymous religious maniac posted me a crisp ten pound note in an envelope every week and Chris the cabbie got over-familiar. I struggled to control his manic chat on air and sometimes he even waited for me in the foyer of the station before the show began – a tall man with chewed nails and virulent loathing of Tony Blair.

'Elo Tess, eh, thought you'd be interested in this book, it's something I'm taking very seriously. A way of galvanising the people!'

This was a man who had told me (and the bit of London that was listening) about his marital breakdown, his infertility and his hatred of the Establishment and I had listened, gaily signing off with 'lots of love' – but now, in the flesh, I struggled to look him in the eye. Too much had been said on-air. I took a sidestep, nodding all the while, surprised by his height and the intensity of his tired face.

'Eh Tess, looking forward to the show! You should get on daytime.'

'Thanks Chris . . . thanks!'

I pushed through the turnstile and headed for the lift. I looked forward to busying in the hour before the show began; time to check my emails, read the first editions and chat things through with Dad (for a more 'mature' perspective) before going live.

But that night Dad stayed awake in vain. I didn't call. I didn't read a single front page. I sat immobile, rigid with disbelief, before my computer screen.

> *Toma Vlad*
> *Re: How are you?*

My heart thumped in my chest, my veins expanded and extended painfully in every limb until my body ached with too much blood. I couldn't hear what my producer was saying, the whirring sound of the computer and my heart in my head so loud. Too loud. Oh my God, I have got an email from Vlad! Oh. My. God.

I am going to click on it. I am lining up the arrow. Thank you, Lord. Thank you.

Dearest Tessa – I'm sorry I haven't written for such a long time. I have been busy with exams (I'm a student at a quite good university in Iaşi). Alin was admitted into Med school and we're planning on some fun.

If you still want to keep in contact, I hope I'll hear from you soon.

Love,

Vlad

P.S. Dog OK – Mum has called it Păpuşă (doll), after you.

'Look! Look! He's got in touch!'

It was nineteen hours since I first opened Vlad's email. Of course I'd printed it off immediately and kept the piece of paper in sight throughout the show, occasionally picking it up to read again.

Dearest sorry contact hope love Vlad

I took it to bed with me but I didn't sleep and now I thrust it, the paper soft and slightly soiled from too much fingering, at Claire. She read it and said nothing.

'Well?'

'He doesn't give you much to go on, does he?'

Claire didn't see what I saw. She saw a poor excuse for correspondence from a boy clearly at a loose end after his exams. And she looked up at me and saw a tired face, luminous with inexplicable joy.

'Have you replied?'

'No, not yet.'

What I didn't tell Claire was that I wanted to hold on to this feeling, the euphoria of having finally been contacted after ten months, for just a little bit longer. As soon as I wrote back I would be waiting again, and I couldn't face that. Not yet.

Iaşi

Vlad tipped his chair away from the computer and signalled for five more minutes at the dude with headphones. He'd known not to bother. Why had he? Vlad's inbox was empty and he'd failed to resist a sudden urge to send a second mail.

He'd entered the cramped computer dug-out on an entirely separate mission: he wanted quantity control for his small harvest of Liberty Caps sourced on the hill behind his grandmother's garden. He didn't want to overdo it. As he flicked impatiently between search engines, occasionally losing the connection, he realised I'd not replied to his email so sent another and immediately wished he hadn't.

17 September 2000 09.27
Dear Tessa – I'm really sorry I didn't keep contact this summer, believe me. This is my try to make you change your mind. I will perfectly understand you if you won't reply.
Hope to hear from you,
Vlad

Then his session timed out and the dude didn't do freebies, not even for five minutes and certainly not for someone he didn't know. Vlad left feeling frustrated, poor and powerless.

Elena had returned to Iaşi from the countryside the same day with a clutch of eggs wrapped in paper and a container of soured wheat stock. Back in the flat, alone and settled, she turned over Uncle Bogan's assurance in her head. Vlad had got onto the best course in Iaşi – that was what he told the whole family. According to Bogdan Robotics and Computing was the degree most likely to get you a proper job; something modern, technical, with good pay.

Elena was pleased. She had always known Vlad was her brightest son. And now, in her place beside the sink, she allowed herself a moment's pause, a brief second of rare contemplation to think about how things might have been different for her. If only. How she privately, fleetingly, wished for her time again so that she might skip the polytechnic school and what came next. Elena, her father's oldest (and favourite) daughter, had gone off early to the big city. Walking over the hill holding her mother's hand – she remembered as if it were yesterday – through the yellow toadflax and dried stubby grasses that prickled her bare legs, and on to the small station and new life that she'd not chosen, arriving hugga mugga with all the other fourteen-year-old girls and boys in the same situation, spewing out into Iaşi.

There had been obligatory schooling – general science, maths, Romanian, Russian – all straightforward enough to leave plenty of time for the technical learning by factory foremen. They barked and commandeered great gaggles of girls teeming through the vast interior of the panelled complex, standing and staring at the appointed stop-spots.

'And here, comrades, is where you will learn to be socialist workers securing the future of a great Romania!'

There was washing and treating, spinning and colouring, cutting and sewing, packing and exporting. Each floor with its own smell and rhythm; the tang of bleach, looms clack-clacking, motes of cotton dust and an inconsistent *thum* driven on by pedal-powered sewing machines. Elena's head buzzed with the noise of over-whelming production and that first night and every night for months after she kept her eyes down, in the canteen, up the factory stairs and across the maze of blocks to bed. Always she scanned the ground just in case. In case she chanced on the surprising shimmer of fallen coins – just enough for a trainfare back home.

Marcica, the next sister, joined her two years later but trained instead to be a school teacher. For Elena, however, one of the first generation sucked early into the city, it was too late and work would always be among the rows and rows of Floor One, alongside her designated pedal-powered sewing machine and sister comrades all pressed in blue, save for the obligatory yellow headscarves, a sinister splash of colour that said where they were from (men's pants, Floor One) and where they were going (men's pants, Floor One). And that was how it was for thirty years.

Elena, still standing at the sink, remembered training herself not to think – for what good did thoughts do? She had learnt to be, not to feel, and so it was. But as she rubbed around the rim of her frying pan on that warm September day, with firm fingers and a dash of detergent, she felt suddenly and enormously glad Vlad had got on the best course in Iași. Well done him.

London

Again at work, again in the middle of the night, I sat in front of that second email from Vlad. The sight of *Toma Vlad* in my inbox was marginally less impactful the second time around. Now I was experiencing and savouring the tangible sensation of delight fused with power. Finally it was my turn (it had been a long ten months). By withholding my response I was now the perpetrator of pain. He wanted *me* to contact *him*. The second email proved that. And my failure to respond immediately proved my love was ordinary – how disappointing.

Of course I was going to respond; indeed I had thought of little else since the first email eight days earlier. I'd already begun several long-hand letters. I wrote numerous drafts in excited blue ink. I used lots of jaunty exclamation marks, and chatted about this and that. They were not so very different from any of the other letters I'd sent. I still had nothing much to go on. But my style was more assured. In the final draft I wrote he was *special* and signed off, *Your friend always, Tess xxxxxxxx* – and: *Well well well well done in you exams! Now you can take over the world! Xxxx P.P.S. Now your exams are over can I come and visit? Or maybe you fancy a trip to London???*

I asked Hina to add a footnote. 'Please, just write a bit at the bottom. Please!'

Hina sighed. She felt compromised. She didn't know this boy Vlad – not any longer, not for six years – but she knew all about my obsession. She'd watched me shred my mind for the best part of a year (and hers in the process). And I wanted her as my conspirator; to write a little message to take the sting out of my covert longing, to keep things friendly, upbeat, *normal*. I needed Hina's seal of approval – I near begged her for it.

161

'Oh all right then.' And in beautiful calligraphy she reluctantly wrote:

Dear Vlad or should I call your Mr Toma for I see from Tessa's photographic evidence you have grown into a fine strapping young man! (Sorry to sound like your auntie.) You must come to London as soon as you can – I promise NOT to drag you on a sight-seeing bus but would love to catch up. Tess is your UK agent. Hope you're happy and well. We'll see you very soon I am sure.
    Love from Hina

'Tessa, only very young girls and old women are meant to find adolescent boys attractive.'

'What d'you mean?'

'You know, flat stomach, downy cheeks, vulnerable reckless beauty – it's hardly breeding material! The look doesn't last.'

'I'm not looking for a breeder.'

Hina smiled, her eyes moving up from the letter. 'Not now, but you will be.'

'What?'

'Oh come on.'

'What are you trying to say, Hina?'

'Sure, go back to Romania and get Vlad out of your system. But don't pin all your hopes on him.'

'What if he doesn't leave my system? Anyway that wouldn't be fair. He, I mean . . . he's, well, young.'

'That's half the appeal, isn't it? The taboo of a reluctant new boy? Do you think men worry?' She puckered her lips.

I threw my pen at her. Hina was testing me. She'd do this sometimes; prod me with the conventions of my class and the contradictions of desire. I wasn't sure where being Asian and Muslim left her and sex in modern Britain, so I was the open book and she the wide-eyed adjudicator; sassy, smarter than me and all too good at forcing honesty – even, self-reflection.

I had tried Ben, knitting, Red Bull, Antonia Fraser – but nothing helped me through the nights like thinking of Vlad. And Hina knew that, although privately she struggled to get beyond the idea of him as the thirteen-year-old boy who she once showed around Oxford and subsequently sent a Mr Bean Christmas card to.

Xmas '95

Dear Vlad – How do you know when you've passed an elephant? You can't shut the loo seat.

  Ha!

  Love,

HINA x

Iaşi, December 2000

Vlad was meant to be in college. Everybody else was at work but he couldn't face the Robotics and Computing course. It was relentlessly dry and his fellow students obscenely keen; a desire to get on, up, out seeping from their shining pores as they burrowed into their books and spat back logarithms and mechanical equations. There was a place in the world waiting for each and every one of them, thought Vlad, resenting their focus and wondering how he was going to stomach the next five years. The following day he and Andrei ducked class. And the next. And the next. Fuck it, thought Vlad. And the next.

There he was home alone without even a hangover as an excuse, staring at Ion Iliescu who was smiling as usual. He had good reason to smile, beaming out from the TV screen at his people, elected president for an inexcusable third time. Vlad felt sick just watching him, this grinning fool, a schmuck who trotted out any ridiculous line to get his grubby mitts back on the tiller. Here was a wolf in sheep's clothing, educated in Moscow, flirting with Brussels. In disgust Vlad flicked off the TV and let himself out of the flat before his mother returned from work.

On his way he checked the Toma letterbox. Nothing. No Christmas card from Mrs Dunlop or Tessa. It annoyed him that the

163

silence after three months still stung. After he sent me his second email Vlad checked his account almost daily, but two weeks went by with nothing and he got pissed off. Small beer and single cigarettes from the kiosk below his block were sacrificed so he could pay to feel shit about himself, logging on to an account that wanted to sell him a penis extension or a yeast infection remedy, an account with no acknowledgement from me. How foolish he felt for having let himself believe for a second in something so clearly impossible. He snapped shut the metal flap on the letterbox, vowing he wouldn't check it again.

Unbeknown to me my letter with Hina's additions hadn't reached Vlad. A postal worker in Bucharest must've fancied the four sample CDs obligingly declared on the front of the foreign package.

So there it was – the chain had been broken. I sent a follow up email a few weeks later. And again another one in December, but by that time Vlad had stopped logging on; he would not play the hopeful fool. And I didn't write again. What was the point if you didn't get a reply?

London

I was to present a lunchtime show on the radio come Christmas Day. A chance to demonstrate my potential, the editor assured me, keen to finish off his festive schedule. So I agreed, wondering how I would manage so far from home at my favourite time of year. I'd never missed a Christmas in Scotland.

As it happened the radio station was deserted, but across London solitary fans rang in and played a silly guessing game with their silly hostess. I went back to the basement after broadcast and listened to the civil servants share their festive spirit above my head before I caved in and rang home.

'Hi Mum. Happy Christmas!'

'Hello darling! Happy Christmas! Heavens it's beautiful here, we are laden down with snow and there's more to come.'

'Mum, I'm only happy on-air.'

164

'Sorry sweetheart?'

'I am only happy on-air – I can forget all my worries and talk to my friends.'

'Friends?'

'My regular callers. They need me.'

'They're not friends, though. You don't know what they're really like.' Mum clicked her lips.

'How do you know what anyone's really like?'

'OK darling, chin up. So sorry you're not here but I must scuttle now – got a million things about to boil over and your father's bawling as usual.'

'Mum. Before you go . . . '

'Yes?'

'Did you send Vlad a Christmas card?'

'What? No, no – I didn't. You're not still hung up on him are you?'

'No. Yes. Oh forget it. Happy Christmas.'

I put down the phone. I couldn't bear hearing the festive clatter – my brothers banging their snowy boots on her kitchen floor and Dad leaving to collect the village waifs for their annual Christmas dinner with the Dunlops.

'It's a jolly lonely time for people without family,' was my mother's festive mantra.

I wanted some Christmas cheer. I wanted someone to collect me in a Maxi and feed me turkey. But most of all, I wanted to talk to Vlad. I wanted to scream, hit, kick, love and laugh with him, at him, everything about him. I wanted Vlad (or at least what I could remember of him).

I was a drunk eyeing the bottle. I'd been sober for fourteen months but was cracking. I lasted one more week. But I needed a hit. The feeling didn't go away. It got worse. I needed to do something. I communicated, that was my job. I talked to strangers on the phone, that's what I did. Fourteen months. Fourteen months of waiting. It had to stop.

'Hello?'

'Alo?'

'Vlad? Vlad este acolo?'

'Nu, nu este. Cine-i? Taysa?'

'Da. Tessa.'

Oh shit. What a fool I felt, caught in the act of longing by his mother.

'Ok. Sorry. Pa, pa.'

'Pa.'

I put down the phone, burning red, hating myself, resenting Vlad. Elena put down the phone bemused.

She had presumed the call would be from one of Tuca's many sisters with more instructions on the business of death. What a month it had been. She perched briefly on the arm of the sofa to take stock. Grandpa Gheorghe, Tuca's father, was dead; found frozen and floating in his pyjamas, tangled in the willows that bent over the water's edge. Gheorghe had been missing for several days. In the bitter cold Tuca, Vlad and Dumitru searched for him every night. A priest was paid, prayers said, a clairvoyant called who'd predicted water and so it was. Mad and drowned (on his way back to fight the Russians, apparently) after eighty-four years of life. Elena sighed; he had always been obsessed with the war but things got so much worse when his memory began to fail.

And there Elena remained, on the edge of the sofa, contemplating death and dear old Grandpa Gheorghe. I suppose given the circumstances it was understandable she forgot to tell her son that the foreign girl called.

At least I've always liked to think it wasn't deliberate.

Two Weeks Later

'Alo?'

'Vlad?'

'Yes.'

'It's Tessa.'

'Oh hello. I didn't . . . '

'You didn't write to me.'

This was not my planned opener. The words spilt out, edgy, angry. I couldn't hide my hurt.

'I did. I sent an email. Two.'

God, his voice was lovely – all crackly and deep.

'Emails don't count. And you didn't call. I called you!'

'Oh . . . did you?'

'It's like you're in this black hole. Impossible to contact. Miles away.'

'I . . . it's been, Granddad . . . '

'I'm thinking of coming over.'

'When?'

'Soon. When I can. Why didn't you write, Vlad?'

'I dunno.'

'I'll call you when I've booked my flight.'

'OK.'

'Bye Vlad.' I was about to cry – I had to get off the phone.

Vlad replaced the handset, confused, shocked at the storm that had shaken the silent room where nothing moved – but he felt different, so totally different with a dry throat and small prickling sensations in his fingers. He sat back down, his thoughts swimming. Where the fuck had that come from? What had just happened?

I called again. That's what.

CHAPTER TEN

Iaşi, March '01

He was at the station ten minutes early. It was 5.30am and the train from Bucharest arrived on time, its thunderous bulk slowing alongside the platform. He had already seen me when I caught his eye. I was by the window, bags alongside, fresh painted smile wide and my hand out, reaching to pull down the pane and push open the door.

'Hi! Vlad. How are you?' And all before he was in earshot as he ambled slowly towards me, hands thrust deep in his pockets, skinny frame wedged into an inadequate coat.

'Hello.' He looked up shy, hesitant. 'How are *you?*'

'Well! Very well. A bit tired!'

I kissed him, leaving a smudge of pink on his pale cheek. And then I looked away, thrown that he wasn't as I had remembered. Had I imagined someone bigger, more majestic perhaps? My disappointment embarrassed me. What had I been thinking?

We sat almost silent in the taxi, occasionally stating the obvious to each other. Yes, spring was some way off. Yes, the cars were different – Renault now owned Dacia, foreigners were buying up everything. Yes, all part of the transition. Vlad paused to stare out of the window at his city.

'Is difficult for my country.' And more than that he could not say; it was too early and he felt, sitting as close as we were in the taxi, strangely disorientated.

I was silent, almost shocked. The boy I had so intensely nurtured in my imagination was alien to me, dangerously thin and sharp with a strong nose. I shuffled up on the seat, keen to give us space, wishing I'd not leapt so far ahead. How vividly I had invented him and us in private sleepless moments. Already I'd kissed every inch of his slender body, undressed him in the broad light of day, laid with him as the crickets whirred and clicked. In my head we had done everything together and now I was sitting, hot with shame, next to a stranger.

When I woke, for a brief moment I couldn't remember where I was, how or why I felt so trapped between tightly pinned sheets. And then I knew immediately, suddenly staring down the sheen of the eiderdown, aware of someone puttering about in the neighbouring room, putting and placing and somewhere else the buzz of a foreign TV. Vlad said I had slept for hours – four to be precise – my train journey having left little room for rest in the night. Half the day had gone and Elena was back already from the factory.

Vlad adjusted the sound on the TV and served scalding, sweet coffee, his gait upright as he left the room and re-entered, his eye catching briefly on my bright mouth before he settled a safe distance from me.

Was Elena entirely surprised at my reappearance? I couldn't tell; she had the same unchanged expression even when I presented her with a brushed cotton apron from a plush London department store. She took her time undoing the ribbon and gently easing off the shining lid, thinking as she did so what a fine box for little Laura, somewhere she could hide all her childhood secrets and much more besides.

'Mulțumesc.' She nodded in approval at the cheery pinny with its images of animal life and handsome front pocket.

'Thank *you*!' I added and groped for what came next, looking around the room for inspiration. Vlad sat quietly with cupped hands, an intermittent translator between his mother and me – a role that for the time being suited him well. He didn't have to think as the moments passed. Through her son Elena talked about the weather (cold) and I inquired about a painting on the wall.

The artist had arrived unannounced in her factory and laid out his work on the floor – he must have been a friend of the foreman. Elena had never seen so many colours. She stood resolutely beside her favourite, paid her money and took home her prize on the trolleybus, averting her eyes from all the curious stares.

'It's a bit too much, yes?' Vlad watched me take in the lurid orange painting. 'Back then we lived in a colourless world. There's no word for *tacky* in our language. Maybe that will come.'

Elena, having shared the story and keen to return to the stove (for the girl must eat), excused herself. In the confines of the kitchen she supped from her caldron of borsch, leaving it to heat as she fried off chicken in a pool of oil. And as she worked she wondered what I was doing once again in their small life. She pondered on where I kept my pots of money to come and go with such assurance and gifts. Who was this woman that she could breeze about the world as you like – here today, gone tomorrow? And shouldn't Vlad be at college?

Vlad and I sat for ten minutes alone, possibly more. We were together on the narrow sofa, Vlad's arm along the wall, and he turned towards me leaving us no choice but to acknowledge the other and chat. It was gauche stuff. Maybe he commented on the illegible hand scratched out in my letters, and I on his mean weight. Did he never feel hungry? I stretched out a hand. I had a sudden urge to feed him, a desire to watch him gorge on hot, filthy food. The smell from the kitchen didn't help. And I knew in that moment, what I had maybe always known: Vlad and I could never be friends. He was very thin and he was too young and he was not the man I had imagined. He was a boy, but I loved him.

Just like that our time was up. Mihaela rang the doorbell with Alin in tow – word was out the British girl was back in town.

There were red carnations for me and kisses and well meaning phrases while Elena bustled and strove to feed the sudden swell in numbers, all of us talking, some in two tongues, laughing, stabbing at the air with an excitement and a frantic need to be understood.

170

'Hey so good to see you, Tay-sa!'

'Vlad never told us you were coming. Vlad, why did you keep Tay-sa a secret? Uh?'

'Elena – stop for a second, come and tell Tessa how it is in Romania these days.'

'Mama, sit down a minute.'

'What do you want to know? That the prices leap up each day, that inflation is killing this country. Killing it! Everything is so expensive.' Elena surprised herself. But that was how it was.

'Pah, the EU! You think they will help us? You wait, is all for nothing. Our politicians have hungry pockets.' Alin rubbed his shaved head with a hand, embellishing his aunt's observations, smacking away my optimism.

I shrugged and smiled at Mihaela, only half-understanding, and all the while craving distance from my dishonourable intentions. Could they tell? Did they know the real reason for my visit?

Smack – and a clutch of skittles fell, another wobbling, recovering to wobble again and fall.

'Half-strike! Half-strike!' flashed on the screen.

'What? Tessa, the devil has you on his side! How do you do it?'

'I've played before!'

All around was crashing music and the smell of sealers, adhesives – or, as Vlad explained with meticulous precision, *volatile organic compounds*, the bowling hall so new it had yet to penetrate the air beyond its heady plastic shield. We were playing at playing and I outplayed the rest.

We had accessed new Iaşi with my millions of befuddling lei and Mihaela's enthusiasm. She longed for anything that might bring her closer to an idea of a world she *dreamt* of but was yet to touch. I helped. She could touch me, on the arm; sometimes she reached to take my hand just as I wanted to take Vlad's.

Then there was ping-pong and pool in a dim hall with smoke and disco lights. It was a warehouse, or had been a warehouse, and

Vlad lit a cigarette and examined his next move – the pink or the blue? I was distracting him, just being there charging him with something other than his usual disinclination. I had come back. I kept my word and came back. And he was a bit drunk; bolder, too, but unsure about his next move.

Until suddenly we were outside. It was all me – I can't pretend otherwise. (I couldn't wait. I'd crossed a continent.)

Alin and Mihaela went home in the other direction so that left us. I led Vlad by the arm up some concrete steps and then I turned and kissed him. I had his lips pressed against me, and I could feel when my tongue found his. I held him, gingerly at first and then a little tighter.

That was us standing on the steps, surrounded by wild dogs; I was above Vlad and he was kissing upwards, looking beyond at the stars.

'You trapped me!' He pulled away first, astonished, adrenalised.

'You let yourself be trapped.'

'I had no chance.' He smiled and touched my lip with a finger.

We walked home slowly with our heads together and our arms wrapped each around the other, and back in the flat we risked more kisses in the little kitchen. I was against the table with its spuggy legs and Vlad planted a tentative mouth on my cheek, forehead, lips. His breath was moist, sweet and uncertain; his arms loose and his neck soft and warm like the muzzle of a foal.

'Shh.'

'Sorry.'

'We should go to bed. Your parents . . . '

And that was how it began. A nervous debut; unsure, unexceptional even. Like many first kisses, I guess. It was real – flawed, wet and tender.

Vlad quietly unpacked the folding bed in the middle room, already in his thin Romanian pyjamas and I brushed my teeth, jumping up and down on the cold stone bathroom floor displeased by the sudden bright light.

I stopped by his bed in the middle of the flat. I lay next to him briefly and we kissed some more between starched sheets.

'Do you . . . do you want to go further?'

'No, no. It's OK.'

Nobody tells you how embarrassing the beginning bit is. Maybe that's why women go for older men. It didn't help that we could hear Elena snoring through the wall like a little piglet.

Poc poc poc went the irregular beat of batons on mats, women bent over their daily duty in the morning sunshine. *Poc poc poc* sang their work as they rhythmically drove out the dust. Vlad watched them as he took his first coffee on the step beneath his block. He saw them that morning more clearly than he'd ever seen them before, all bundled up for the winter that was past; their stooped shapeless forms, their careworn faces and knotted scarves, banging their mats as if their lives depended on them. Maybe, thought Vlad, he should offer to bang his mother's mats.

He sat on the step in Elena's new apron – a gesture of his uncommonly good mood, perhaps? It had remained stiff and new on the peg in the kitchen as if to remind him that he had not dreamt the night before – I was indeed asleep next door and we had kissed, had we not? He ran his tongue across his lower lip and carried on sitting outside, his coffee long gone, with a large giraffe painted across his chest bearing its teeth in an inane, impossibly large grin.

By the time I woke the temporary bed was neatly folded away and Vlad was back inside, seated in a small chair in the corner of the room. Vlad and the apron – I was struck by this little piece of England on his whippet thin body – and the smile on his face that gave him away. To see him made me flush. We sat together shyly on the upright sofa and watched Madonna strut on the telly.

'Do you like Madonna?'

'No. She doesn't look like a nice person.'

I wasn't sure that nice was really the point of Madonna, nor was

I sure why I felt the need to talk about Madonna or indeed talk at all, but I couldn't help myself.

'Do you not have to go to college today?'

'No, I couldn't be bothered.'

I reached out and took his hand. 'Does that mean we've got the day together then?'

It was four in the afternoon. Monica sat up and vigorously rubbed the sleep from her face. Baby Laura sat beside her in a bonnet and tights, her small gold earrings winking in the electric light.

'You OK, Monica? You look tired.'

'I got in from work at eight this morning.' Vlad's sister-in-law stared at his hand in mine. I withdrew my arm, feigning an itch, taking the time to stare around her cramped home.

There was a collection of stuffed animals and a plastic doll in a box on a ledge that framed the bed. In one direction was a balcony looking at a wall and a small strip for cooking, and the other a tiny washroom and the door. We were on the fourth floor in a block of bedsits, although Vlad didn't know to use that word.

Dumitru excused himself to buy bottles of Tuborg beer and peanuts from the kiosk outside. Monica stopped rubbing her face and padded across the room. She began heating water in an *ibric*, for what exactly she was not sure. It was too late for coffee, too early for food. Still, she was keen to make the right impression. She had heard about this London. Her high school friend Viorela had gone there and come back with stories of quick money and stupid men, her bag crammed full of white fluffy slippers, miniature soaps, shampoos, cellophane-wrapped cookies with chocolate dots and sachets of sweet, hot drinking cocoa.

'Will you go back?' Monica had asked her, a mouth full of biscuit.

No, Viorela wouldn't go back because she couldn't get a visa and the hotel where she worked wouldn't take her back without one, and the house where she stayed was rough and there was no lock on her door. But she didn't tell Monica that. Instead she shrugged.

Maybe she would go back, she said. Maybe, which was enough for Monica who liked the cookies and the new thin Viorela, who had lost her swollen country figure and had an adult look in her limpet eyes. Monica wanted a bit of what Viorela had, and now here was Vlad with his funny British girl who never stopped talking in her one hundred Romanian words and kept taking photos of Vlad on the balcony.

'Mulţumesc! Smile!'

'Super!'

'Mulţumesc!'

'I like your country very much.'

'Noroc!'

'Thank you!'

'Goodbye. Pa pa, pa pa!'

How I tried to be likeable in those early days and Monica liked me back, but she was tired and I was foreign. She shut the door behind us and Laura hammered her pink angry fists against the wall, furious she'd lost her audience. Her mother bent to restrain her and calm her down with sweet tea from a beaker. Then, settling on the balcony, Monica smoked a final cigarette before going to work where she sold alcohol, corn puffs and tobacco until the sun came up and she went home, sliding between the sheets, still warm, where her husband had been lying some twenty minutes earlier.

'Let's go somewhere!'

'What? Where?'

'I don't know . . . somewhere!'

Vlad looked at me. He didn't go places – that was not something he did.

'It would be nice to get away.'

We had done two days of chatting, cracking nuts, squirreling kisses in secret moments, visiting and chatting some more but we lacked privacy and the nights were difficult. When we tried to lie

175

together the camp-bed creaked and we were scared his mother might find us. The flat was very small.

And so I planned an excursion and that was how we found ourselves serenaded by a tomcat of a man with a large head and bulky frame. Vlad as a rule didn't do deals with gypsies – not unless he had to. But here he was humouring his crazy blonde who'd insisted on an adventure and that required a car apparently.

'I saw Hertz at Bucharest airport . . . '

That was Bucharest airport, however, and we couldn't find its equivalent in Iaşi, try as Vlad might with his self-conscious phone manner. We even asked Uncle Bogdan, which led to Mihaela and Alin gate-crashing our romantic break away, and so we were all standing at the bottom of Hotel Unirea (having been to the top) looking at a Daewoo. Vlad thought maybe he should haggle, but for how much? And anyway I was conducting the affair, a bit, he thought, like a bomb going off in a crater, shaking up the order, throwing my arm across the gypsy's leather shoulder and pulling out unnecessary dollars. He and Alin stood back, watching the performance; mesmerised, appalled.

I'd not driven on the right before, and Vlad was full of foreboding.

'Tessa, the infrastructure is very poor in my country.'

'A South Korean car from a gypsy and you want to go to the mountains. We will never get home.'

'You will never see your $100 deposit. This is a very bad idea.'

I got my way. Vlad relented and wrapped up the salami sausage from his mother's fridge before leaving her a note. 'Dear Lord, dear good Lord – bring them back safely from this mad plan.'

We were heading for Vatra Dornei, which was Vlad's idea; he'd been walking in the nearby mountains with friends. They'd not seen another human for days. There were open fires, fat berries and startled roe deer. Did they even hear a wolf? Yes, if they had to go on an excursion then let it be Vatra Dornei.

'Sounds great, Vlad!'

'Ce fain! Vatra Dornei,' said Mihaela, crossing herself as we careered past Iaşi's many churches and the building sites for many more. 'Vai!'

She insisted on sitting beside me in the front. I was the unelected leader, clipping the wing mirror on a stationary car before we cleared Iaşi. And I was the sole driver.

'Stringent rules in Britain!' I shouted over the noise of the radio. 'Getting my test was a nightmare . . . ' It all felt a little bit naughty. 'Oops!'

Vlad leant forward between the seats, cautioning about the horse and carts moving slowly, the potholes (deceptively deep) and the police (extremely corrupt). He was feeling alive today. He wasn't ready to die.

'Careful, Tessa. Slow down! Slow down, I said!' He wanted to put out a restraining hand but not with his cousins in the car.

The steering wheel pulled hard left; Vlad put his head in his hands.

'What is it with the potholes in your country?'

It was near dark by the time the boys had changed the wheel, ripped through on the broken road. Mihaela stood by the immobilised car and said a little prayer and then asked if we could share a room at our destination.

It was the police who stopped us next. Just a spot check, they insisted, pulling up from nowhere on the Moldavian highway and pushing their heads in the driver's side. Vlad said nothing, furious with them in their blue breeches and infuriated by me. Hadn't he said this was a bad idea – why did he have the uncontrollable urge to stroke my head? Fucking hell and Alin started arguing, getting out of the car and posturing, making things worse.

In the end I showed the pair my licence and my passport and smiled a winning smile but it didn't stop the fine. What for, exactly, none of us were sure. (Carrying dollars, maybe? Being foreign? For stopping when they told us to?)

We set off subdued, the freedom of the moment squashed. I

turned up the music and we took a narrow winding route through the hills, the sun sunk, the black forest almost invisible.

It was the radio that died first and then the battery. The car stopped just like that, in the dark.

'Told you,' said Vlad. 'Told you so!' His each and every prophesy materialising as if by magic, dominoes falling one by one. He got out and kicked the side of the Daewoo before walking into the night, angry with himself for being so angry – but why couldn't I try and understand that Romania was not like England? Fucking gypsy! Fucking car!

We never reached Vatra Dornei. Instead we spent the night in a log cabin, which Vlad spotted, quite by chance, twinkling through the woods like a fairy house. We drank vodka in a bar that never closed and I gently explained to Mihaela that I wanted to share a room with Vlad.

Mihaela didn't understand but Alin did, and he took his sister by the arm and led her into their pine-panelled room.

'Duh Mihaela, Tessa and Vlad are having it off.'

'What do you mean?'

'He has gone for the easy option – he has fallen in love with a Westerner.'

'Vai,' said Mihaela, her eyes as large as saucers. 'Vai, but she is *my* friend.'

'Christ, you're as dumb as the rest.' And he turned his back on her and smoked out of the window.

Vlad and I spent our first proper night together, though not fully undressed. The breath of one on the other, a shy hand, a new touch was enough such were our nerves and the disturbing nature of intimacy. And the pine-panelled walls were paper thin.

CHAPTER ELEVEN

London, April '01

I was in the chemist on Clapham High Street. I was waiting for my photographs, itching to relieve my craving, desperate for some small tangible morsel of my Romanian adventure that I could hold up and show off – my life with Vlad for the world to see.

There he was standing on Monica's balcony looking wise and vulnerable, like an anorexic owl in a pullover. And again with Alin changing the tyre, smiling, pleased at their manly achievement with so little experience and girls watching on. Then a picture of Vlad and me together the night we first kissed, leaning in and laughing at the arm outstretched, snapping the moment in the gloaming. And finally there was my favourite: Vlad staring down the lens from the narrow couchette in the sleeper train to Bucharest, a starched pillow behind his head, the whites of his eyes exposed beneath the irises in that disarming hangdog way of his and small points of pink in his cheeks from our time together.

I was a clumsy leader, unsure of what to do and how to go about it. I had even asked if he wanted a blow job. I sat up on the couchette and asked the question as if offering him a cup of tea.

'Tessa,' he replied gently. 'I cannot imagine that would be a pleasure for you.'

How I loved Vlad in that moment! My dear sweet Vlad. Clatter-boom, clatter-boom on the train all the way through the night to Bucharest to say goodbye.

But all too soon our holiday was spent and Vlad was thousands of miles away, my poor boy in his poor country. I needed to talk about him if I couldn't be with him and so I talked and talked.

'Hmm,' said Hina (on the phone from her grown-up job in publishing). 'So the brown-eyed boy came up trumps.'

'Yes! I can't explain how exactly, just I can tell you it was so, I mean so . . . there is just something. His essence, I can't put it into words . . . '

'That's love for you – inexplicable. So when are you going back?'

'I don't know, I promised Annabel I would go to Mexico with her this summer. Hey I've got amazing photos, will you come round? When can you come round?'

Annabel was my most sensible friend. Talented, balanced and old-fashioned in her tastes, she liked nothing too out of the ordinary – which, in our tiring alternative world, made her exceptional. She was not, however, entirely receptive to the idea of Vlad.

'Did you . . . did you have sex with him?' Annabel didn't, but may have wanted to wrinkle her nose at this point, as she poured over my photographs not seeing or even trying to see what I saw: a solemnity, a deep unshakeable integrity. My sweet boy.

'No, not yet. It was, you know, more innocent than that. It was nice, though.'

Annabel was visibly relieved and I immediately wished I'd lied and told her we had lots of sex, especially the wrong way around in the train – clatter-boom, clatter-boom. She didn't understand and I could tell she couldn't be bothered trying. But I wouldn't let her spoil my moment. Instead I filed her in a category along with my mother: conventional, and waiting for me to pass through this latest funny phase.

Iaşi

Vlad travelled through the night with me to Bucharest and then back to Iaşi through the following day, feeling sleep deprived and incomplete. He'd stood at the airport, leaning on the silver bar beyond which he was not permitted to go, his big boot like a black boat perched on the rail, one hand raised in an acknowledgement of us. I moved away to push my passport through the glass panel at the official who stared and smacked my book with a rubber stamp.

When I turned a final time Vlad was already walking in his upright way towards the exit, wondering how on earth to get back through the maze of Bucharest.

I'd cried big noisy hiccups on the plane. Between gulps I told a young air-hostess about my new, fragile love and she gave me a small bottle of Moët and a free make-up sample to take the pain away.

Vlad didn't cry; he didn't even move save to spark up a cigarette on the noisy train north. He pushed his thoughts very deep down inside himself so they didn't force up anything unexpected. Still, he was occasionally caught out; unravelling fringes of paranoia his tired mind could not control – the panic he may never see me again, that somehow he may have put me off, the fear of something so utterly unknown, unplanned, so uninvited and raw. The journey dragged – how could it take this long to get home when our ride through the night had been snatched away so quickly? Him telling tales of Vlad Tepeş (the Impaler) to his (almost) naked blonde in slow Romanian, stroking her pale skin and telling of unknown cruelty and bloodlust in his troubled land.

'Why do you not come again, Lord Tepeş?'

It was a little later in our relationship he came to regret his considered response to my offer of oral sex.

It was near dusk when he finally let himself back into the flat. He knew his mother would be home, in the kitchen busying away at the stove.

Elena was indeed in the kitchen. She'd seen her son walking towards the block, his head down, his dark features drawn in the evening light. She thought how troubled he looked and felt huge relief he was home again. Elena did not, however, ask why he'd gone all the way to Bucharest. She didn't presume to question her nearly adult son. It didn't mean she approved. She didn't, but it was not her way to comment.

And Vlad knew his mother wouldn't question him. Elena would keep her thoughts to herself, as she always had. He knew no one more discreet. Under the communists she'd been the ideal comrade – a silent worker bee minding her own business. He'd been just eight when the two of them rushed back from town one morning – Vlad clutching his new prize Motorcross, a pitifully simple game with plastic pieces and coloured card – and that was when they saw it, in fresh black paint across the side of a block, screaming out from the grey: *CEAUȘESCU ASASIN*. It was right there in front of them – unimaginable defiance! Vlad stood riveted, rooted to the spot, his mother now tugging at his coat, cursing under her breath.

'We should not have seen this, keep your eyes down. Come on Vlad! Come on!'

When she got home she told no one, especially not her husband, and swore Vlad to do the same. It was the very next, cold December day that saw Ceaușescu airlifted from the roof of the Communist Party's Central Committee in Bucharest, his game finally up. But old habits died hard. Still Elena told no one what she'd seen.

Eleven years on, the world around her changed, she remained as circumspect as ever. Vlad knew she wouldn't ask any questions about where he'd been but that didn't make the evening pass more easily. She dutifully placed fried chicken in front of him and a hunk of bread, pausing briefly by the fridge to let him know I'd called.

'I think she'd arrived in London already – she sounded upset.'

The foreign girl was, Elena decided, prone to tears.

London, June '01

'You see, people in your country is crazy! Yesterday I drive to Manchester to drop off a computer – six hundred this cost the company. Six hundred pound!'

'Where are you from, Grigor? Romania?'

'Ha, close! I am from Bulgaria. Eh, you see now though I have British passport, I pass the exam, pay my money – everything.'

'Well done you! My boyfriend is Romanian.'

'Hey we say in Bulgaria you have a thief boyfriend! We have

the guns and they have the thief. You wanna hear my joke on the Romanian thief?'

Grigor looked back at me in his driver's mirror, his face all beaten and red, incongruous against the suave greys of London's Regent Street.

'This is so bad a thief, when he die he not get to heaven. God say to him, "You get out! You think you get paradise. No way! Get out!" And so he go down in hell and then Satan wants to punish him real bad so he puts him on a stick and tell his slave, "Turn this Romanian over the fire good and slow. Very slow, make him a-scream." When he comes back the slave is turning fast, fast, very fast and Satan say, "Hey! What you doing? Turn him a slow!" And the slave say, "If I turn him slow, he keep stealing potatoes out of the fire!" '

And Grigor slapped his leg, pleased as punch with his performance and then, in case his foreign audience had missed a trick, added, 'You see in Romania and Bulgaria we cook potatoes in open fire . . . '

I liked Grigor and his potato joke. I liked him so much I took his number, just in case I wanted to talk more about Bulgaria and hopefully Romania, too.

'You know why I left Bulgaria?'

'No – why?'

'Not just the mafia, is too many communist slaves left over and no one not even say thank you!'

'They don't thank you much in Romania either.'

'Yes because they have not been told to say thank you! In my country will be another twenty years, maybe more. Then I go home.'

Grigor, I decided, would never go home. He left me on the pavement, beeping the horn of his black Merc. I'd been deposited outside the radio studio with my insatiable appetite for anything Romanian temporarily quenched, and a whole four hours of open line to plough through before I could return to thinking about Vlad and his world – the only way to ease my aching need.

I didn't tell Vlad my new Romanian joke. His family telephone had a faulty bell so it didn't always ring their end. I would spend hours curled up on the floor with the receiver under my ear, letting the foreign dial tone ring out until I could bear it no more. And when I eventually did get through often Vlad wasn't home and I found talking to Elena agonising.

'Nu, Vlad nu este acasă.'

What could I say to that? On the rare occasion Vlad answered I did all the talking. I couldn't gauge his thoughts from the few words he offered. (Were his family in the room? Was he shy? Did he want me off the phone?) And Vlad couldn't picture what I was talking about so said even less. He had no money to call me with and I began to feel less sure about his feelings, while Vlad never felt sure of mine or the possibility of us. All over again and every day he was slipping a little further from me and I couldn't figure out how to catch him in the abyss. Did he want to get caught?

Once, Vlad tried to email me from the internet room between the blocks the day after he returned from Bucharest.

Hey Tess – I miss you like I lost part of my body, like people who lose limbs and can still feel them – do you know what I mean? I slept for some of the train trip north and so escaped a little of the burden of paranoyically (is there such a word?) missing you, a thing I am currently doing. I love you.
Te pup pe frunte (I kiss you on the forehead).
Vlăduț

But he didn't send what he wrote. He read the email through twice and decided it was lame. It presumed too much and I was so far away he couldn't imagine seeing me again. Our time together already felt like a dream and dreams couldn't be trusted. Vlad, as a rule, didn't dream. So he saved the email in his draft folder and Googled *Cannibal Corpse* and *Industrial Metal* until his time ran out.

The basement, Clapham
27th June 2001 5am!

Vlad – I'm allowed ten minutes to write this then I've got to go to <u>bed</u>. Is it because I can't have you that I think about you? More and more every day, made worse because I don't even know when I'm going to see you again. You've become an official obsession. Is it just the idea of you I'm in love with or is it really you?

All I want to do is be with you – see you, hold you, love you. This wasn't meant to happen. I was meant to come back from Romania minus the obsession I arrived with. It has just got worse instead. Vlad give me a look into your dreams for the future – I need something to hold on to.

A Romanian lady of eighty-two rang up my show tonight. She spoke Romanian to me; she was a refugee fifty years ago. I am breaking all my radio rules and am going to meet her on Thursday. The other Romanian bloke (the one I told you about called Ion) – I'm trying to shake him off. The Home Office are on his back. He came around to the flat the other night, and keeps trying to get me to help him. Anyway an eighty-two-year-old is a much safer bet. Hina thinks I've lost the plot. Can I blame it on you?

Vlad please write to me. You can write anything, I find it reassuring to hear from you, know you're thinking about me, us.

When is the best time to ring? When are you alone? Ever?

My ten minutes is up – maybe now I've written to you I'll be able to sleep.

Big of big love,

TESS xxxxxx

P.S. Enclosed is a picture of us together. x

P.P.S. This is an illegible scrawl. Don't worry if you can't read it – so long as you know I think of you every day, every hour.

Vlad read the letter on the way back from college. It had sat in his pocket all morning. He wanted to read it alone, preferring to avoid any questions or attention a foreign letter would attract, aware he could marshal his feelings better when by himself. Vlad generally found reading through my pages of pleading obsession unsettling. They made him feel helpless and he didn't like that. He stared at the photo taken at dusk, the two of us arm in arm, Vlad with his legs standing stiff and self-conscious and me with a look that knew there was a camera on us, and a man passing by on a bicycle, then the blocks and the bare spring trees. He flicked the picture over in his hand.

Who took this, Vlad? Very apt it's at a distance. I hate distance.
Tess xxx

He re-read the letter. Was love supposed to make you feel so impotent, he wondered, and buried the letter back in his pocket. He didn't like the idea of me meeting random Romanians in London. He didn't trust his fellow countrymen, especially those who skulked off abroad looking for quick hits and the high life.

This was one of the few things he took the time to tell me on the telephone, frustrated by my cavalier attitude. I was touched he cared and told him so.

Vai! Vlad shook his head. He'd been brought up not to trust; that was how it was, his mother explained very early on and in the same breath reminded him never to take anything that wasn't his from anyone. Understood? Vlad had and did understand. In that way he was like Elena. Even in the desperate final winters under Ceauşescu she managed survival with honesty. Pulling on men's knickers, the ones she had sewed herself, over her own in the factory toilet was her sole concession to the national game of take. The security man with big hands at the entrance gate wouldn't find them there. Marcel, Dumitru and Vlad were never short of underpants.

It was Elena who rescued my letter from the floor in Vlad's room. She stashed it but not before she'd studied the photograph –

186

her son arm in arm with the foreign girl. She stared at the image, sensing she was looking at something that wasn't intended for her eyes but unable to resist, drawn fully into our narrative, sitting on her son's bed with his story in her hand.

Elena didn't tell Tuca what she'd seen, or how many letters I'd sent. Maybe one a week? Certainly one every fortnight. She couldn't see how any good would come of it and yet a small part of her felt sympathy for the girl who always rang with the same desperate eager edge in her voice.

'Alo! Scuzaţi-mă! Vlad este acasă?'

'You should write to her, you know,' Elena told her son one summer evening, after another of my calls looking for an absent Vlad. She stared at the wall above the sink and continued. 'It is not fair to say nothing to a girl.'

London

Eva lived in a large art deco block of municipal flats set back from Maida Vale's noisy slog. Beside her door on the eleventh floor there was a mezuzah of thinly spun silver minus its prayer, and maybe I presumed to guess her story before she answered my knock.

Eva took me in with the eyes of a listener, struggling to realign her idea of the girl she heard on the radio with what stood before her.

'Hello. I'm Tessa.'

'Yes, I see that,' she replied in clipped, immaculate English. 'You're younger than you sound.'

She sat down at the small kitchen table and I took my place on marigold swirls that bled across the ottoman.

'So does your Romanian know you are visiting an old Jew?'

'I'm sorry?'

'I assume there's a man in the picture. You talk a lot about the country in your programmes.' She looked across at me, the skin on her face hanging in delicate, papery folds.

'I, well, yes . . . but no he doesn't know exactly.'

'Ah. Be sure to tell him.' She stood to sort through plates and snacks. 'I've made you egg plant salad.'

'Thank you.' I spooned the sludgy mess onto bread and Eva began talking, the stories of her life slowly fanning out in front of her.

There was a villa in the old quarter of Bucharest – all gone now, she said with a flick of her wrist – a bookshop and a tavern and then difficult (violent) politics and the war, and she puckered her lips momentarily, lost in thought. Her father died in a labour camp beyond the River Dniester. Eva got up to consult an old map. With a manicured finger she found south Transnistria in what was Greater Romania. There she was split from her sweetheart Ariel when the Russians poured in and Romania swapped sides in the war. He tried (and eventually succeeded) to make it in a boat to the Holy Land. She went back to Bucharest with her sister.

Eva paused as if to remember how the pieces then fitted together, where her place was amid the chaos. Ariel swapped Tel Aviv for London in the 1960s, where she'd established herself as an engineering fellow having paid her way out of Romania. They rekindled their love in the capital but it was too late for children. Ariel had since died and now she lived alone.

'I spend my time with the radio and my prayer book. And I'm brushing up my Hebrew. I thought I might take a trip to Israel before my health fails.'

'Have you been back to Romania?'

'No, what would I go back for?'

We changed the subject, moving to discuss my curious callers and late nights on the air. When I finally stood to leave, full of coffee and sweet chocolate, she stood with me and clasped my hand in hers.

'Thank you for taking an interest.' Then she added, almost as an afterthought, 'Remember men do not share our sense of urgency. But I can see you are a determined girl. I wish you luck.'

5th August 2001

Dearest Tessa – A promise is a promise, so here I am at my desk trying to write a fine letter for you (I'm sure it will be boring rather than fine). I will put at the end enough Romanian to cool your thirst.

Hey, what can I say? Not much. You know how it is around here – nothing ever happens. It's so hot, and I hate the summer; I am waiting for the autumn, because the weather will calm down and, of course, because I'll see you again. (Won't I?) So in order not to destroy a young, unstable immature mind, will you come and meet me again? Please . . . ? (That's your official invitation.)

I can only look forward to meeting my blonde goddess who made me lose interest in any other girl, no matter how beautiful or smart. You should feel loved, don't mind the distance. You should also always be aware that I'm deeply inside the continent and in love. (Reading that again sounds like poor English, but I'm sure you'll get my drift.)

I can't wait for us to meet, for you to be bossy – it won't annoy me – for us to sit without worrying about the time and drink together Romanian beer, and you will have an upset stomach and talk about life as I sit and smile at you, pure and simple.

What else? Nothing, except the <u>fact</u> that I love you.

Only yours,

VLĂDUŢ

P.S. I kiss you on the nose.

Five months late on the doormat one hot August morning, in a thin brown envelope with a large watery Romanian stamp: my first and only love letter. I read it slowly, word by word, savouring each mini-bite. I cried quietly to myself, and when I look at it now I see the ink has run, as if the page was left out in the rain. (I still know every word by heart.) It was worth the wait and of course I read it down the phone to Claire, Hina, even Annabel.

'At last,' said Hina. 'Vlad has woken up.'

'It's a *cute* letter,' was the best Annabel could manage. I was touched she tried.

That night, for the first time, I told my listeners I was in love with a nineteen-year-old Romanian and we talked together about long distance love for four hours until the sun came up. Eva called in the last few minutes, and, pausing only occasionally, told her tale to our little corner of late night London.

It was the best phone-in programme I ever presented.

The morning of the letter was also the morning I booked my flight to Romania: 16 September 2001, flying BA from Heathrow to Bucharest, £249 return. Then I rang Vlad.

'OK,' he said.

'Just OK?'

'Great. I'll come to Bucharest to meet you.'

'Are you sure?'

'Yes.'

'Great. Hey, love you Vlad.'

'Um . . . ' He checked around the room. 'Love you, too.' His voice dropped to a whisper; even his parents knew *I love you*.

London, September '01

Two weeks before I flew the head of the radio station called me into his office.

'We've decided we're going to try you out on the daytime schedule.'

'Wow! Great! Thanks . . . '

'2-4pm – the mid-afternoon show. When you're back from your holiday you can get underway properly.'

'Thanks.'

'OK, Tess. Well done.' Nick clearly wanted to leave it at that, but there was something about him with his well-travelled tan and well-cut suit that made me brave.

'Will I get a payrise?' I too had developed an expensive overseas habit.

He stared at me. 'Tessa,' he said with a chortle, 'you're very well-paid for a girl of your age.'

'But . . . '

'And daytime shifts are much easier.' He returned to his computer. The conversation was over.

The week before I flew, I had my roots bleached and found a green surfing jacket on discount for Vlad, its cotton lining decorated over and over with the three green leaves of the marijuana plant. Always a keen forward-planner, I bought a box of condoms from the chemist at a cost of nearly a pound each. No wonder there were so many teenage pregnancies, I tutted during my final late show. Betty in Bermondsey rang and agreed. Edith called and said she worked in the last condom factory in London. Apparently they'd blow them up to make sure they weren't faulty. It closed sometime after the war.

'Because of the pill,' said Edith.

'I don't like the pill,' I said. 'I think it's the reason why four million women in Britain are fat and grumpy.'

Edith agreed. She'd had five children (she didn't get free condoms once the factory closed down).

Iaşi, September 2001

Vlad was wondering how he was going to get to Bucharest with no money, although really he already knew the answer. He would travel in the loo and hope like hell the guard didn't find him. Just in case, Vlad would need some cash. To bribe was against his principles but, hey, so was poverty. Still, at least he'd got his hands on some grass. He liked the idea of getting stoned with me. It might calm me down a bit and that could only be a good thing, he thought.

It was as he sat contemplating these thoughts in front of the TV that out of a clear blue sky into two tall buildings flew two aeroplanes, one then the other, and the narration was suddenly panicky, the translation intermittent. Vlad spent the rest of the day in front of the TV, occasionally switching over to Euronews then back again to Romania's attempt at keeping up, cutting between different American images of the same horrific scene.

His mother stayed in the kitchen, preferring the radio, crossing herself. Who would fly? Why on earth would you go in an aeroplane? People must be mad.

Vlad continued to sit, hating humanity, hating religion, hating America for pumping the world so full of shit – and worrying that maybe I wouldn't come to Bucharest, after all.

London

'Well done, really good effort!'

Nick was shaking my hand; he was slightly pink in the face. The Twin Towers had given him something of a managerial headache – hardly ideal with a novice presenter on-air who wasn't sure how to pronounce *Al Qaeda* and only levelled the excited squeak in her voice on his say-so midway through live broadcast. By Wednesday I had mastered the special voice that correspondents draw on for major catastrophes and by Friday everyone in the building had received an all-staff thank you email for their 'hard work during an unprecedented week'.

Bin Laden could not have spread the global terror and speculation without his international team of media cadres. I was flushed and flattered.

'Thanks Nick, I'm back on Wednesday – we can discuss the new show then.'

'You better not go to Bucharest this weekend, darling.' Mum raised an eyebrow across the kitchen at Dad, the telephone tucked under her chin as she chopped carrots.

'Why not? Of course I'm going. It's all booked.'

'It's a very dangerous time to fly.'

'But not to Romania.'

'I don't know. Those funny far-off countries, the governments are planning retaliation. We don't know what's going to happen.'

'Mum, you're muddling communism with fundamentalism. Romania is probably the safest country in the world right now. I'll be much safer there than in bloody London.'

'Gosh, you are a stubborn girl.'

'No, I'm not. And I'm not going to let the terrorists ruin my holiday. Anyway I know it's because you don't really approve of me going to see Vlad.'

'That's nonsense, darling. I've nothing against Vlad.'

'Well *I* bloody have,' Dad huffed somewhere in the background. 'Some good-for-nothing Romanian yick!'

'And you can tell Dad to piss off! I'll call when I get back.'

I hung up and immediately felt remorse. I'd send them a postcard from Bucharest to make up for swearing.

Bucharest, Otopeni Airport

Vlad's train had been on time, and by 7am he was at the airport pressed against the wall. In disgust he watched the waiting crowd, scavenging birds gathered to swoop – taxi drivers, porters, wheeler-dealers, all and sundry pushing up against each other every time the automatic doors breathed to release another shoal of travellers.

He was dog-tired, nervous and out of cigarettes, and some hours passed before I landed, bouncing along the conveyor belt, buoyed up on my week of adrenalin and demands, primped and plucked, ready for my weekend away.

Out and into the wall of noise and cardboard names, me walking tall – and where was Vlad?

'Taxi! Taxi! Hey blonda, taxi!'

'Hotel, hotel, you want good price? Hey you, English?'

Vlad saw me first. He didn't move – he couldn't – the flight from London caused a scrum and I was, as he had known I would be, a target; too long and pale with shiny blonde hair and expensive denim. So he hung back and waited to catch my eye with a small gesture and a raised brow.

'Hi! Shit, this airport's so hardcore. Sorry about the delay, security

193

is mad in London. How are you? Hi Vlad!' Still he hung back and, impatiently, I pulled him to me and that was how our weekend in Bucharest began, his cheek forced against my mouth.

'It is difficult, isn't it?' Vlad would say much later that night, in the sag of an old mattress, still holding the smell of its former occupant. 'It's difficult at first to be together, after so long.'

I nodded, unable to speak, my brain full and dimmed with pungent grass and relief that each of us had finally grasped the other as we lay together in our dark room. The first day had indeed been difficult, and disappointing.

Was it my insistence that we should talk about the war that got his goat? Maybe. I was pumped. I couldn't see beyond the world of news – I wanted to find American telly and stay plugged into the constant gaggle that 9/11 demanded. Vlad found my pronouncements distasteful and self-important. He didn't buy a 'War on Terror'. He didn't understand my complicit belief in everything I'd been told, which I then repeated. And he resented the (smug) hangover from my radio promotion.

Sure, I was offish in the beginning. Once again my imagination had run away from reality, and this time my letters and calls left me exposed. I'd got caught up in my own romantic dialogue, an idea of our love that existed only in my head. I'd conveniently forgotten how much of a kid Vlad was – his adolescent frame effortlessly thin, his clothes ill-fitting, our conversation stilted – and I considered his conspiracy theories juvenile.

Vlad also made mistakes, letting slip early on that his first year at university had come to nought.

'You failed?'

'I guess.'

'Well, you either did or you didn't'

'I just didn't show for the exams.'

'You didn't? I don't believe it! You failed!'

He couldn't understand my rage that he could've been so careless as to waste a precious year, which must now be re-built before we could move forward. He was nineteen and rudderless. He didn't do macro-thoughts or long-term planning; he didn't understand my mental wall charts and timescales, my tick-lists and four-year prognosis. Sure, he was anxious that he might perform to please me later that night and maybe anxious he didn't appear a hick amid the crush of Bucharest, but it hadn't occurred to Vlad that my happiness depended on his success in life more generally.

'Christ. How long do you expect me to wait? I'll have hit the menopause by the time you graduate.'

'This is conditional love,' he said, visibly hurt. We were sitting in a shoddy pavement café, drinking beer.

'No it isn't, Vlad!' I cracked my bottle down on the table. 'Love isn't a fucking Eminescu poem; I can't make this work alone, you know.' I was nearing thirty. Of course I was obsessed with time. I was bitterly disappointed, too – Vlad should have been four years away from graduation and now he was five – again. Five ! How do you kill five years when you're in love? I hated love.

So it took us time to sand away the edges; the beer helped, me perching on his bony knee, staring into his giant eyes, and then shutting out the world once we'd paid for our room.

'Tomorrow we will move,' I said. Neither of us enjoyed the monumental receptionist with her morbid stare.

Vlad said nothing. He didn't enjoy transactions in Bucharest, especially not with me; my mouth flapping, wallet open, bag splayed for all to see.

'Oh it's fine, stop worrying! I live in London.'

When we turned the key it was a huge relief, our earlier anger forcing us to be gentle with each other; quickly we were in recovery mode, apologetic – even, passionate. For once I was not poisoned with anxiety, that this was a man trying to plant me with his seed and his agenda, and Vlad said he trusted me – which was naive and hugely attractive. We giggled like teenagers as we struggled with the condom and with no plug in the bath to wash away our efforts we took turns to splash under the tap. There was no room service so we went to sleep hungry and stoned, our legs tangled with just a sheet for cover.

And the next morning when we woke the whole day stretched out in front of us like a shimmering light you could never quite touch.

'It's like minding a child.' Vlad laughed when I had to double-back through the X-ray machine, having forgotten my bag the other side. 'If you get on the plane it will be a miracle!'

And so I hugged him again and pushed more lei into his shirt pocket.

'Buy a ticket home,' I said. 'Travelling in the loo is gross!' I blew him a kiss, stumbling through the machine backwards, knowing I wouldn't cry for him until he was gone and I was airborne.

It was after that moment when I left his sight Vlad found the hardest, as if there was a sudden eclipse and he was standing in the shadows alone. He found it difficult to focus and failed to care about the guards who watched him with ill-humoured curiosity – that one of theirs should be so young and play with such an expensive toy.

He headed back through Bucharest, unmoored, not ready for home. It was only when he arrived at Gara de Nord that he sensed something; just the merest suggestion of a movement, for the briefest of moments.

'Hell, the Vagina of his Mother! Damn it!'

He brought his fist down hard against the station wall, pressing his forehead against the marble. He'd been robbed, every single lei pinched. And more shaming, still, the thief had taken the time to re-fasten his breast pocket.

'What do you mean he's in Bucharest? Why didn't he tell me?' Marcel was standing in the hall of his flat leaning on the freshly tiled wall, watching his neat wife as she crossed the floor, unbuttoning her coat.

'He met with Tessa.' Elena's voice was flatter than usual. 'I told you she visited us in the spring when you were working in Prague.'

196

'Yes but . . . why was she in Bucharest? Tessa? Why didn't they call me?'

There was silence at the other end of the line. Elena said nothing. Marcel furrowed his brow and reached for a cigarette.

There was a particular phrase in English, Marcel would later think, that summed up his mother's silent mask and what it hid – and the phrase was *headfuck*. He'd often heard it used in American movies. This was surely a headfuck?

'So he, erm, OK . . . ' Marcel took his time. Like his mother he was careful with the words he used. 'When's he due home?'

'I don't know.'

'What about college?'

Elena sighed. 'That's his business.'

Marcel shook his head and they signed off, retreating cautiously from the affairs of others. Tessa with Vlăduţ. Surely that wasn't why the foreign girl had invited him to Scotland all those years ago? Baby Vlad travelling into a roaring fire. It was not possible. She was a woman, after all. Marcel continued to watch his wife as he slid down the tiles until he reached the floor, feeling slightly sick. Was this his fault?

'Marcel, what are you doing? Don't sit on the floor – you'll get dust on your new trousers. Marcel!'

20 September 2001 11.13

Subject: Shattered and Dismembered

Hey Tessa – pretty impressive title, isn't it?

I just been through your emails. May I say they are quite unexpected, as I left Otopeni without part of me (something inside me just seemed to have been left behind), thinking: Oh, that's probably the last time I'll ever see her . . .

Now to read how you feel – it's even more painful knowing I am missing out on your love, my love.

I LOVE YOU. Big kisses everywhere,

Vlad

And yes, I am trying to smoke less . . .

It wasn't a sudden decision; for my part, at least, it evolved from our September meeting. After our rocky start I felt convinced we could never again leave it so long without seeing each other. And so it was that Bucharest became our own illicit hideout whenever money and time would allow – and even when they wouldn't. The city, with its disreputable (and inhospitable) air, became ours for brief snatches of time. I invented doctor's appointments to duck work, I racked up ugly credit card debt on airfares and telephone bills, and I spent hours talking Vlad through our future together: we could run a vodka bar in London; become tourist guides on the trail of Romania's brown bears; simply hold hands and hope for the best.

Vlad lived more in the moment – always surprised when he heard from me, but always at the airport to meet me. Our bittersweet stays in Bucharest hurled us together just as they ripped us apart. Leaving got harder and the pressure to be perfect for each other in those precious few hours took its toll. Often I walked up the rising corridor of Otopeni airport to Departures full of fear and regret, knowing I could have loved better. Vlad worried, too, especially when he twice arrived in Bucharest with toothache.

It was after five months and as many trips to Romania, as I booked a Saturday flight to return on the Sunday, I knew something must give. I couldn't keep drip-feeding my engorged craving, demand every time outstripping supply. It was too painful and too expensive and I always I wanted more. No, if we were to move forward and, crucially, if Vlad was to believe like I did, he would have to visit Britain.

It was his turn, after all.

CHAPTER TWELVE

London, March '02

The Home Office Immigration website was terrifying. Intimidating. Official. Eons of bureaucracy and expense. It was lonely, too; a huge man-made construct, a millstone around my neck already tethered by Vlad's instinctive pessimism, his poverty and better ability to tolerate our fragmented situation. I boggled for hours until the jargon made me cry. The huge invisible block that lay between me and the boy I loved was like a tumour – unpredictable and potentially dangerous to tamper with. To fight it I needed to choose my moments carefully. I had to be feeling robust and at no point must Vlad be frightened off.

It was the following week on the radio when again the discussion turned to illegal immigrants that I found help. Michael, a lawyer, came on the show to field calls. His round face lit up and he waved his hands around to emphasise his point. At the end of our hour together I gushed.

'You were brilliant. A real natural!'

'Thanks. No problem. Anytime!'

'Ooh before you go, could I ask you a question . . . in, erm, confidence?'

His response was blunt. Bringing foreign nationals into Britain legally, especially young men, was getting harder. Romania was still out in the cold – it would be a long, difficult process.

He looked at his watch. 'Money helps, if you can prove you're solvent, reliable – a mortgage is good. Mind you unless you marry him you shouldn't admit to your relationship. They'll worry about elopement.'

'Elopement?'

'Well, if he gets a tourist visa they'll want to be sure he'll go home at the end of it. That's unlikely if you're, well . . . ' He raised an eyebrow.

'Mum it's just . . . it's Vlad. I think it would be good if he came over here. I think it would motivate him.'

'Tess, you can't go rushing into these things. You can't just rip him out of his own country because it suits you. I know you – you're like a bull in a china shop.'

Mum had waited for my Vlad phase to pass and when it didn't she privately allowed her doubts to be met with a degree of admiration. Her daughter was nothing if not determined. There must be something about the boy.

'That's why I was thinking of a holiday,' I continued down the phone, on a roll. 'So he could come over here and meet everyone.'

'Hmm, I guess it wouldn't do any harm.'

'I knew you'd think it was a good idea! I don't suppose you could be his official host could you, Mum? Only it would look much, well . . . less suspicious.'

'Sorry?'

'Don't worry! I'll pay, but I need you to write a letter of invitation to show immigration. And some bank statements. I mean, as a retired school teacher it doesn't look . . . you're not very likely to be his lover.'

'Sorry darling?'

'It'll be easy, I promise. So will you be his official guardian? On paper . . . please?'

There was a brief moment while Mum gathered herself, thankful her gruff husband was out marking cows. 'Why is everything so complicated with you, Tessa?'

'Because I'm your daughter. Please?'

'It is legal, isn't it? I don't want any trouble.'

'Oh yes, it'll be fine. Thanks Mum!' I'd asked Mum before Vlad. Later I would think this was insensitive.

The following day I signed up with four local estate agents. I needed to get on the property ladder.

Iaşi

Vlad put down the phone. He felt cornered. Marcel had rung out of the blue, asking, almost insisting, that the next time Vlad was in Bucharest he stayed with them.

'No it's OK, we . . . we have somewhere to stay. I'm not sure if I'll be down again.'

'Just come for supper. We're really easy to find, by Park Sebastian. Hey, come on! Come for a catch up.'

'OK. If I'm down again I'll tell you.'

Vlad resented the promise as soon as he made it, preferring things as they were; our world separate from the rest of his life. But now, like a bright, broken yolk, the bleeding of one into the other seemed inevitable and messy. And that, thought Vlad, was regrettable.

Once back in Iaşi, his trips to Bucharest assumed a surreal quality. Sometimes he struggled to believe they really happened; each, he supposed, was the last. Surprised was how Vlad felt when he headed back down to the capital to unpack our allotted hours in the hotel we finally settled on, Floreta de Aur. It was unlikely; modern and simple with tennis courts that were always empty and floors that squeaked under his rubber shoes. The sheets were rough but clean and it was in the north of the city where scented trees beat the traffic and flower girls sold bright posies. From there we would walk or sometimes catch a tram. Vlad was always astonished (and embarrassed) at my audacity as a tourist. I didn't just want to see Ceauşescu's villa. I wanted to go inside and touch the gold taps, until a man with a gun pointed me away. And as we suffocated under vast slabs of white marble in the People's Palace, he winced when I demanded answers.

'How many men died building this?' The guide blushed. 'Is it true the workers shat on the floor because there were no loos?'

201

'I see you like rumours,' he said, hurrying us into the next enormous space.

Only later did Vlad allow himself to be amused. 'That poor guy, he was dying in there, under your fire.'

'He was a terrible guide. What was he doing working in your main tourist attraction?'

'And you think he got his job because he's good at it?'

Sometimes we wouldn't get to where we were going, each distracted by the other, instead breaking off to return to the hotel.

'Hey let's go to that Athenaeum tomorrow, the one that looks like a cake.'

'Are you never satisfied?' Left to choose, Vlad liked the crackly TV and post-coital cans of beer best of all.

'No, never! Not when there's a whole city out there!'

Bucharest, April '02

We were in the old part of the city where the villas had verandas and trailing vines, the dogs that barked had owners and the dusty streets were wide, with ample space for parked cars – a meagre section of a Bucharest that was once, before the war, affectionately known as 'Little Paris in the Breadbasket of the East'.

Romania's monarchy was of German descent; one of Queen Victoria's granddaughters married into it. Marie wrote epic, heart-wrenching memoirs about her adopted country. Next came a playboy prince with his unsuitable Jewish lover. No one then foresaw the future.

The British Embassy, a white neo-classical building with re-assuring clean lines and numerous armed men in uniforms littering the street, in glass kiosks, outside the gate, just standing there – we stood for hours, too, waiting for the doors to open, to take a number and come back later.

'How much later?'

The guard shrugged. Four hours, maybe more.

Vlad wasn't sure he could drink any more coffee, or look over the form again, or go through the story another time.

'Just one more time! Please!'

It was the waiting, and the uncertainty, not to mention the sheaves of paperwork. His hand shook slightly as he shuffled them into an order of sorts. Mrs Dunlop's bank statements, a handwritten letter talking about her long-term interest in Vlad, her hope he'd attend her sixtieth birthday party – and all in her unmistakable hand. The five Christmas cards she had sent him down the years as evidence of their sustained relationship, Vlad's student card to prove he had something to return to Romania for and, finally, his application form.

'Good good, you'll do fine! Remember the whole process is designed to intimidate.'

I smiled nervously. Vlad was tired, he had rings around his eyes and his face was grey; he looked curiously inappropriate and not entirely unlike the many other waiting faces circling the embassy.

'You'll be fine!' my voice boomed across the table – hearty and loud.

'Tess?' Vlad looked at me over his McDonald's coffee. 'We don't really have to go to your mum's sixtieth, do we? I mean, can't it just be the two of us?'

'Come on, it'll be a laugh. Everybody's coming. Mum loves a party – she's having it on a Scottish island!'

My mother celebrated the corners of her adopted country with a fervour I've never encountered in a native Celt.

'South Uist is a magical haven,' she exclaimed, starry-eyed.' Her enthusiasm was infectious; twenty-five people were coming. I couldn't wait.

We returned to the embassy – Vlad silent, me exhilarated, happy to be back in Romania beside my boy, at last fighting together to be together. Brimming with hope and adrenalin, my chatter was constant. I explained that immigrants already in Britain queued in Croydon; how the press took pictures of their desperate faces. 'Visa or no visa our government just take their money,' I said brightly, grateful we were in Bucharest. It felt less personal, the scrutiny less insulting. 'I reckon it's probably cheaper applying from Romania, too. Don't you think?'

But Vlad wasn't listening; he couldn't get over the cost for something so uncertain and didn't like the way the guards looked at him. Nor did he like the smell in the queue, the bittersweet stench of fear, each applicant waiting to front up to their destiny behind a glass screen. Some got invited back for a second interview. One broke down on the floor. Another whooped with joy.

'God this is like waiting in A and E. I hope you get a woman. And I hope she isn't premenstrual.'

Vlad looked embarrassed. He wished I'd go now and stop creating a fuss. He worried I'd draw attention where none was needed.

Instead I started talking to the only other British person in the queue. John was pink and round like a scallop. Liver spots flecked his arms and there was a gold chain nestling in the springy hair on his chest. He wanted to bring Liliana to Britain. Liliana was at least twenty years younger. There were smears of shimmering blue above her eyes and her small frame was tightly parcelled into a belted leather jacket. They'd met on a cruise ship where she'd been a masseuse. I imagined her neat painted fingers pummelling John's fleshy back and felt slightly sick. John was not getting his mother to sponsor Liliana; I suspected his mother was probably dead. They were going to come clean about their relationship.

'Are you married?' I asked.

'One day I hope,' said Liliana in strongly accented English, clutching her John.

'They won't get in,' I said to Vlad.

'Why not?'

'I just know they won't. Bet they don't have Christmas cards.'

She'd even complimented him on his English. Vlad looked up into the spring sky – unbelievable, that was so easy! She'd smiled right at him. It was like she wanted him in her country.

'So you last went to Britain when you were thirteen. Wow, that must have been an experience!'

'Yes it was.'

'And this Mrs Dunlop, she's a family friend you say?'

'That's right. I think the word in English is eccentric.'

The perky civil servant smirked behind her panel. 'Well Vlad, I'm going to give you a six-month tourist visa. Have a great stay!'

He almost ran down Jules Michelet, pushing in through the swing doors of McDonald's, waiting until he was standing over my table, grinning with a force that lifted his face and lit up his eyes.

'I did it, I'm in!'

'Haha! No way!'

And we kissed across the cartons and the fries, knocking a chair over and laughing, overjoyed at our luck.

'Wow! A six-month multiple entry – they must really like you!'

'Hmm, I think she did . . . '

We kissed again.

'Oh and you were right. The other couple didn't get their visa. I met them on the way out. Liliana was crying.'

'That was a fun night.' Vlad and I were in a taxi on our way back from Marcel's flat.

'Did you think so?'

'Yes, I like you brother. He's sweet. He hasn't aged a bit.'

Even Vlad felt privately surprised the evening had been so easy. Marcel was pleased to see his brother and relieved our pairing was less appalling in reality. He listened to the embassy saga and was visibly impressed with Vlad's British visa, taking the time to scrutinise its handsome detail and calligraphy. His wife – dark, well proportioned, a Bucurestean – was less convinced. She believed there was an insurmountable power balance between us and told Marcel so several times after we left.

'It won't work, you'll see. In the end she will tire of him.'

This Silvia said as she sat over her laptop adjusting the proportions of an electronic mast to be installed on the West Coast of Africa the following week. We had left her behind schedule and her drum-tight pregnant belly meant she was more tired than usual. Still, it had been worth it. Silvia very much enjoyed showing off her flat.

'God, she loved it when you gushed over her kitchen. She purred like a cat. You know she had a ship bring over all that furniture from Africa? A ship!' Vlad shook his head in disbelief.

The flat was indeed worthy of exclamation. Behind the ubiquitous concrete façade Silvia had created a little piece of cosmopolitan paradise; bamboo furniture from their time as engineers in Africa, exquisite Czech glass found when under contract in Prague, and a variety of carefully sourced fixtures and fittings (a few with the unmistakeable stamp of IKEA, which had just opened on the outskirts of Bucharest).

Silvia was a charming hostess. She made us chicken in a bag, gave us French wine and intermittently pulled on her husband's cigarette. She had enjoyed Cameroon, where she taught her maid to shave her legs and persuaded her to eat not crossed-legged on the floor with fingers, but at the table with a knife and fork.

'It is so backward and dirty there.' She laughed and I sat and listened, trying, failing, to stay quiet on the subject of unborn babies and smoking.

'It's just, in our country, they don't recommend it.'

South Uist, July '02

'Tess is coming with a car full of young tomorrow! And Dunc's arriving from Edinburgh with Jessie.'

Mum toyed with a shopping list beside her sister Angie. The first week in Uist, she decided, had been a roaring success; wild walks, lots of chat, bridge – even the weather had been kind. Only Dad was in poor form, hating being away from his lambs, ugly ulcers on his legs knocking the edge off his humour.

'So we'll be a full house tomorrow!'

'Who's this Romanian chap that Tessa's bringing?' Uncle Pete looked up from the paper.

'Oh you know Tess, loves a challenge. Vlad is one of her projects!' Mum laughed.

'Bloody long-term project,' Dad grumbled in the corner. He wasn't looking forward to meeting a semi-adult Vlad.

Mum added beer to her list and wondered, not for the first time, about the sleeping arrangements for her new arrivals.

Danny drove us – reliable, Christian, an old family friend. Vlad and I were crushed in the back with Annabel and Claire. Hina had the front seat. Everybody was in a holiday mood – everybody, that is, except Vlad. I was, he'd decided, different with my friends; noisier and less relaxed, I wouldn't let him be. None of us would. Every conversation was turned to him with a question, a polite cock of the head, a small sideways glance. What was it about these grown-up girls with their ordered chat and smug chauffeur?

Twice Annabel asked him what it was like to live in Budapest. ('Or was it Belgrade?') Claire would keep bringing up the gypsies. Only Hina saved the day by offering her cigarettes and smiling at him softly.

'Don't worry,' she said, 'the Dunlops know how to make us Black and Tans feel very welcome.' Vlad knew whatever she meant was well intended so he smiled back and accepted the cigarette.

I didn't like Vlad smoking, and I knew my mother would hate it. I hadn't realised how much I'd dislike it until the first thing he did at Heathrow was light up; anxious, desperate, longing for the comforting burn of tobacco. What felt naughty and poetic in Romania, I decided, looked tawdry and immature in Britain. As did his shaved head, which appalled me.

'I was drunk,' he explained. 'It was a bet.'

'But you knew you were coming to stay.'

'So? You don't love me without hair?'

'It's not that. It's just . . . '

Vlad stared at me with a relentless gaze all the sharper for a lack of hair to hide behind. I was the cad, a shallow dandy that I cared so – but I did. He'd arrived looking like an East European convict and this was meant to be our big moment, a chance to introduce my world to Vlad as someone to believe in – my first proper boyfriend, thank you very much. But of course it was never going to be like that. The chasm was too great, my hopes too high. We didn't mention his hair again. Or the fact he had failed a second attempt at first year in Iaşi. God, why did it have to be so hard? Why couldn't Vlad buck up?

Only as we sailed north in a rented Peugeot did it slowly dawn on me that he'd been right. Of course his first trip to Britain as my boyfriend should've been just me and him and the buzz and clatter of London. Beautiful, silent Vlad in my private space would have been enough for a first time together. But distance distorts and I was impatient to show him off – my love, my obsession, my shaven smoking foreign boy.

The house was imposing and Georgian with black sash windows staring out to sea. There was a dry-stone dyke flecked with lichen and white painted stones flanked the gravel path beneath a wide grey sky. It had been the longest journey of Vlad's life.

'We're here! We're here!'

Vlad peered out of the window. He felt like he was on Death Row, waiting, crouching beneath his seat belt as everybody scrambled from the car.

'Darlings! Well done! Hello hello!' Mum ran to her guests, arms out, the dogs dancing at her feet. Soon it would be his turn, and sure enough there he was being embraced, scooped up in a curious rush of nostalgia as Mrs Dunlop took his hand between her rough palms and leant forwards to kiss him purposefully on both cheeks.

'Vlad, good to see you! Must have been quite a journey. I do hope these girls let you get a word in!' And before he knew it she'd moved on to take Hina with one arm and me by the other to show us the view from the front of the house.

'Isn't it heaven! Absolute heaven and not a soul for miles.'

Vlad stood rooted to spot, staring at our trio, temporarily astounded by the similarity between mother and daughter.

Mum had ushered us into the conservatory and was introducing her young guests to her old ones. 'And this is Vlad. Gosh! Haven't you grown?' She stood back checking him properly for the first time, Vlad's cheek stained with patches of dark crimson. Aunt Angie smiled.

'Mum!' I protested in a violent whisper.

'Well darling, he has. Come on, don't be so sensitive!' She was having too much fun – not even her daughter's adolescent boy could get in the way.

'SO VLAD, HOW WAS YOUR JOURNEY? WAS-IT-LONG?'

My aunt began shouting, loudly, into Vlad's face. I winced. He wondered whether he should shout back.

'HOW WAS YOUR FLIGHT?

He said nothing. I nudged him.

'Fine, his flight was fine. Wasn't it Vlad?'

Vlad said nothing.

'Aye aye, now who would like a drink?' My father arrived to fill the door frame but did not, I noticed, look at Vlad – who I was answering for once more, though this time he'd not been asked a question.

'I would like a gin and tonic and Vlad will have a beer.'

'No daughter of mine will drink gin!' Dad was still not looking at Vlad, standing as he was raking his hand through a mop of curly hair, aware of where Vlad stood in the room but still unable to bring himself to look. I turned to Danny.

'Danny, can you get me a gin? Make it a large one. And a beer for Vlad?'

Briefly I hated the men I loved most. Both of them. I had made a mistake and neither was going to let me forget it.

For Vlad, most punishing of all were the dinners; the first an ominous taste of what followed night after night. Even the preparations overwhelmed him. Why, for instance, was I upset when he wedged the cork back in the freshly opened red wine? Did it really matter who sat where? If every oil painting was lit with lamps, were twelve candles really necessary? How many knives? Where to put the forks? Vlad didn't recall such efforts at Strathallan. What kind of holiday house was this anyway, with its endless silver and dust?

'Mum borrowed it from my godmother.' Still my voice was not warm. The shaved head mattered so much more than it should've done.

Vlad asked no further questions as the room swelled suddenly with expectant, loud diners, fresh in from boules and golf.

'Oh, so this is Vlad! Jings you could do with some flesh on you! Eh! Extra potatoes here for the anorexic Bulgarian!' My vast younger brother Duncan, buoyed by a rare birdie at the ninth, mauled Vlad's shoulders in a bracing grasp. Duncan's work had something to do with conflict resolution in the Balkans; like Dad he disarmed through attack. Vlad didn't want extra potatoes. Duncan had not yet said hello.

Why, Vlad wanted to know, could he not sit next to me? Instead my mother, twirling late into the room every bit the birthday girl, graced him with the seat beside her. My heart sank.

For Vlad the only moment of respite came with the fillet steak, a single velvet and bloody experience that he would never forget. As a child a paucity of meat had seen it revered as better than fine pudding but it was in the hub of that Uist dining room that he really came to understand how sweet meat could be. If only he'd shared this thought with his exquisite hostess.

*

210

Hina's parcels were always beautifully wrapped in pastel paper with pretty matching ribbons, and Claire (again) opted to give Mum a sponsored Oxfam animal. But it was Vlad's gift that turned heads.

'My, what's this?' From a yellow plastic bag Mum extracted, with thespian poise, a pair of orange polyester pants.

'Pyjamas,' said Vlad quietly, wanting to die.

The pyjamas were held aloft; slightly shiny, cut for short legs and large thighs.

'They are lovely! Thank you, Vlad. How thoughtful.'

'Vlad's mum works in a pyjama factory.' I tried to make it better. I made it worse.

'Ooh, a pyjama factory.'

'Really!'

There was just time for Aunt Angie to catch her sister's eye before conversation resumed noisily at the other end of the table. Vlad glared at me. We were hurting. Why couldn't he try? Why couldn't I shut up?

'Tessa, where's Vlad gone?'

'How would I know?' Vlad, mid-meal, had left the table.

I found him in the porch staring out to sea. 'We don't really go to the loo in the middle of dinner over here.'

'I didn't go to the loo.'

'Oh?'

'I went for a cigarette.'

'We don't do that either.'

'I thought you didn't want me to smoke in front of your parents.'

'I don't, but . . . '

'You don't like it that I smoke, you don't like my hair, you don't like it when I say nothing, you don't like what I do say. What do you like, Tessa? What the fuck to do you like?'

'Don't swear.'

'Fuck off.' Vlad walked outside into the dim evening light, wishing he had another cigarette. 'And for the record, Tessa, I'm not your performing animal.'

I can't pretend I was proud of myself that first night. I sat late and alone in the sunroom, drinking Dad's Laphroaig and petting Chokkie, who was very old and kept farting.

'You care more about what your family think than you do about me,' had been Vlad's parting shot as he stormed off, shoulders hunched, head forward.

And as it happened that week I did. I hadn't realised I'd feel that way until we were en route for the island and by then it was too late. I cared hugely about my family (loving beneath all the brouhaha, but occasionally cruel) and longed for them to accept Vlad (especially Dad). It hadn't occurred to me that Vlad might not accept them. Or that there was a potential for real hurt in the crossfire. They were my family, after all. Of course retrospectively the one I should have stood to protect was lone Vlad, but I too felt vulnerable beneath the brutal scrutiny. I was weak and vain. I wanted my boy to be a hit. I had hoped for the impossible and cared too much when he wasn't. I'd seen Aunt Angie's looks and understood Mum's dry laugh.

I couldn't deny it. I cared deeply what they thought, but it didn't stop me loving Vlad. At the end of that first night in Uist woozy on whisky, I eventually stood for bed, determined things would be different the next day. I would give Mum and Dad hell and try to be nicer to Vlad.

Things got easier. They couldn't have got worse. Vlad didn't forgive me, but he came to find aspects of the holiday bearable. He could handle the touch rugby on the beach (he was quicker than my brother), Uncle Peter didn't ask him to play golf (thank God), and he couldn't swim so braving the North Sea was out. His favourite time of day was mid-morning playing Boggle with Hina in the sunroom.

'Mum you know that Duncan and Jessie are sharing a room. How come Duncan gets to share a room and I don't?'

'Darling . . .' She gave a little laugh and wafted her hand in the air. Intimate matters were not a family strength.

'I just don't understand why Vlad and I can't share a room. What's the problem?'

'You always make such a fuss. Jessie and Dunc, well . . . I mean, Vlad is very – '

'Very what? Very what, Mum?'

'Very young, darling.'

'He's twenty, and guess what – we are having sex! I'm sorry if you find that idea so awful.'

Vlad spent the rest of the holiday on the floor in the snug. We'd not had sex since he arrived in Britain.

London

It was Vlad who eventually called his mother; cupping the phone in his hand, aware that despite the shower his skin still smelt of chlorine. How many chemicals had they put in that pool? Why was Tessa so obsessed with the idea of him learning to swim? Where was his mother?

'Alo Mama. It's me. I'm in London.'

There was a silence on the other end of the line. Elena had wondered where her youngest son was – she'd presumed with the foreign girl (Marcel mentioned a visa). It was typical of Vlad to leave without so much as a goodbye. It made her feel sad inside but she didn't expect an apology. After all, it was up to Vlad now.

'I'm OK. It's all OK here.'

But Vlad knew something was up. His mother's voice was thicker than usual. He pressed her gently.

'It's just your father. I've come back from the countryside and he's . . . he's . . . '

'Drunk?'

'Uhm.'

'I'm sorry, Mama. I'll be home soon.'

Cursing his father Vlad put down the receiver, struck by how old his mother had sounded. And vulnerable.

We were, at last, together and alone in London recovering. Uist was behind us but not forgotten. Vlad couldn't forget my disloyalty; that I had left him exposed and unloved.

'Not true.'

'True Tessa!' He flared his nostrils, caught me by the wrist and we made love in the small back room of the flat.

Later and spent, we lay together on the bed, hoping to trick time that would keep moving on without us. Vlad occasionally wondered how he compared to previous men but he never asked about the others. It might have turned the attention on him and his past and he didn't want that. Instead and mostly he enjoyed us and how we could be together, now we were shot of my invasive audience. And he took the time to marvel at his new altered state – weak, hot, satisfied, brimming with affection.

'Your flat is . . . ' Vlad started, smiling, staring at the damp patch on the ceiling, 'smaller than I imagined. And messier. You are very messy.'

'Is it disappointing? Do you wish I lived in a penthouse?'

'No. I couldn't care. I love you whatever – you know that don't you, Tessa?'

Vlad didn't mention his conversation with his mother but internally ached with the thought he'd left and not told her where he was. Had he been embarrassed – or in disbelief? Either way Vlad didn't share. It was something his mother had got used to. Maybe it's what gave him his mystery – a silent survival streak that I had briefly forgotten to love.

'Ach!' said Dad, finally home in Rannoch, tending his Rayburn, trying to ignore the pain in his legs. 'Ach she'll eventually shed him, Anthea. He can't even hold down a degree. Useless, underweight little bugger! She'll tire of him – I'm sure of it.'

He didn't need his wife to point out for someone so young Vlad had been around for a very long time.

We stood in the chrome, tiled, tiring airport.

'Don't go.'

'I have to.'

'I know.'

'But it will be hard this time.'

'I know.'

'I love you.'

'I know that, too.'

Vlad and I understood that what came next was uncertain, vague. That he somehow had to find a direction to move in. He had to grow up. It was up to him, I said – for the umpteenth time – and watched as he moved behind the Perspex wall to smoke a cigarette before his flight.

'Can't you just do without?'

'No.' Vlad smiled and lit his cigarette.

I didn't like looking at him when he smoked. I found it hard. It reminded me of being a child and watching Dad inhale deep lungfuls of smoke. I would protest and will him to exhale. I couldn't bear the idea of someone I loved so much being filled with poison.

'I just hate seeing you smoke, that's all.'

Vlad laughed. The moment passed. He held me goodbye and went to catch his flight.

I stayed standing beside nicotine's Mecca full to bursting and watched the retreating figure of my boy, thin and walking away.

We didn't talk for a week. (Again the bell was broken on their telephone.) When Vlad finally picked up there was a surprising lilt in his voice.

'Hey Tess, guess what?'

'What?'

'I have registered to study Physics in Bucharest. I take the exams in a couple of months. It's a four-year course.'

'Cool.'

'You don't sound like you think it's cool.'

'I do. It is. Dad has cancer.' There it was, blurted out. Cancer – the ultimate show-stopper.

'Oh. Oh no . . .'

'Can you come and study in Britain?'

'What? How?'

'I need you here.'

'But . . .'

'Are you still smoking?'

'Tess. Not that – '

'Sorry. It's just . . .'

'I know.'

I put down the phone in tears, guilty, wretched.

Mum had called all three of us, her children, from the car, pressing our numbers into her mobile phone with an inexperienced finger.

'Oh.' I was standing in my little flat. I could hear my neighbour stir below. 'Are they sure? What kind of cancer?'

'Myelofibrosis.' Mum pushed out the word as if it was an unmanageable piece of gristle. Over the years she would get better at saying it. Eventually it would roll off her tongue with a disarming fluency.

'What's that? Where's Dad now?'

'It's bone marrow cancer. He's in another appointment. Will you call him tonight, Tess? He loves your calls.'

'Yes. OK. Of course. Why's he got cancer? Will he die?'

'I don't know, darling.'

I rang Dad. For the first time I dreaded talking to my big, shocking father. I'd been a coward. I could have pushed him sooner. There were little signs – his temper, the deliberate way he sat down, the basket he used to carry logs into the house. But I didn't want to know. And neither did he.

'Aye aye, daughter. Anthea no! Not fish! I wish they'd leave the bloody things in the sea!'

'Dad?'

'I've only got one thousand, five hundred dinners left and your mother insists on ruining one of them by giving me fish. I hate the stuff.'

'I'm sorry about your news, Dad.'

'Ach that's life. They've given me up to five years. I'll be around a while yet.'

'Do you think it was the sheep dip?'

'What? Bloody nonsense, and what the hell difference does it make now?'

'I looked on the internet and – '

'Leave that Goddamn machine alone.'

So that was that. Dad asked no questions. Characteristically he was all blunderbuss and black humour. I felt disloyal trying to ascertain whether cigarettes or pesticides or sheep dip were the cause. Dad said there was nothing he could do about it. He would receive increasing numbers of blood transfusions and take pills and slowly get worse and that was that. He'd known there was something very wrong for years, but why fuss?

None of which stopped me looking. I filled the hours scanning the net longing for answers, miles from Dad and Vlad, between jobs and radio slots and visits home. I had an irrational urge to order and attribute. To understand and eliminate. I had a new obsession – how could this have happened? – and there was the internet; my inanimate companion day or night, or both.

Myelofibrosis: symptoms include bruising, fatigue, pneumonia, diarrhoea, anaemia, engorged spleen, engorged liver. Slow death. Incurable. Condition rare. Causes uncertain. Benzene may contribute. Causes unknown.

I couldn't stop. I couldn't find the answers I wanted.

Did you know there are fifty poisons in cigarettes? Benzene is present in cigarette smoke and accounts for half of all human exposure to this health hazard. If you smoke you may die. Do not start, it is VERY addictive. Call this number to STOP.

Every night like a greedy child I gobbled up more of the same horror story, my sick father trailing in my mental wake. 25% of British men smoked – it was the country's biggest killer. 69% of Romanian men smoked – was there anybody left? In Romania men died younger than elsewhere in Europe. Oh my God. Vlad smoked therefore he was going to die. Vlad was going to die as well. Nothing I read told me smoking would not maim or kill. Nothing I saw told me Dad would live. Dad was huge and indestructible and he was dying. Vlad was thin and poor and he smoked. Nothing I saw told me it was easy to give up. Every webpage scared me. Everybody agreed with me. Smoking killed. Every smoker was dying.

Bucharest

Vlad would never admit it, but visiting me in Britain had forced a change. Briefly, after the acute disappointment of Uist (possibly because of it), in that precious final week hunkering down together in London anything had felt possible. We ate hot curry in the local Indian, peered out of the pod in the London Eye and sat together watching *Spider-Man*, munching ice cubes from cola buckets. We were in love and free to enjoy it.

On his return and still buzzing with vital memories and good intentions, Vlad surprised himself, calling Marcel, asking a favour (two, in fact). Yes, he could stay with his brother in Bucharest when he took his exams. Yes, if he passed he could live in their flat.

And so Vlad cut out alcohol (and glue and grass), and began studying. He'd enjoyed Physics in high school. He liked the fresh equations, the crisp logic and the science that clipped along unfettered by the need to conform to the vocational world.

'Why do you want to study *physic*?' tutted his mother, still bemused by Vlad's two wasted years. Uncle Bogdan shook his head. 'What job can you get with such theorising?'

But Vlad didn't listen. I'd told him any science would do. A science made him sound brainy.

'Brainy?'

'Yes, believe me science gives you credibility.'

Vlad didn't ask any further questions, lest he did not enjoy the answers. Instead he registered to sit the August entrance exams at the Institute of Physics in Bucharest and braced himself for life minus Andrei, Dragoş and Iaşi.

That was how he came to live in his brother's flat in the capital (empty save for a baby and a mother-in-law – Marcel and Silvia had landed another contract in Cameroon). Vlad passed the exams and took his place at the Physics Institute in September, catching a bus through Bucharest every morning beyond the workers' blocks to the flat fields of Wallachia; great wastelands filled with plastic bags on the edge of which sat the Physics Faculty. Vlad spent his free time with his little nephew, and listened to music. He only left the block for essential shopping and to join the post office queue if there was a package to collect.

He never opened his parcels from England until he was back in the flat, hidden from grey, polluted Bucharest. The contents invariably left him bewildered. A Nicorette patch. Nicorette gum – two packets (or three). Mouthwash. Multivitamins. Fruit drops or Polo mints. A scribbled note, sometimes on the back of a postcard.

Vlad – sorry, please forgive me, I can't help it. I am worried about you. I worry that away from your mum you'll not be eating properly and smoking a lot. I miss you. I am trying but I don't think I can wait four more years. How did they manage in the war?
Love,

       Tess xxxxxxxxxxxxxxxxxxxxxxxxxxxxxxxxxxxxxxxxx

What, Vlad wondered, had changed?

London

It's with some regret I look back at that uptight, irrational autumn, unable to see the good and instead seeking out the hopeless and the off-putting.

I tried pills but they made me feel stupid. I tried a councillor but I didn't get on with her scatter cushions or the beads around her neck.

'It is very normal what you are feeling. To worry about those you love.'

'No, it's not! The reason I'm here is because it has been drawn to my attention that I'm not behaving normally.' I may have raised my voice. I didn't go back for a second session.

A dose of 7.5 mg of Zopiclone nightly was what the doctor prescribed on my third, tear-filled visit. A sedative, a chemical black-out wiping away the thoughts spinning uncontrollably through my head and rudely poking me awake at an impossible hour.

During this deranged, sleepless storm and out of the blue my agent found me a new job. I'd briefly taken my eye off the glitzy appeal of a media career and pulled away from a creeping, almost shameful desire to become a TV presenter – and that was how I landed my first on-screen job. I didn't give a stuff at the audition. *I was a character*, the series editor decided, and so it was that I accepted a contract in Bristol to become a regional presenter.

I thought it might distract me but it didn't. It made things worse. I broke my radio contract, found a lodger, packed a bag and got in the car. Vlad was in Bucharest, my parents were in Scotland, my life was in London and I was going to be a regional presenter in a city I did not know.

Bristol has a world famous bridge (popular for suicides), spacious city downs and the 'finest suburb in England': Clifton. It has two trendy universities and the wonderful West Country burr. But all I saw was my programme editor worrying about this woman he'd employed who wafted around spilling into tears and upsetting contributors. And I saw smokers. Above all else, I saw smokers.

I was taken to one side within the first month. 'Tessa there have been, well . . . ' My boss looked anxious, like a prep schoolmaster who needed to hit a child he didn't want to hurt. I felt sorry for him. 'It's just . . . people are finding you very hard to work with. There have been complaints.'

'James, can we move tables please?'

'What? Yes. Why?'

'I've got a wobbly chair.'

I had a smoking neighbour. I nearly lost my job.

'Darling, you've got to pull yourself together. This is nonsense! Vlad is working very hard in Bucharest and you have a new job.'

'I know, Mum, but I can't stop thinking about his smoking.'

'But he's a young boy. Leave him be.' Mum sighed.

'It's no good. I can't see the point to anything when everybody smokes. They're all killing themselves. Dad is going yellow and I keep thinking of Vlad in that block in Bucharest smoking and smoking.'

'Tessa! He's twenty. Listen to yourself. Please. Anyway my grand-mother smoked all her life. She would drift around the house and as children we'd try to catch the ash before it fell from her cigarette.'

'And what did she die of?'

'I don't know, darling. But she was very old.'

Mum eventually got me off the phone and shook her head at Dad. 'I'm very worried about Tessa. She's more potty than usual. She's calling me several times a day to talk about smoking.'

Dad looked at his anxious, thin wife over the top of the paper and wondered if worry was genetic. 'For Christ's sake, Anthea, tell her to get a hold of herself! I have no intention of dying yet. She'll frighten away that good-for-nothing Romanian of hers if she's not careful.'

It was at that moment, sat across the table from her indignant husband, Mum had a brainwave. Later the same night, she picked up her pen and wrote to Vlad for the first time in years.

9th November 2002

My dear Vlad – Firstly to say how good it was to see you in the summer – I was touched you came so far to celebrate an old hag's birthday. The pyjamas await a Scottish winter! And I believe that congratulations are in order as Tess tells me you have got into Bucharest University – well done you! Physics, my word that does sound impressive!

As you also no doubt know dear Donald has been given a life sentence of sorts with a jolly nasty cancer that no one seems to be able to cure. He is, needless to say, managing remarkably and without complaint. The same, however, cannot be said for his devoted daughter who seems to think that his condition has been caused by cigarettes.

From what I gather Vlad you have borne the brunt of her inexcusable smoking obsession but as a mother who has currently lost her daughter I wondered if I might beseech you to consider (temporarily) stopping smoking. I know this is unfair, but I don't know what else to do. I realise that to even ask you is most horribly remiss and understand fully if you toss this letter to one side as the mad ramblings of a silly old woman.

With much love and hoping to see you soon,

Ants xxx

In the envelope she enclosed a copy of Allen Carr's *Easy Way to Stop Smoking*.

Bucharest

That weekend Vlad collected not one but two packets from the post office. Back in the flat he sat, staring at their curious contents. After some hours and half a packet of cigarettes later he decided being in love was very tough indeed. He also decided he would try and manage without his main and most comforting companion in Bucharest.

On hearing the news I broke down in tears. 'Thank you, Vlad. Thank you!'

'You owe me one. By the way I feel like shit, I have a cold and my chest is contracting.'

It did make a difference. I can't pretend it didn't – as if a huge weight had been miraculously lifted from above. I was freed (temporarily – something else would come along!) from the vice-like traction of obsession. Hurrah! Vlad would live. How I owed my mother. I would buy my father a Stilton. I would make it up to them.

It turned out I didn't need to – they were my parents, after all. Vlad, however, wasn't happy, and felt his forced renunciation of cigarettes was unjustifiable emotional blackmail. A step too far, but one he bore out of love.

When Mum heard the news, the conversion happened overnight. Just like that she became his staunchest ally. 'I would do anything for that boy,' she asserted in front of family sceptics and Dad's disapproving grunts. 'I am devoted to him. He's very good for Tess.'

As far as she was concerned Vlad had made the ultimate sacrifice. He did something for me that Dad never did for her: he gave up smoking.

One Month Later

'What? Study in London?' The line wasn't great. Vlad wondered if he'd misheard.

'Yes.'

'No.'

'Why not? Please Vlad. I can't wait another four years. We'll be . . . I'll be, well . . . old.'

'Văleu! You said if I gave up smoking that would be it. No more requests.'

'It's not a request, it's an opportunity. You'll love it. The prospectus looks great!'

'You have the prospectus already?'

'Yes.'

Vlad felt exhausted. God. Had he not just come to Bucharest?

'No Tessa. It's too much. I don't think . . . ' He didn't finish his sentence. He no longer knew what to think. Except how badly he wanted a cigarette.

I put down the phone. I'd gone in too hard, too fast. Predictably one obsession replaced the other; a non-smoking Vlad was great, but I wanted him with me in London. To live next to him, to share my life with him, to have a relationship together – I wanted it all. I always had, from the moment I saw him again, but now I couldn't wait.

It seemed, however, that for the moment Vlad could. He didn't want to come to Britain.

Bristol

I received a letter from Iaşi. It was in Romanian, sent from Monica, Dumitru's wife (Vlad's sister-in-law). I spent the rest of the afternoon deciphering her loopy hand and foreign sentences.

Dear Tessa – How are you? We all have our health here and Laura starts nursery soon. She misses you since your visit and Vlad too as he is in Bucharest. I have been unemployed for some months now. The economics here are very bad. You can imagine how hard it is here without money or work. I would like very much to come to London and work in London. I could be a carer or a cleaner. I would be happy to do anything. I was hoping you could help me? My friend said there are lots of jobs in London but it is difficult to get over there unless you know someone. I was hoping you could help. I will learn English. I will not be a problem. Write back as soon as you can. As for Laura she will go to nursery and Elena will look after her. I hope you are well. I send you love and wait to hear from you.

With a sweet kiss. And Dumitru kisses you, too.

MONICA

I re-read the letter, wishing Vlad could be more like other young Romanians.

Monica did not hear from me. And I did not hear from Vlad, not for some weeks. I kept Monica's letter – I still have it. Her plan to leave her little daughter shocked me.

It shocks me less now. She didn't plan to leave her daughter; she planned to leave her country and that meant leaving her daughter. Monica eventually bought an Italian dictionary and found a job in Florence. For six years she worked in Italy as a chamber maid or, in Elena's words, 'wiping the shit of foreign men'. Laura had nightmares for the first year but gradually she got used to life without her mother.

CHAPTER THIRTEEN

Iaşi, Summer '03

Elena couldn't believe her ears. Vlad was leaving? He was flying to London? Next month?

'Yes yes! Mihaela, can you explain to Elena that it will be better for him? With a British degree he can choose to work anywhere in the world.' I'd opted to bypass Vlad – he wasn't being forthcoming.

'Văleu!' Elena shook her head. 'Alas,' she kept saying. 'Alas.'

'But it's a great opportunity!'

'My mother does not see it like that.'

Elena was now only just listening. She heard the disjointed, excited conversation but already her mind was elsewhere. 'A man belongs in his own country!' That is what she wanted to say. 'Each man in his own country!' Maybe she also wanted to bang her fist on the table, much as my Aunt Angie had done when I told her our news.

'Guess what!' I'd announced at Granny's ninetieth. 'Vlad's got into London's best university! Can you believe it?'

Angie, who'd been worrying about levels of immigration for some time, decided to set things straight. 'If your Romanian boy is so special he should stay in his own country!' Thump-thump went Angie's plump fist, thumpty-thump up and down on the extendable oak table. 'Our country is too full!' Thump, back down onto the same table where she'd reared her two handsome children. Thump, a perfect little pink fist.

But Elena didn't thump; nor did she comment. She rose briefly from her stool to turn down the borsch and call Laura in from outside.

So that was that, she thought. Her boy was going to live in London with the foreign woman.

Vlad hadn't wanted this. He couldn't put his finger on exactly why. After all, the Prospectus sold student life in London as shiny and enticing, the labs astonishing, the equipment new – spectrometers, particle counters, lasers. There he would be a scientist conducting his own experiments. A lithe Asian girl smiled out from the picture beyond her safety goggles and hagib. *UCL is an international community.* This was an establishment proud of its heritage and diversity, the Physics and Astronomy course a market leader, second only to Cambridge.

But it wasn't a fear of the unknown that held him back. It was more fundamental than that. It was me, or at least the idea of being dependent on me.

'How much?'

'£12,000.'

'In total?'

'No. For the first year.'

'Holy shit!'

At the time we'd been staying in a neo-Gothic, almost kitsch hotel in Sinaia – a picturesque ski resort complete with old King Carol's castle and royal connections. English-born Queen Marie would come here to absorb the solitude and scale the mountainside on horseback, while Ceauşescu liked it as a place to entertain dignitaries and shoot bears.

I'd intended the trip as a romantic weekend away after Christmas. Somewhere I could warm Vlad up to my idea, only Vlad didn't ski or shoot bear and he had toothache. And the waiter kept staring.

'No Tessa! It's too much money.' So much in fact that Vlad couldn't work it out in lei. 'Do you even earn that?'

'I'll find ways to earn the extra money. You'll see. Anything is possible!' I bit into a large garlic sausage.

Vlad caught his breath. He was acutely aware of the optimistic smile on my face. *Anything is possible.* Not once in his entire life had Vlad ever considered that *anything* might be possible. That's not how it worked in his head or country. Success surprised him.

'It's not a good idea – I think it is too much,' he said again above the rattle of the accordion, and took another swig of beer. He pushed back his chair and looked about the room in disgust. 'I hate this restaurant! It's full of rich, corrupt fuckers. All the fat pigs in this room are corrupt.'

'It's that Latin machismo of yours that's getting in the way. No one needs to know I'm paying for you.' I squeezed his hand. 'No one!'

But Vlad knew. After I had flown back to London, he consulted an English Dictionary for the first time in years.

Machismo: a strong sense of masculine pride: an exaggerated masculinity.

There was another two months of brooding before Vlad signed the UCAS form. Purlease Vlad, I wheedled down the phone. Purlease! I filled in the application for him with lots of flowery sentences and sent it on to Mr Barnes (still at Strathallan) for a reference in compulsory English. He was delighted to be able to help, naturally.

When it came, the conditional offer was stiff – 80% in all Vlad's summer exams. I cringed; he groaned. UCL, *London's Global University*, did not recognise Romania's examination system – there had been no rush of former communists to the capital's exorbitant seat of learning.

But despite his reservations Vlad studied hard that summer, got the grades (he even enjoyed a couple of the papers) and there was a record score in his International English exam (he wrote an essay on how to give up smoking). I telephoned through the results and UCL firmed up their offer in writing. I stuck the letter on the wall in Bristol – my landlady had a rule about bluetack but I couldn't help myself. My Vlad at UCL! Who's a clever boy!

As for Vlad, he almost started looking forward to the change. After all, it meant we'd be together – which was the whole point. He sent me a final email the week before I flew out to meet him.

Tess I love you.

I loved talking to you on the phone yesterday; I found our conversation very entertaining.

I love your sms messages although I think you will build an astronomical bill.

I love the fact you're a dreamer — someone has to be.

I love the thought of coming home to you.

I wait for you with an open heart.

Vlăduţ

With Vlad's mother told, the British embassy in Bucharest was our last port of call. Both of us wanted the train journey south to last forever; feeding on cold chicken schnitzels, leaning out of the window and waving at the pastoral scene, watching the poplars blow silver in the wind and counting the hours until the sky went pink.

Bucharest, in comparison, was a dirty come-down and the British embassy an arbitrary exam at the end of a spirited summer term.

In the queue there was a couple speaking a little loudly, and laughing too. Vlad bristled. They were British and on a gap year. They stood in front of us as we waited to apply for a student visa outside, on the pavement.

'Ya,' said the young boy. 'Hugo said he'd come but he got stuck in Serbia. Daft idiot! He was absolutely hammered on the local juice and missed the train.'

'Oh God, Bodge! This queue is taking forever. Who *are* all these people? You're such a dope for losing your passport!'

Bodge looked out over the crowd surrounding the embassy. 'Excuse me! HOW LONG BEFORE OUR TURN, HMM?' He pointed ostentatiously at his silver watch. 'HMM?' The security guard with a gun shrugged. Bodge asked again, louder this time.

The couple's unregulated noise showed up the anxious faces that queued beside them. Their lack of humility in that moment was an affront. We were in Romania, after all.

'Who *are* all these people?' the girl asked a second time. 'God, this is awful.'

I squirmed and turned my pale Anglo-Saxon face to the pavement. I wanted to say something, to tap the pair sharply on the shoulder and explain. 'These people are looking to do what you have done. To take a break from their country. And they all speak English.' Vlad was glad I didn't. He wanted to punch them in the face. Five minutes later they were fast-tracked.

There was a problem. I could tell from the line of Vlad's back. It was erect and his neck had coloured, a creeping blush moving up from under his collar. He was mid-interview and in trouble.

'Do you guarantee that you will leave the United Kingdom after you have completed your studies?'

That had been the final question on the form.

'Tick yes, obviously! I urged. Just tell them what they want to hear.'

I was Vlad's guiding hand and also his official sponsor. Mum had stepped back. Vlad had got into UCL, after all. Even bogus students made it into Britain, didn't they? I signed myself as Vlad's (platonic) sponsor and Mum agreed to provide some extra paperwork. What could possibly go wrong?

Vlad must have got a man beyond the glass, one who didn't like his young single male status. A status *without dependants*.

It was a small gesture, little more than a twist of the wrist. Vlad was summoning me. I stood up promptly and smoothed down my taupe skirt.

'What are you wearing?' he'd asked in horror that morning when I emerged from his brother's flat.

'It's my Establishment look.' I twirled in my mother's fawn cashmere throw, a velvet headband, inherited pearls and a little light lip gloss. Very understated, I thought. Should I be called for, I was prepared. I could not possibly be fucking Vlad.

'These bank statements don't demonstrate a regular income. Who exactly did you say was sponsoring you?'

232

Vlad felt sick. 'A girl, a woman, family friend. Erm, she works in TV.' Christ, he was losing this. Where was the smirking woman with the pert breasts? Who was this faded man with a snail for a mouth? Vlad wished he'd worn a tie.

'TV?'

'Yes. I think so.'

'You think so?'

It was during the silence that followed and in desperation Vlad decided to pass the game over to me, the reason behind his undignified presence in front of a glass screen he wanted to smash. That's when he bent his wrist in my direction. 'My sponsor is here with me if you would like to meet her?' Did he mumble? Most probably.

Before the civil servant had a chance to answer (if he heard) I was there in front of his face, grinning through the glass, a red bow for a smile and a voice raised above the rest.

'Hello!'

Vlad almost jumped, stepping back to make way, astonished by the change in the air around him, the shift in demeanour of the man whose mouth was pinker and wider now and whose arms unfolded to reveal a slight stomach.

'Hello, how can I help?' I pushed out a perfectly formed plum. Vlad watched agog, riveted and repulsed as his mature sponsor grew into her role.

'Ya, that's right – we're keeping an eye on him. He's done awfully well and got into University College London. One of the best, you know.'

The bureaucrat nodded and warmly, almost apologetically, explained that my bank statements did not reflect a regular income, or the means to sponsor a student to the tune of £12,000 a year.

'Ya. You see I work in the media and they're terribly slow payers. Most irregular. It's really more of a hobby.' I gave my head a little toss.

'Well, we'll need more evidence of your financial means.'

'Of course!'

With a flourish I deftly flicked through the pile of papers.

'Vlad should have drawn your attention to this. Such a quiet lad, aren't you?' I pushed a thick, rich sheaf of paper under the counter. 'I think you will see there that my grandmother is a woman of some means. £80,000 in that fund alone, and she has many more. We love to help in different corners of the world – three musketeers are we!'

'Yes, well, this looks in order.' The civil servant glanced up and smiled. 'What was it you wanted? A one-year visa?' I had made a friend. He didn't smile at Vlad, just me.

'That would be great. Hmm? Eh Vlad, you lucky chap! You better behave yourself in London.' I looked through narrowed eyes at my charge, who stood still, unable to speak, watching as I said a final farewell to our bureaucratic gatekeeper. 'Thanks awfully.' Swish went my hair. Only the glass panel stopped me leaning in for a kiss.

'What worries me most,' Vlad said later, once I'd removed the pearls, headband, lip gloss, 'is that you really seemed to enjoy your little performance.'

'Yes, you know I rather think I did.'

London, Two Weeks Later

'Darling, calm down! You know the boys. That's what brothers are for.' Mum was distracted. She thought (not for the first time) her daughter was over-reacting.

'Grooming, Mum! Duncan said I was grooming Vlad. That's sick.'

'Oh come on, sweetheart. Where's your sense of humour?'

I'd lost my sense of humour. I'd forgotten to put it down on my list.

> *Driving lessons (ring for provisional licence)*
> *Dentist (private?)*
> *Bicycle*
> *Bank account*
> *Extra swimming lessons*
> *Part-time job*

'Bloody hell, Tess. Does the poor guy know what's about to hit him?' Duncan found my list (it was pinned to the fridge). Vlad's arrival was two weeks away and I was in preparation mode. The lodger had been moved out.

Douglas, who hadn't seen Vlad for eight years, turned the whole thing into one big joke. 'Does Tessa want me to come and tuck him up on an evening? Tess, can I come and play rubber rings in Peckham pool?'

Only Dad remained uncharacteristically quiet. In part accounted for by near constant nausea, but exacerbated by his daughter and her plan, of which he did not approve. He'd refused to put any money towards Project Vlad but he did comment on Listgate.

'Go easy on the lad, Tessa. If you wanted an all-singing, all-dancing, public schoolboy you should have found one.'

'Just because you have cancer doesn't mean you can say what you like!' I yelled down the phone, and immediately wished I hadn't.

But I duly crossed *Extra swimming lessons* off the list. They could wait until the following summer.

Vlad's plane landed in Heathrow on time and he stood in a queue behind an enormous Nigerian woman in swathes of lurid cotton. Was it something he'd said? Maybe the way he looked?

'So you're here to study.' It had not been a question. The immigration official raised an eyebrow under his turban, snapped the Romanian passport onto the desk, called a colleague and Vlad was led away by the shoulder into a small room where the dregs of London's newcomers were scanned for nasties.

Finally it was Vlad's turn. The neat woman taking the X-rays almost apologised as she pressed the white machine against his crooked chest. His impeccable English helped – so too his scrappy, boyish look, which only certain women would ever understand as attractive.

Some four hours after arrival he was set free with a clean bill of health. He did not have tuberculosis, although his breathing was somewhat constricted as he followed my scribbled instructions on how to cross London.

After his fleeting visit to the capital post-Uist a year earlier, Alin had pressed him to talk but Vlad hadn't been forthcoming. Tucked away in my curious corner of the capital he'd been preoccupied with us and the traumatic ebbs and flows of new love. Even the London Eye had proved an unwanted distraction; he was shocked by the £20 tickets and dismayed by the relentless grey. All cities, he thought, were the same from above.

'But what is it like?' pressed Alin.

'Big,' shrugged Vlad.

Rattling across the western suburbs of the capital, he saw his new home through sharper eyes. The human juggernaut that pushed in and out of the carriage at every station stop – their multi-coloured clothes, multi-ethnic faces, multiple modes of being and sitting or standing. He was squashed up in a sea of otherness thousands of miles away from the Romania he knew, where difference was limited and simple; you were from Bucharest or Moldavia, a gypsy or Romanian, city dweller or peasant.

Vlad was not one for reflection or regret, but as he sat in the crush he did wonder exactly why he'd decided it was a good idea to leave his homeland.

Iaşi

Elena left the ward without turning back, her upright posture giving nothing away. What a fool Tuca was, burning up in the midday sun on the roof until there was nothing left in his head except nonsense and steam. He had fallen from his perch onto the cracked earth below, his skull just missing the sharp concrete edge of the step. For the love of God! Stapling sheets of aluminium at forty degrees was a young man's work, but then no one worked like her Tuca.

She'd called Marcel in Cameroon that same morning. How else could she pay for her husband's care? He'd be sure to wire the money. Marcel was always as good as his word – and now, recently promoted, he had plenty cash. This was a relief. In the bed next to Tuca was a pale man with a broken arm. She could tell from his colour he'd been in the bed some days – the sheets were soiled and the sick arm stuck out at an unfortunate angle. Elena tried hard not to look. Hospitals were no place for the poor.

Thank the Lord that Dumitru had come home. How else would she cope with a husband who had a torso the colour of a ripe plum and two broken ribs? Dumitru had been working in Italy. He'd taken the tourist bus that only went one way, kissing his small daughter on the forehead before he left.

'Be good for your granny. I will come home with candy in my pockets!'

'Tata, don't forget to send me rollerblades like Gita's.'

But Dumitru didn't like living abroad. 'Naşpa!' he spat on his premature return. 'I don't like Italians, they are racist. And I don't like Romanians in Italy – all they do is talk about money.' And with that he resumed his life in the bread factory, dropping his little daughter at school every morning. It was his wife Monica who went back to Florence.

Yes, Elena was glad she had one son at home. Maybe there was something to be said for not studying, after all. As for Vlad, he would be in London by now. Her baby had upped and left just like that, as she had always known he would, to live with the foreign storm in her sparkly life. Two of her boys in foreign lands with strange tongues, and a crackly phone line to connect them. And as she stepped across the hospital courtyard she couldn't help but shake her head in wonder. For years the communists had tried to crack the family with their cruel factory rotas, youth camps and ceaseless queuing – and now, finally, belatedly, they had got their way. Her defunct country was haemorrhaging young to the potent greedy West. What hope did a mother have?

London

Vlad unlocked the door, squeezed past the bicycle and let himself into the flat. There was a note on the kitchen table.

Hi Vlad – you've made it, well done! Call me when you get in otherwise I'll worry. I'm in Bristol till tomorrow – sorry! Make yourself at home.
Lots of love, Tess xxxxx

Vlad sat motionless on a kitchen chair and stared at the note. He sat there long enough for a small mouse to brave a scamper across the floor, under the oven, re-emerging along the (soiled) kitchen unit where it stopped briefly. Vlad had never seen a mouse in a house before. Not even in the countryside and especially not in the city. He didn't expect to see one in London. It was a loud sudden noise from the basement that frightened the mouse back under the sideboard. It frightened Vlad, too. A curious, aggressive moan; almost a grunt followed by another and another prolonged agonising release. Vlad kept on sitting – silent, appalled. What was happening downstairs? Was someone hurt? Christ!

I rang the flat. And I rang again and again until Vlad picked up.
'Alo?'
'Vlad?'
'Yes.'
'I've been worried sick. What time did you get in? How are you?'
'Fine. Yes.'
'How is it? Welcome to London! Sorry I didn't have time to clean the flat.'
'It's fine. I've put some music on as I could hear two men having sex downstairs.'
'Oh, Ian must be home. Yes, that can get a bit noisy. Just bang your foot on the floor. I'll be back tomorrow, help yourself to anything you fancy – there's money in a pot by the bed. Love you, Vlad!'

Vlad put down the phone. *Bang your foot on the floor!* Vlad had never banged his foot on the floor of a flat in his life. He found the money in the pot and took out a fiver, feeling slightly grubby. He didn't like taking money from my pot but he really needed a beer.

I was stuck in Bristol; at least, that's how it felt. How utterly gutting! Vlad was in London and once more I was in the wrong city.

'Tessa, I think it'd look better if you tried to sound like you meant welcome when you said it!' Kathy managed a watery smile.

'Hello and WELCOME to *The West Country's World*! Tonight Mike Brown goes in search of the ultimate caving experience and Wild Boars are back! I go tracking big pigs in the Forest of Dean.'

'OK – once more, shake it up a bit, and when you've finished walk out of shot.'

We didn't finish for another two hours. I missed my train back to London, the city I wasn't meant to live in because I was a regional presenter in the West Country – a regional presenter without a local accent, a point that was picked up on by the Nations and Regions Exec.

'The viewing figures are down, Tessa.' My boss pushed his glasses back up the bridge of his nose as he examined small dots in a table. It was an inauspicious start to the day.

'Well no one watches telly in the summer,' I said lightly, hating telly, hating Bristol.

Please *please* let the figures go up next week! I'd change my accent. I'd cut my hair. I'd do anything – I could *not* afford to lose my job. I had commitments.

'Vlad, are you OK?'

It was the fifth time I'd called. I couldn't bear to think of him all alone on his second day in London.

'Yes.'

'If you're bored you can take my bike out for a roam around. Just remember to cycle on the left. I'll be back tomorrow and then we can make a plan.'

'Plan?'

'Yes, I'll help you find a part-time job and we can go and register you at Uni. Hey, I miss you!'

Vlad made an indistinguishable noise. He didn't like the sound of a plan. He'd never had a *job*. Right now he couldn't imagine being of any use to anyone. God, what was he doing?

'Tessa?'

'Yes?'

'What's the password for your computer?'

'*Bigknickers* – all one word.'

'Thanks. See you tomorrow.'

Vlad spent the rest of his day drinking coffee and playing online chess. I spent the rest of mine telling Kathy how much I loved Vlad.

'Come on, Vlad – focus!'

'I don't like this. I don't like lying.'

'You cannot get a job without a couple of white lies. Welcome to the wicked world of capitalism.'

I played with the font at the top of Vlad's soon-to-be CV. I was back in London, we were together at last, the bed-ridden euphoria had lasted two days and then the pressing matter of a life to plan got in my way.

'We'll pretend you worked for Dad last summer, doing the books for the farm. He'll give you a reference.'

Vlad wasn't fully listening. He was watching a repeat of *100 Greatest Britons* on TV. 'Your country is obsessed with Winston Churchill.'

'Of course – he won the war. What do you expect?'

'And he handed Romania to Stalin on a plate. He promised that pig 90% dominance in our country. He's not *my* hero.'

'He's a *national* hero.'

'The world is obscenely parochial.' Vlad shook his head.

I looked across at him, marvelling briefly at his English. He'd been in Britain less than a week and spoke better than most of London. I wished he would focus on his CV.

Three years later the same TV format would be exported to Romania. Elena watched every episode. Curled up on the folding bed, she used her phone to vote for the first time. As it happened she picked the winner: Stephen the Great, the medieval Moldavian King who built a painted monastery every time he beat the Turks. Ion Antonescu made number six – an anti-Semite military dictator and bedfellow of Hitler during the Second World War. Nicolae Ceauşescu snuck in at number eleven. National heroes, all of them.

We didn't finish Vlad's CV that evening. In fact we hardly started it. He threw a cushion at the computer when I tried to claim he'd played basketball for the Romanian National team.

'Why not? You're tall and lean.'

'Just because, Tessa. That's why. Just because.'

I liked to think the differences in our value systems were superficial.

Two Weeks Later

'Oh Vlad surely it isn't that hard.' Why couldn't anyone else see what I saw?

'It *is* hard. I've tried, OK?'

Vlad felt exhausted. He'd spent two weeks trudging the streets of South London looking for a job (any job) without luck. Six weeks before college started, the idea was for Vlad to earn a bit of his own money. I wanted him to feel like he belonged and the best way of doing that in London was to work. Maybe the only way.

'It can't be that hard. Everybody else manages.'

'But I don't have a National Insurance number. I don't have any experience! And there are bloody Poles everywhere! Oh yes, and I'm Romanian.'

I was taken aback – Vlad was almost shouting. Ian banged on the ceiling. I stood up and put my arm around him. I felt helpless, like a mother at the school gates. 'Don't worry, we'll find a way. Have you tried the Camberwell job centre?'

'Yes. Twice.'

'And?'

'There's nothing for someone who's only legal to work twenty hours a week. They left me in a queue where a woman was showing people how to write a CV.'

Vlad laid his head on the table, longing for a cigarette and the dull familiar throb of home where there were no jobs for students, and where no money was a given and hanging out the only option. He missed his friends.

'Shit, Tess – I don't know. I don't know how all the foreigners in your city do it. I really don't.'

When I gave it some thought, neither did I – even menial employers demanded the basics: English, a bank account, a National Insurance number. It was a vicious circle.

'Hmm . . .' I chewed my bottom lip. 'I think we need to know someone, you know – on the inside. I'll put out some feelers.'

I called Annabel and Claire and Danny and Douglas. And Mum and Dad. And my agent (just in case). I was a privileged white girl in the hazy world of TV and radio, trying to find my boyfriend a position as a kitchen porter or maybe an industrial cleaner.

'Darling, I don't know – but Aunt Angie says he shouldn't have a problem. Apparently East Europeans are awfully hard workers. She has a lovely pair doing up her kitchen.'

'Thanks Mum . . .'

Vlad and I had managed to (almost) always rise above Romanian corruption, but that summer British bureaucracy beat us. In the end it was thanks to Annabel that Vlad eventually found work, washing dishes in a café in the Square Mile. She knew the owner (cash in hand – no questions asked).

So Vlad hosed water into canteen pasta vats, earned his first pounds and got to know his first Londoners: an Albanian pizza chef with stories about swapping Kalashnikovs for hard currency; a Mexican waitress who'd left her three children behind in Puebla; and there was a dwarf who stood on two stools to reach the taps – she was English.

242

At the end of the second week, Vlad cycled home, taking on the hulking Elephant and Castle roundabouts with no pause for thought, his bottom scarcely touching the saddle, £250 cash wedged into his breast pocket.

He came through the door brandishing a bottle of Co-op wine and a copy of *Metal Hammer*. We kissed and fell back, laughing, on to the sofa. He smelled of fried food and fresh sweat. God love him.

'Good old Annabel – we must thank her. See Vlad! Life's all about who you know.'

'Hmm . . . what happens if you don't know anyone?'

'I'm not too sure.'

September '03

I was at Annabel's house, going through her wedding plans. She was very excited and perhaps a little stressed. I don't think the Atkins Diet was helping her mood – she complained it was making her gums bleed. I worried she might have scurvy.

'I don't care – only three more days. The marquee goes up tomorrow.'

'Great! Annabel, see on your wedding invite it says, *Morning Dress*. Does that include everyone?'

'Yes, of course! I don't want you turning up in tails, though!'

I winced. The whole marriage thing was proving rather costly: hen party in Ibiza; Scottish wedding on the West Coast; luxury present (from a list I hadn't looked at); and now a fancy suit for Vlad. Not to mention the first instalment of his student fees the following week. I would have to call my bank.

Vlad was bemused. 'Why are you going to Ibiza?' he'd asked. 'You hate music and dancing . . . '

'Because I'm a good friend. It's a hen party, Vlad. Don't you have them in Romania?'

'Not like that – of course not.'

He was even more bemused when I took him to Layman and Sons in the West End, where the fitters walked on the balls of their feet and spoke in curious clipped English. I'd been hoping he'd get away with my dead grandfather's suit but Mum assured me it would be too big around the middle.

Vlad didn't want to go to the wedding and he couldn't get over his suit. Four days of dishwashing to pay for the privilege of looking like a cock.

Scotland, Annabel's Wedding

I knew Vlad was drunk – for a start, he was talking. And he kept jabbing the air with his poppyseed roll. On his right was a woman maybe twice his age. They were talking about her daughter's religious education. Uncharacteristically loose-mouthed and repulsed by her buffed face, Vlad rudely dismissed her belief in a multi-faith education.

'Christ, really I can tell you, you are wasting your time. You cannot take your child shopping for God. She will end up with crap in her head.'

So spoke the boy raised solely on the mystery of the Lord and saintly intervention, Vlad the cynical atheist who'd found the orchestrated hush of Annabel's church wedding disquieting. Not to mention that awful poem about love.

I tried to sign at him across the table, then kicked out and caught a stockbroker on the ankle. I took a slug of wine. Please Vlad! Not religion. His neighbour was puce – she'd never been spoken to like this, not by someone so young.

'Vlad!'

But Vlad was busy quaffing *Fleurie* and warming to his theme in an unusually thick accent. 'You think taking her to a synagogue is going to make some difference. I've never heard such bullshit!'

That was when I cut in, when Vlad was finally forced to look up and across at me as I loudly changed direction. 'Did you know,' I declared to everyone in earshot, 'I fell in love with Vlad when he was twelve?'

The table fell silent. There was no more talk of religion.

Vlad and I didn't speak for the rest of the night. I eventually found him having a cigarette behind the marquee with the bride-groom's pretty (young) cousin.

Things didn't improve on the journey home. The UCL term started in under a week; Vlad was distracted (possibly nervous), and I was planning ahead regardless. Friends' weddings can have that effect – indeed, they can be most unhelpful.

'Not all weddings are bad,' I said lightly, somewhere between Newcastle and Peterborough. 'Annabel's was very conventional. They don't have to be in a church, you know.'

'No Tessa! Don't even go there!'

'We'll have to go there at some point, Vlad.'

'No. We won't.'

Yes, I thought. We will. Romania wasn't due to join the EU until 2007 (assuming Brussels turned a sufficient blind eye), and Vlad's student visa ran out in 2005. Oh and I was nearly thirty.

Tick-tock.

London, UCL

It was the air of exclusiveness that struck Vlad first. Manicured green spaces behind gates and bars in black lacquered paint, perfectly pre-served squares with plane trees towering up and over the stuccoed houses; handsome, unscathed four-storey brick buildings with well-polished knockers and flowers that bobbed and waved in each window.

Bloomsbury, he had to admit, was a fine part of London. There were no messes on the streets and the pubs were old, dark and inviting. The university tried a bit too hard with a stumpy dome and columns close together, yet there was something reassuring about the campus. It felt solid, even cool, and the students were not what he was expecting.

'What *did* you expect?'

'I don't know. They're . . . I mean, they're different – lots of foreigners. It's like nowhere in particular . . . '

'That's London for you.'

'It isn't what I expected it to feel like. I didn't think London would be like this. I imagined something else.'

He smiled and gave me a kiss, and off he went on his bike to work in the Student Union bar.

It was much later that same night when he'd had four (maybe five) beers Vlad came home on the tube, walking purposefully, head down, hands deep inside his pockets. The flat, he knew, would be empty. I'd gone back to Bristol. There was the betting shop and the off licence with bars on the windows and the Co-op with a cracked door, which meant he was nearly there, ducking behind the dry cleaners and passing along the side of the concrete play park. He never fully understood why I claimed to love this part of London, or why I insisted on calling it quirky when it was so evidently a bit of a shithole.

'Hey! Waz the time mate?'

'What?'

'Eh bro, take it easy yeah?'

Fuck. There were three of them. One behind him, a hand in his back, one under a cap and now in his pockets, the other in front with a small knife pressed against his kidney, a gleaming silver strip under the street light.

'Hey bruv, steady! Easy!'

'You've picked the wrong person. I have no money. Not a pence.'

'Shut it, yeah? Arms out!'

There he was, powerless, his hands in the air.

'Steady, steady. Easy does it bruver!'

'I am not your BROTHER!'

'S'for the brown innit, bruv yeah, now don't you go calling the pigs. We're on yous, yeah!'

And as quickly as they arrived, they vanished off into the night with one old Nokia phone, three pounds and a blade in their pocket.

Vlad stumbled into the flat, stripping off his coat, rubbing his face in disbelief, breathing fast and shallow – and there and then he did something he never thought he'd ever do. He called the police.

'I think it's amazing what you're doing, Tess. I really do.'

We were standing together in Annabel's kitchen, leaning on the granite surface and chatting between courses – as girls do.

'What d'you mean?'

'You know, paying for Vlad, making this huge commitment to help him. We all think it's, well . . . amazing.'

'But it's not such a big deal. Johnny would do it for you. Anyway, I like working. Did I tell you, I've got a weekend radio show starting back in London next month?'

That was where the conversation ended. Johnny appeared in the kitchen and patted his new wife gently on the bottom. He was all out of things to say to Vlad.

I couldn't sleep that night as I lay next to my boy, his thin body tucked up against the wall. I knew Annabel wasn't alone. Did anyone see Vlad as my partner? Maybe Claire. Maybe Mum. For everybody else his arrival at UCL was an act of amazing (foolhardy) charity. Vlad, Tessa's temporary fetish, was a *very* lucky boy. They chose not to see I was playing an altogether different, self-involved game called *being in love*. Vlad would need a good, British degree to be a supportive husband and – dare I think it – a father, too. There was no getting away from it. I knew I was helping him for me, just as Johnny was helping himself when he persuaded Annabel to give up work four months into her pregnancy. So why was I finding it hard? Why sometimes did I feel mean (resentful, even) around Vlad? I wanted him to show me a little gratitude, although I knew it wouldn't work if he did. Did Johnny ever feel mean towards his gently swelling wife? Maybe the salary of a hedge fund manager protected him from such thoughts. Possibly it was tougher the other way around – harder for a girl who wasn't a banker to pay for a boy. Harder still for the boy in question.

247

Slade was jangling out of several speakers and the shop was mobbed. Christmas had come very early, or was it always like this?

Vlad had finished his first term and needed clothes. I should have given him his birthday voucher early but it hadn't occurred to me. Nor had it occurred to Vlad; that is, until he arrived in London. He'd even been mugged by boys with better (branded) footwear. He resented the acute cloying dissatisfaction he now felt in the boots he'd once learnt to love, the (fake) Levis too long for his brother and several tracksuit tops – nylon and, he realised, slightly shiny. Only the tribes of Poles wore similar harsh-coloured, man-made fabrics. Vlad had, for three months, controlled the swell of desire that caught him off-guard, when he cycled to and from lectures, stood in line for lunch or served cold beer in the student bar. He would not fall prey to the commercial trap that bowed the world's head and kept it working. But he was glad when I gave him a voucher from H&M for his birthday. The cottons, the colours, the cuts – *Merry Christmas everybody!*

'Wow, you look great!' I pulled at the bridge of his new jeans. They outlined and flattered his long legs and gave way to grey, understated sneakers. 'I like the shirt. Was that Hennes, too?'

Vlad looked back into the mirror and nodded. He was glad he'd bothered to get the right size. It was a very nice shirt. Worth £20, he decided. Definitely.

I looked into the mirror and kissed him on the cheek. 'You're lucky, Vlad – only thin people look good in cheap clothes.'

Vlad wore the same charcoal grey shirt to Christmas dinner in Scotland and then, too, I thought how handsome he looked across the table, candlelight marking each of his eyes as he patiently listened to Mrs Waddell talk about village life and her dead cat. Mum was impressed. Dad said little but then as a rule he was saying less and less anyway. He would live on for five more years and with each withdraw slightly; incremental changes only noticeable to family (in the beginning, at least).

This softer, sicker man was, however, easier for Vlad; they met halfway over the chessboard – just small beer and quiet conversation required. To see them sit together on the landing of our family home, staking out their pieces, heads cupped in hands, gave me great joy.

Dad took an interest and Vlad took care with his answers. They discussed collective farming. Dad shared a favourite memory: how he'd picked up two blonde hitchhikers on the Schiehallion Road in the spring of '68 – they'd squeezed into the pick-up between his dogs and asked to stop briefly at the local shop where they bought bread and margarine.

'That won't put any beef on y'bones! Come and feed at mine.' And so it was that Dad acquired two young Czech houseguests. They cleared trees, burned heather and clipped sheep for their keep.

It was a blazing hot day later that summer when Dad ran into the field below the house where they were stacking haybales. 'The Russians have invaded your country. The tanks are in Prague! It's all over the news.'

Honza and Magda immediately returned to their homeland and their family. From then on Dad received a Christmas card every year signed simply, *From Honza and Magda.*

That is, until Christmas '89 when pages of news and love and memories spilled out at the kitchen table. Dad promptly accepted their invitation and went to see the remnants of a collective farm for himself – it was the same year I travelled to look after the Romanian orphans.

'I told them my daughter had gone to Romania. They weren't impressed. Magda said they spit at gypsies!'

Dad moved to block Vlad's knight with his Queen and looked up at his opponent for a reaction.

'Ha! I bet they didn't tell you the only Bloc country that didn't help the Soviets in '68 was Romania. We refused the Russians . . . ' Vlad paused briefly to contemplate his move. 'Checkmate, Mr Dunlop.'

Dad was beaten by the Romanian yick. Very few people beat Dad at chess, but then not many who played came to Rannoch. That Christmas, Vlad provided indoor sport for a man who'd lived his life outside.

'Alo Elena! Crăciun Fericit! Ce mai faceţi?' I was shouting loudly down the phone, stroking my cashmere Christmas prize.

'Alo, bine, suntem bine.'

But Elena didn't sound *bine*. She sounded flat. She was flat, and cold. They'd made a mistake, she decided, joining deaf old Anica for Christmas in the little blue house. The ceramic wood burning stove had a crack in it and smoked them out of the kitchen. There was nowhere warm and electric heating was so much money. She couldn't bear to burn money like that. No wonder Anica spent so much time in bed.

'What are you doing for Christmas?' I tried.

'We stay inside. It is cold.'

'Oh yes! Of course, silly me . . . ' I called Vlad to the phone, my mood crushed.

Elena talked to him briefly, protecting him from her maternal longing, her urgent need to touch and see her son – one or the other of them. She didn't pass the phone to Tuca – he didn't know how to handle it properly and anyway he'd had a drink. Well, it *was* Christmas.

Vlad decided not to mention the presents to his mother. He was embarrassed – so many presents! Even one from my grandmother: a fine blue woollen scarf. He'd never received so much in one day, in one year. He felt tired from the attendant appreciation. He was out of words. What to say when he un-wrapped an *ACDC* T-shirt and CD? Mum had really tried.

'How do you do Christmas in Romania, Vlad?' she enquired, offering him a crisp.

'We don't really. I mean, there are loads of adverts now on TV, and religious people go to church. And we sometimes roast a pig.'

Here Vlad allowed himself a smile. He stroked the dog's head and thought better of describing Mr Frost, St Nic's communist replacement for the country that didn't consume.

London, March '04

Vlad tried to avoid British news. He didn't like our prime minister or my blind faith in our political system. He was secretly pleased there were no weapons of mass destruction. Of course there were no weapons of mass destruction! What had I been thinking? Vlad spent a lot of time following conspiracy theories on the net – even more after he was stopped once, then twice, by the police.

'What for?'

'Dunno. They checked my rucksack.'

'It might be because he looks like a fairground worker,' suggested Annabel, somewhat unhelpfully.

So why then did he feel at ease in London? Why, after the first year, and more so during the second, was it hard to imagine returning to Romania?

I've become like an animal in a zoo, thought Vlad. He couldn't bear the idea of his country's chaos and corruption.

'I belong nowhere now,' he said, staring at Tony Blair on the TV.

A report by the National Audit Office says thousands of Bulgarians and Romanians were granted British visas even though immigration officials said they should have been turned down.

The TV image moved to a reporter standing in the street where Vlad and I had stood so often, outside the British embassy in Bucharest.

If you ask people here what their dream is, they will tell you it is to come to Britain.

The reporter was warming to his theme, pressing his hands together with an easy assurance.

Vlad got up and turned off the TV. The next day the immigration minister lost her job; the reporter, however, kept his. No one knew (or cared) that Italy and Spain were the main destinations for migrant Romanians. In comparison Britain was hard to get into.

'Vlad, we should book our flights for next month before the prices go up.' I began to worry about the next student visa.

Vlad nodded. He missed his home and his family. As long as he was with me in London he realised his life would be cut in half. And I knew it. Doesn't everyone who's married to a foreigner?

Romania, Crucea, July '04

Vlad's maternal grandmother reminded me of a walnut; she had knowing dark eyes set in a sandy face. The day we met she padded around her yard with bare brown feet and stocky legs that had kept her upright for eighty years. In and out she went, up and down, tending to her pumpkin plants. There was baby corn and watermelon, cabbages, potatoes, garlic and geese that hissed and one old communal well. She had a bare electric light in the main room and memories of the Germans and Romanians fighting the Russians on the plain beyond her house. (An explosion cracked the windows and every room was ransacked.) Her chin went out and her mouth went in and the dust made her eyes smart. Her name was Zânica, meaning 'little fairy'.

Vlad and I walked for an hour from the train to reach her house, holding hands and sometimes arm in arm. Up over the hill, passing worker peasants who carried water, through the wild flowers that gave Zânica's bees their tangy honey and into Crucea, her Moldavian village. We ate cold pork and tomatoes in the cool dark of her small croft and I longed for Vlad's granny to like me. I tried to tell her that he'd got a first in his end of term exams, but she couldn't understand my Romanian.

And I stared as grandmother turned to grandson and asked how we understood each other; she puckered her toothless mouth in wonder and then wagged her finger at me. 'They fell out when I was thirty-three.'

'I'm sorry?'

'My teeth, I see you looking for my teeth. They snapped off one by one and I laid them out on the table all in a row. That's how Elena learnt to count.' She gave her daughter a mischievous smile.

We were joined by her sister Elisaveta who lived across the dirt track with her son Valerica. Homebrewed *racu* was served and stories tumbled out in no particular order. Vlad translated here and there, browbeaten by my need to know, and the incongruous scene – his showy girl on the old brass bed beside an ancient aunt and her adult son. And Elena, standing for the most part, watching out over us all in the room where she grew up.

Her eyes prickled just once, at the telling of the sorry tale of Uncle Cristian – Elisaveta's husband. He'd been chopping wood in the forest while his little wife and baby boy waited at home with supper on the table, but he never returned. The felled tree landed on his head and split his skull in two. Elisaveta went to live next to her sister. Zânica cared for mother and son in the old brass bed. She knew all too well how it was to be alone – she lost her husband before they'd even married. Her childhood sweetheart had gone missing for four years, presumed dead. The bell tolled for him in the local church and they had a thanksgiving service. It was months later on the day of St Dumitru Ioan appeared in the doorway of his family home, too thin to be alive with lice dancing on his chin. The Russians had sent him to Siberia, his punishment for being a Romanian soldier and fighting with the Germans.

'But then there was the famine after the war. That was worse.' Zânica shook her head. 'Everyone so poor and everything going to Russia. Once they had eaten the starving cow with no milk, what to do? There were dead people in the ditch.' She pointed a finger out of the window.

Vlad thought maybe this was enough story-telling but I didn't want it to stop; two sisters with so much life folded up inside each of their well-worn bodies.

'Please Vlad, the communists! I just want to understand how it was when the communists came.'

'You've been reading too many books, Tessa. Come on, we've got to go!'

There was only one train back to Iaşi.

'Are you leaving us again Vlad?' Zânica stared up at her grandson. 'Vai soon there will only be old people and gypsies left in our country.'

London, August '04

'Marry me!'

'What?'

'Marry me, Vlad. Please! Christ, don't make me beg . . . '

Vlad was tired. He'd been serving coffee to pregnant women all day in Dulwich Park and his computer had just crashed.

'Not now, Tessa. I can't think about that now.'

'When then? I am not going through that visa nonsense again.'

'I'm going to have to take this apart.'

'What? I'm trying to talk about *us*. Will you leave that bloody computer alone?'

Vlad looked up and sighed. 'Do we have to get married? It's just, so . . . '

'So what?'

'Tessa, we don't even have sex any more. You're always too busy. Working. Or planning . . . '

It stung. He'd meant it to. We had sex that night. And we agreed to get married.

That summer I'd almost been arrested by a man with a gun for trying to take photos of my own embassy while I waited for Vlad. It was the final straw and left me in no doubt – marriage was a must. It had always been desirable but I never craved the formal legitimacy of marriage. I knew Vlad and I were for life, certificate or not, and I certainly didn't want his Romanian name. Or a puffy white dress. But we needed marriage to reduce the humiliating, expensive bureaucracy. Once Vlad graduated he would have no automatic right to work. It took one (focused) night in bed to persuade my reluctant toy boy to marry me. The government did the rest. And if we had to get married then I definitely wanted a wedding. More than I believed possible, I wanted a wedding.

I blamed Dad. Beneath his bluff and brute force I knew ceremony and tradition were important to him. I wanted to get married before he died, but it was more than that. Vlad, from the outset, had been a hard sell and I wanted Dad to die knowing, despite his misgivings, I'd made a good choice (the right choice). And for that, he would have to meet Vlad's family – good people all of them.

Sure, I told Dad about Elena, her tolerance and kindness and her family with their extraordinary lives. I saved for him the stories about the collective farm; tales of Vlad's grandfather with his huge coat, under which he smuggled heads of corn from the barn to feed his hungry family; the great uncle whose whiskers twitched as he hopped up and down trying to convince his audience that life was better under Ceauşescu. He'd looked after the collective shop – for him life had certainly been better.

But stories can only ever get you so far. I wanted my father and his family (my family) to see it all. I wanted Dad to understand what made Vlad who he was before he died. I longed for his paternal blessing, even though his macho style prohibited such schmaltz. I knew, if he could, he'd make the trip – but only for a wedding. And the sooner the better.

'God Tessa, no! Not a wedding! They won't even be able to talk to each other.'

Needless to say a *multicultural* wedding in Iaşi was Vlad's idea of hell. Apparently opposites attract.

CHAPTER FOURTEEN

Scotland, September '04

Vlad travelled to Scotland on the through-the-night bus. He insisted; he still couldn't get over the cost of train travel. Mum agreed to meet him off the coach in Pitlochry. Claire, Hina and I were heading north a day later after work. We were going to celebrate my birthday.

With no chance of sleep Vlad stared out of the window at the lorries lumbering up the motorway like a procession of elephants. It wasn't the marriage that troubled him. He'd always known we'd have to marry if we were to stay together. How else to duck out of that student promise he'd made to immigration? And he loved me. He wasn't sure he believed in fate but he never questioned whether we were meant to be together. We were and he wouldn't have it any other way. But a wedding? Oh shit, with Annabel and Mrs Dunlop and his drunken father – he couldn't imagine a wedding. Nor did he want to.

The coach had swung in and back out of Glasgow, and was strumming up the last leg of the journey. Vlad felt fuzzy with fatigue but clear about what he must do when he arrived. After all, it was my birthday the very next day.

The rain ran in thick rivulets down the window and the sky was that special Scottish grey, but Mrs Dunlop was there just as she'd promised, keenly peering out from under her hood and waving wildly as soon as she saw him.

'Yoohoo, darling! Well done! What a slog. How was the journey?'

'Oh it was fine.' He kissed his hostess on both cheeks and, as he swung his bag into the boot of her car, 'Mrs Dunlop, I think I need to buy Tessa a present for tomorrow – do we have time?'

'Of course. What fun? What were you thinking? There are some lovely knitwear shops.'

When I finally arrived with Hina and Claire, Mum was more animated than usual. She would keep humming and broke into a spontaneous skip during the dogs' walk.

'Are you OK, Mum? It hasn't been too much work has it? Having all of us to stay?'

'No no!' Her face was rosy. 'It's lovely to have you girls here!'

'Then what's up?'

'Oh darling, it's just . . . well, you mustn't say I told you.'

'No! Of course not!' A lack of discretion was a keen family trait. I leant in.

'Well, when Vlad got off the bus do you know what he said?'

'No, what?'

' "Mrs Dunlop, I would like to do a spot of shopping for Tessa's birthday." ' She rolled her tongue around and tried to take off Vlad's accent. 'Do you know where he wanted to go?'

I was nonplussed. Pitlochry, a small highland town, was not renowned for shopping.

'To the Little Gem Box! We went to the Little Gem Box.' Mum's eyebrows hit her hairline and she made a strange tooking noise in the back of her throat like a hen. 'I, erm . . . I tried to steer him in the right direction. There was one with a pink stone but I didn't . . . well, it wasn't to my taste!'

I smiled. Mum loved an event to look forward to and she'd enjoy telling her friends. *It's such wonderful news – they met so young and have come such a long way together. It's too romantic for words.*

She would skim over the difficult bits, the age gap and the awkward calls, just as she skimmed over the rocks in her own marriage. After all, nothing should get in the way of a good story.

Vlad shuffled up and shoved the box at me. 'I bet your mum's already told you,' he said with a lopsided grin.

'Yes she has. Of course!'

'You can change it if you like. It only cost £25.'

It was a silver ring with a pale blue oval stone. I put it on my middle finger and spun it round.

'I think we might need to make it a bit smaller to convince immigration, don't you?'

He laughed and put his hand on my shoulder.

'Thanks Vlad. It'll all be OK, I promise. And I'll try and be less hectic.'

Did we kiss? I hope so.

'Ahem everybody, I have an announcement to make.' I tapped on the kitchen dresser. Claire stopped pulling Dad's hair and Hina briefly looked up from picking moss off her freshly gathered chanterelle. Vlad frowned. He knew what was coming – Christ, it was like being in some shit teen movie. How his fiancée loved a show!

'We are all going on holiday to Romania next year because, wait for it . . . Vlad and I are getting married!'

'Ooh!'

'Vlad, you brave boy!'

The girls (me included) whooped and kissed, and Mum clapped her hands. Vlad, meanwhile, looked like he wanted to climb inside the kitchen dresser. Dad, for the briefest moment, said nothing; he stayed where he was, rubbing his head with his hand. We avoided eye contact. And then, pushing himself to his feet, one hand on the Rayburn and the other on the table, he joined in.

'I guess we'd better have a dram. Anthea, where's the whisky?'

Mum was on cue. Dad towered over the room. He took his finger of whisky, added the same of water and lifted his glass.

'So!' he bellowed. 'Here's to the most reluctant bridegroom I've ever seen and his virgin bride!'

'Thanks Dad . . . '

After a second whisky even Vlad started to enjoy himself.

Iaşi

'What do you mean she's dead?'

'She was crossing the road to go to church and got hit by a car.'

'In the Vagina of the Big Mother of God! That bloody road, it shouldn't be allowed. Jesus!' Vlad reached a hand out to steady himself. 'Dead?' This wasn't the conversation he'd anticipated when I insisted he called home.

'Yes Vlad, dead.' Elena sighed. She was still numb. It was a shock but then Anica was so very deaf – and that road! Bloody men driving cars faster than their minds. She wrapped the phone cord around her index finger.

'I shall fly back.' But even as he said it Vlad knew he wouldn't go home. He was in the wrong country. Term started next week. He had no money. The funeral was the next day.

'No Vlad, really, there's no need. I can manage with Dumitru.' Elena's mind was already elsewhere; the food, the priest, the logistics and what to do with the little blue house and the animals. Alas, so many animals for one old woman!

Vlad was silent on the other end of the phone. He was never quite sure what to say when life threw up a big moment. Thankfully his mother didn't demand he say anything. He was very fond of his grandma and now, out of the blue, she was dead; old jam on the lethal road to Russia, and he'd not be there for her funeral. Vlad, the Londoner, whose granny died in a different world.

He hadn't forgotten the reason for his call, but he did decide against telling his mother about our wedding. Moldavians took death very seriously, and Elena was no exception.

She put down the telephone and shook her head, sad that two of her sons were so far away and sadder still at the shocking demise of poor old Anica. Tuca's family's had such bad luck.

Hers had escaped lightly in comparison, her father the only real loss and then they'd done him proud. The whole village turned up to see dear Ioan into the ground, his pale waxen face still handsome after seven years of escaping cancer. She and her sisters had cooked and cooked and dressed their father in his finest suit and folded his hands across his chest, their filial love ensuring everything was as it should be before he was lowered into his afterlife. And eight days later they cooked all over again and the local priest entered the house with his holy water, which he flicked and flacked around the room to banish any lingering spirits. On the fortieth day once more they gathered to cook and remember. Elena wasn't sure if she really believed her father's soul was being nourished from above by their caldron of borsch and cabbage parcels, but she found the idea a comfort and gulped up the steaming scent of fine food. On the first anniversary of his passing she wondered where the time had gone and was glad to stop and remember; indeed, it was only the seventh year Elena dreaded. To dig him up seemed somewhat macabre but her mother insisted – the spirit of Ioan must be freed. That was how it was in Moldavia.

The priest duly arrived with his stole and basil branch and all the brothers and sisters crowded around the coffin, which Tuca dug up with the speed and agility of a practised gravedigger. The result was disappointing. Her father was not there any more, and his suit looked shabby; only the polyester shirt had kept its form and colour. His grey skeleton didn't smell fragrant like St Parascheva's and, unlike her, his flesh had decomposed. Her dear father was ordinary, after all.

Her mother Zânica stroked her long chin and wiped away a solitary tear. 'To Great Lord,' she said. 'He looks thinner than when Russians released him. I did not think it possible.'

Rannoch

'So Vlad! What did your mum say? Is she pleased? Will she help us with the wedding? Did you tell her you asked me? I bet you didn't.' I burst into the sitting room, over-excited, in love.

'What? Oh.' Vlad, ripped suddenly from his own thoughts, looked into my expectant face and decided against telling me about his grandmother's funeral – just as he hadn't told his mother about our wedding. Never one for a commotion, Vlad would break the news in his own time.

Chicerea, Two Weeks Later

Elena walked up the baked brown courtyard towards her husband. She shielded the sun from her eyes with a hand and briefly paused to watch him at work. His hands and shirt were stained with ruby juice as he busied and skipped between his barrels, brimming with fermenting juice. Her man Tuca, the Dionysus of his time – adjusting the press and a weight here, another turn there. Despite herself she felt a surge of affection. Since his retirement Tuca rarely came back to the block in Iaşi, and with Anica dead Elena knew it was only a matter of months before they left the city for good.

'Hey Tuca! Don't you go drinking all the wine this year . . . '

'Eh? Hai my little gypsy if that isn't the best thing you've ever tasted I'm not a man!' He wiped the sticky juice that ran down his rough-shaven face with a sleeve. There he was, her jubilant god of wine.

'Did you hear me, Tuca? No drinking the wine. You have a wedding to provide for!'

'Eh?'

'That's right, a wedding. Vlad is getting married to Taysa. The foreign girl is joining . . . '

But before she had a chance to finish her sentence Tuca had jumped towards his wife, gripped her by the waist and started spinning her though the geese.

'Put me down you damn fool! Put me down!'

'Taysa, our Moldavian Rose Taysa! Ah, next year – a great year already! We are all a family now!'

Bucharest, March'05

'It's so sad,' she kept saying.

'It's not that sad,' I insisted.

It was the spring before our summer wedding and Mum was in

Bucharest. We were on our way to Iaşi and had decided to break the journey up. I thought she'd like to see some sights. But the capital was not quite ready for her. It was a cold March day and the rain was relentless, fat white fingers of cloud sat between the blocks. The concrete façades were cracking after forty years of intense hot and cold, and the sporadic signs of growth were not enough to swing it. In fact, they made things worse.

The palace was shut to visitors and for a dog lover Mum didn't respond well to the strays. 'Gosh Vlad, you really are remarkable!'

Vlad pulled his hood up and said nothing. What exactly had Mrs Dunlop expected?

'It really is much further behind Poland. Your father and I stayed in such a lovely little village there last year.'

I was beginning to regret the whole idea of involving Mum. I thought planning the wedding would be a distraction; give her a break from Dad and the animals. I'd forgotten that Romania didn't really do breaks for people like my mother.

That said, things improved on the train north; the views became more rural, the simple villages easier on the eye and clusters of goats and sheep with bells, tended by a single shepherd, delighted her.

'Look look!' she'd cry, jumping from her seat. 'It's biblical, positively biblical! Oh do look!'

Elena came into town for our late arrival in Iaşi. She'd starched the sheets and cooked and cleaned – everything was spic and span. Of course, the meeting of the two mothers was more or less a silent affair – apart from my noisy projections. Everything was about the look and manner. As Elena served my mother, she quietly noted her tired, friendly face, careworn hands and girlish figure – not what she'd been expecting. Later, when Elena climbed into bed beside Laura and Dumitru, she realised she couldn't remember what she had been expecting. Someone younger, perhaps – and more perfumed.

Mum, tired from the train ride and frustrated at not being able to talk properly to her little hostess – *What a remarkable woman darling and so like Vlad!* – also turned in early. We shared a bed. Missing her hot bath, Mum scrabbled and turned and I didn't like it when her feet touched my legs.

It was a long night and I wasn't ready when she bounced up early the next morning waiting for the day's agenda to begin, keen not to miss a trick. Elena was ready for her, however, bustling in the kitchen. Of course I should have been there to intervene – how predictable that I wasn't. A lifetime of toast and homemade marmalade washed down with a little weak tea didn't leave Mum best-placed to savour the delights of a Romanian breakfast alone. She baulked at the calves' livers in a pink sauce and couldn't manage the treacly sweet coffee and solid slice of bread. Then, with her silent hostess standing over her and the meal untouched, she worried terribly that she might have caused offence.

Elena didn't mind, but in the sharp morning light she was shocked my mother was so thin. Weren't westerners meant to be fat?

It was some hours later before we set off to find a venue for our wedding guests – a curious quartet picking our way between the blocks, with Laura straggling behind. The wedding venue I wanted didn't exist and Mum's persistent craving for a cup of tea and a biscuit diverted the search. Elena could not understand why or how my guests were coming for so short a period of time, at such vast expense.

'Have one party here and one in Scotland,' she repeated like a parrot.

'No Elena. I want everyone to mix. I want them to see Vlad's home.' But she didn't understand. She tutted, firmly gripped my mother's hand and kept walking.

Mum, meanwhile, became fixated with the idea of flowers.

'We must have flowers, darling. Lots of them.' I could tell she wanted to break up the grey for Uncle Peter and Aunt Angie. I snapped at her for caring.

Vlad was weathering his own internal storm. He wasn't ready for this. He didn't want it. He couldn't face it and he missed his Iași. Had he really been gone that long? Like mushrooms in the night, villas with gaudy roofs and railings had muscled their way onto the cityscape, his billiards den sacrificed for a plastic shopping mall, local traders wiped out by a Carrefour Supermarket. His mother was yet to visit the new French food paradise – she didn't like change.

We eventually stopped in the elegant university end of the city, where there was a hopeful wedding venue with a veranda and a stage. Mum sampled the chicken in soured cream, keen to make up for breakfast. Elena refused – she couldn't get over the cost. Why pay to eat when there was food in her fridge? Vlad said nothing. He didn't like the waiter with his cocky swagger and pink *Fuck Barbie* T-shirt.

We stayed in Iași for two more days. Things got easier; that is, until Vlad announced there would be no priest at our wedding. Elena shook her head in disbelief.

'Vlad, you must! Especially on 24th June – that's the nativity of St John the Baptist. You cannot risk no blessing. Vlad!' And she dropped her spoon to cross her chest in horror.

'The day was hijacked by the church, Mama. It was a pagan festival first.'

Vlad held on to this midsummer solstice. Let everyone believe fairies spent all day searching for Ladies Bedstraw to sneak wreaths under their pillows. He could handle a pagan love-in (he wouldn't even mind a bonfire), but he couldn't countenance holding hands and dancing in a circle with a greedy priest in a smock with flapping pockets.

'Mrs Dunlop can have her flowers. We will cover the terrace in wild flowers.'

But Mrs Dunlop was no longer listening. Unable to understand, infuriated by her failure to communicate with Vlad's immaculate mother, she'd taken refuge in party games. Laura was being intro-duced to Hunt the Thimble with lots of arm gestures and wild expressions. Elena was forced to find her thimble. She left her vituperating son to stand in the doorway and watch her elderly guest leap between the folding bed and lace table, one hand covering her eyes, the other with fingers counting while Laura hovered, mesmerised in the centre of the room, unsure quite what to do with her granny's *degetar*.

'Ready? Are you ready?'

'Am I getting warmer? Tessa, what's *warm* in Romanian?'

'Cald? Hot hot! Ooh ouch!' And on she went until she finally found the thimble, clenched tight in Laura's hot little hand.

Rannoch, April '05

Mum put the phone down feeling bothered. It wasn't like that, she knew it wasn't, but somehow she hadn't been able to say so. Aunt Angie had a way of getting in there first.

'I mean, Ants, how can you be sure he isn't just marrying her for the visa?'

'What?' Mum was taken aback.

'It's quite well known, darling – you read about it all the time. I just don't want to see Tessa getting hurt, that's all.'

'Tessa's more than capable of looking after herself.' She paused. 'And I won't have a word said against Vlad.'

The subject was politely dropped, no more said, but it rankled. The Tomas were such a lovely family and she'd been made to feel so welcome. Why was she not quicker off the mark with Angie? Damn her sister.

When we talked later that night Mum was surprised at my phlegmatic response. 'Don't worry. People are always going to be funny about poor foreigners. I've got used to it – there are lots of Angies and Shelias.'

I met Shelia on one of my many flights to Bucharest. She was going skiing.

'We couldn't believe it,' she told me. 'I mean, we found this deal. It really was ever so cheap, wasn't it Gav? To Romania! Who'd have thought? I didn't even know where Romania was!'

Gav smiled behind his Dick Francis.

'Nice to go somewhere new!'

Then it was my turn. I told her about Vlad. When we lived apart I found talking to strangers helped and this time, all geared up to see him, I really went for it. I made Vlad sound like an exotic eastern dream. I even exaggerated the age gap. I told her one day I hoped we'd marry.

'Oh,' said Shelia.

Oh? She didn't look as impressed as I hoped she might.

I talked some more, and Vlad became the spitting image of Goran Ivanisevic.

'Hmm,' said Shelia, still unmoved. There was a pause. 'So this boy of yours, what will happen? Will you move to Romania to live with him?' Gav peered over his book. They were both eyeing me intently. It was a look I'd seen before.

'No, I . . . I mean, I don't know if I could do that. Romania is much poorer. I'm hoping he'll come to London.' I nearly apologised – I felt genuinely sorry. I wished I could've surprised them with the answer.

Shelia smiled thinly and Gav went back to his Dick Francis. The conversation was over.

Chicerea

Elena got the gist of what I'd tried to say. The line wasn't good and I would shout the same few words over and over, but she put down the receiver knowing what she had to do. Look for somewhere else. I didn't want to share the wedding terrace. Did she know anywhere? Surely she knew somewhere good for a wedding.

She sat at the table and gave it some thought. She'd got married in Chicerea in 1971. Anica had boiled five chickens and the church on the hill was packed with locals. She and Tuca had danced around the altar in their holy crowns – just as it should be. God save us all.

But no, Tessa was looking for somewhere flash and central. In

266

the city with over one hundred churches she was looking for somewhere godless and convenient for her foreign guests and thin mother. To the Mother of the Lord, what will become of them all?

Elena shook her head and moved to shoo a hen out of the little kitchen. And there and then, quite suddenly, she had a brainwave. Why hadn't she thought of it before? The Strand – ah yes, the Strand! She put her hand to her mouth to cover the surprise. Yes, the Strand! Imbued with an unexpected urgency she crossed to the mirror, combed her cropped hair and strapped on a pair of sandals. She would go to the Strand and have a look. If she could've carried a tune Elena would, at that moment, have broken into song.

Tuca had been a handsome man back then; pristine pressed shirts, neat grey flannels and a fresh aroma of tangy lemons. She'd met him through her colleague at work (the one who sewed the cotton section into the base of every pair of pants). Elena had been just nineteen. Every Friday Tuca would wait for her outside the factory, with one red rose and a crooked arm to escort her to the Strand. Trailing roses and honeysuckle, the woodpigeons competing with the live accordion, there were symbols and fiddles and proper harmonies. Tuca would sometimes take to the stage and, with his beautiful baritone voice, serenade her – holding each note as if he were holding her in the palm of his outstretched hand. They married three months later and that first winter together they continued their weekly outings to the Strand. The lakes froze over and men and women skated arm in arm and drank hot lemonade. Elena had no skates but she loved to stand and stare with her man. Marcel was born the following summer and that was the end of their romantic outings. She had never been back to the Strand.

The tram took her into the centre of town. Elena didn't want to make a scene. She would just have a peek from a distance before she decided what to do. The Palace of Culture was being renovated. Iaşi's fairy castle was eerily quiet when she approached its fussy façade. Head down and minding her own business, Elena picking her path carefully down the side of the giant building. She could feel her heart beat fast and hard like a trapped bird in her chest. She was almost young again in that briefest of moments, preparing herself to look down at the panoramic of her beloved Strand.

Stock still, leaning on a trunk of walnut tree, Elena couldn't believe her eyes. What had happened? Where was it all? The lakes? The lawns? But how could this be?

'Eh woman! What are you doing? You're trespassing! Lady!'

Elena jumped back, apologetic, appalled at her own audacity. 'Scuză-mă, scuză-mă . . . ' And then, because she needed to know, 'Don't be upset, but please tell me what has happened to the Strand?'

The guard looked at Elena. He saw a Moldavian woman, almost his contemporary, and his tone softened.

'What, you don't know? The land was sold to a millionaire. They're building a luxury complex; hotel, flats – you know! For rich people.'

Elena nodded silently and looked once more out across the building site with its mechanical hum and clatter. What a fool she felt.

Romania, Transylvania, June '05

At last I was presenting something proper, working my way through Europe's legends for the Discovery Channel (it was a shame the commissioner insisted on including a psychic). The wedding was a month away and there I was in Romania, looking for the 'real' Vlad Dracula, who'd died some five hundred years earlier.

What serendipity! I was so high that week I thought I might fly off the side of the mountain. Not even Romanian bureaucracy could break my spirit. But aware that it might, I paid the Romanian production assistant bundles of dollars to stand in line to get another document translated and stamped in the Bucharest embassy.

No, I am not married in the UK. Yes, I am the citizen I say I am. Yes, I live where I say I live. Yes, I have money – look, see all my pots of money. Now can I get on and marry one of yours?

'Tessa, when are you coming to Iaşi? You have to have a medical.'

Vlad was unusually assertive on the phone. He didn't like his wife-to-be roaming around his country, the country he didn't trust. 'Oh yes, and there's a train strike.'

'I should be done by Friday. Don't worry, everything will be fine. Tell your mum not to worry.'

I spent my last days as a single woman flirting on (and off) camera in the land of vampires. Trevor the psychic lay on the ground and panted while old women spun yarns about their national hero and held my cheek, exclaiming over my sparse Romanian and wishing me matrimonial good fortune.

'She marrying a Moldavian! Vai, have you met my son? He lives in London.'

'She's a sweetie, listen to her Romanian. Lucky man! May you have many children!'

'Trevor, how many children will I have?'

'I told you to come north sooner. All your stupid family are arriving and there are no trains.'

Vlad was tired. He'd not just been paid silly money to film on a mountain top in Transylvania. He'd been looking for a venue without success. But he'd booked Hotel Traian for twenty-five people and made me an appointment with a doctor.

'I don't need a doctor.'

'Tessa, we need a stamp to say you've had a blood test.'

'No Romanian doctor is getting anywhere near me with a needle.'

'It's OK – we'll bribe.' Vlad sighed. His mother said she had a dear doctor who'd do us a *favour*. Elena had been surprised at my indignation over the prospect of a medical. Was it not a standard procedure for every young couple? She and Tuca had their samples taken.

'But why?' I asked.

'To check we were compatible. To make sure we didn't have handicapped children.' And on hearing the words spill out of her mouth she stuck out her tongue. The stupidity of it all.

Rannoch

Given the destination and distance involved, and Dad's unpredictable condition, Mum looked forward to the wedding with a degree of apprehension. She took out four hundred pounds' worth of travel insurance and days in advance packed three cases, ticking off her list as she worked:

Chemotherapy pills, anti-nausea tablets, warfarin, sterile gauze swabs, toothbrushes, toothpaste, microporous tape, large cotton pants, several checked cotton shirts, that lovely cream jacket that made him look like Noel Coward . . .

'Donald, do you want me to pack your talking tapes in case you can't sleep?'

'For Christ's sake, Anthea. Anybody would think we're going to the moon!'

Dad, stubborn as ever, travelled as he always did; his ubiquitous tweed jacket, a passport and toothbrush stuffed in the inside pocket. He counted twenty-five pills into a screw of paper and promptly forgot to take them. But then his daughter *was* getting married.

Bucharest, Otopeni Airport

I'd told myself so many times, a rail strike could just as easily have been scheduled in Britain. The truth is, as far as I could see (and as long as they weren't subjected to petrol rations), the communists had done public transport rather better than the West. However, Romania was being rocked by the world of the free – even the publicly-owned railways were not immune. There was just one scheduled train on the afternoon of Thursday 23rd June 2005 and that was at 4pm. My twenty-five British compatriots were arriving on a random clutch of flights. Needless to say, those on the cheap flights missed the train and had to pay to fly on to Iaşi.

Most arrived in time, stepping out onto the airport foyer victorious and inescapably British – inordinately tall, a predominance of elderly gents in straw hats and slacks (two uncles, one godfather), led by my irrepressible bosomy Aunt Sally, floating through the double doors in royal blue.

'Darling, how exciting! What fun!'

My group were certainly eye-catching and just a little out of place. I would have turned to smile affectionately at Vlad, but I didn't because we weren't talking. Prior to my own I'd never really given weddings much thought. I certainly didn't care for most of the matrimonial paraphernalia people go for in Britain; however, I did insist on quality wine.

'What do you mean? We've got my dad's wine.'

'Vlad that home-made stuff isn't going to be OK for my god-father, is it?'

'Sod your godfather.'

It went downhill from there. He didn't join me on the train south to Bucharest. I made the picnic for twenty-five alone. I hired the minibus to get us across the city alone. I travelled to the airport alone. Indeed, Vlad had only just materialised at Otopeni. He'd been on an extensive wine-tasting session with Andrei and Dragoş. He looked terrible. He smelt worse.

Iaşi, 24th June '05

There wasn't a big day, as such; more an alternative one – at least, from the British point of view. While for the Romanians our wedding was a novel anti-climax.

Don't get me wrong I knew enough to understand what was expected as a bride in Moldavia. I should have been helping my mother sew a dowry of hemp mats, crimping my hair that it might slide neatly under a nylon bright white veil, and investing in the most important costume of my life: a dress. Even in Siret two years after the Revolution you could buy a wedding dress in the local shop, flouncy and nipped at the waist. Back then it wouldn't have cost you much more than a packet of Marlboro Lights. But I'd always baulked at the prospect of a submissive pantomime (Romanian or not), and Vlad agreed. So I bought a simple floral dress off the peg in Selfridges and felt pleased I'd get to wear it again. And there was no photographer (did we forget?) so what I looked like was a bit irrelevant. Especially as our marriage didn't take place in the eyes of God. I never wanted Romania's punishing God at our wedding and nor did Vlad but Elena didn't believe us. Not until the day came and the legal ceremony was over, quick as a flash – so insubstantial it almost felt rude. Where was the thin silvery rattle of incense burners? The Byzantine chant of the faithful? The sublime, shimmering beauty of an Orthodox church?

'Upon my life, God save our children.'

Instead our curious collection of relations sidled awkwardly into a marble administrative office and watched as Vlad and I agreed with everything a woman wrapped in a Romanian flag said.

'Da,' replied Vlad when she asked about love and commitment.

'Sigur!' I managed a noisier affirmative – it got a titter.

The registrar looked vaguely overwhelmed in the face of her foreign audience, although she assured me she'd conducted one mixed marriage before. (Apparently a girl from Iaşi came back to marry her Italian – it didn't last.)

She said her final piece, we signed a certificate, and it was over. Before I knew it everyone was clapping and Elena and Tuca, swept up in the moment, were moving towards me, arms out-stretched, misty-eyed. They reached around my middle, and together held me tight. Everyone clapped a bit more and I kissed Tuca on the top of his head where the hairs parted, the scent of his scalp salty and familiar. I closed my eyes and breathed deeply, unsteady suddenly and surprised by my own emotions.

So we were married at last. But I was still angry with Vlad.

'Hey Tess, it's going well isn't it?'

My husband looked extremely handsome in his black suit, bought with Aunt Angie and Uncle Peter's wedding cheque – but at that moment, in the middle of our wedding party, I had an overriding urge to hit him. We'd just got married, I'd nearly cried with joy – I'd even forgotten what we'd argued about – but I was still furious. My head hurt, my throat ached, I had a bruise on my shin where I'd walked into the hotel bed leg, I hadn't slept for three nights and cousin Alin had just asked me if I was pregnant. Pregnant! Cheeky blighter – I'd only just tied the knot. Playing hostess to twenty-five Britons, including three men with terminal conditions (solidarity in numbers), had taken its toll. And then there was the small matter of dragging a reluctant fiancé behind me.

'What? Of course it's bloody going well, Vlad! I've spent the last year telling you it would.'

'I know,' he said, pulling me to him, 'and you should be pleased you were right.' There was a catch in his voice.

Vlad eyed the long string of pearls, the ivory edge of my push-up bra. He didn't see my bruise or my ambushed eyes. He saw my silky dress, and the pink tips of my ears. Was it then that I forgave him? He reached to kiss me on the lips. It was touching he was so very happy with me, his wife, and what we'd achieved in that small terraced restaurant behind Hotel Traian. If we didn't go for the religious bit I liked to think we threw a good party. Against the odds. Even his speech had got a couple of laughs.

'We don't do speeches in our country,' said Elena, matter-of-factly.

'Well, we do in ours.' I'd forced Vlad to sit down with a pen and paper the day before. And sure enough his joke about the country wine and Uncle Peter's palet got a giggle (on my side).

The older Romanians looked bewildered. Elena was right; they didn't do speeches, especially not in a language they didn't under-stand, so I got up and told everyone in Romanian I loved Vlad. And then I said Elena was a mighty and patient hostess and that was when I noticed she was crying.

After Dad's speech Elena was still crying, so I crossed the floor to console her, gently pushing Marcel's wife out of the way. But being there in front of her made it worse. Elena looked up at me. 'You've stolen my boy!'

'Ce?'

'You've stolen my boy. You've stolen my boy!'

On and on she went, repeating the same short sentence at her long, pissed daughter-in-law who just smiled down at her with bright teeth and foolish blue eyes. 'Sorree. Elena, don't cry . . . '

She looked small and broken, quite different from the woman who'd hugged me three hours earlier. 'You've stolen my boy!'

And so I had. An outsized cuckoo, I had flown into her country and stolen her boy. I had come to look after the orphans and now I was leaving behind an abandoned mother. Our wedding was not the beginning – for Elena it felt like the end. A most unholy farewell.

But then you can't please everyone. I have a wedding photograph of Vlad and Dad, standing side by side against the yellow flare of a municipal corrugated wall, and there's a striking similarity between bridegroom and father of the bride. Broad open faces, wide smiles and dark wavy hair – both of them pleased as punch. Faithless to the end they escaped with the shortest wedding service of all time; a record five minutes set them up for the rest of the day (and night). Hallelujah!

Even my mum didn't need God to have a good time. Was it the Romanian arc of flowers, each bundle individually wrapped in cellophane and held high about above our heads? Possibly the surprise, flaming wedding cake? The white glittery scarves (a special, inclusive gesture to welcome the parents of the bride)? Or maybe it was the warm summer air filled with the aroma of garlic sausage and lime blossom? She couldn't put her finger on exactly why, but by the evening of our appointed day Mum declared the wedding her favourite of all time. Could it simply be that her daughter was getting married? Or, as likely, that she'd found her nimble match in Tuca Toma? How they danced! A delicious fusion of reeling and tap, waltzing and folk, Romanian and Scottish; the old showing up the young, who in turn cheered and laughed. Such crazy fools.

There was also a lewd demonstration of what Scottish men wore under their kilts led by my younger brother, an argument with the restaurant owner who insisted on us paying millions of lei in cash at three in the morning, and Dad's cousin with bowel cancer had to go to bed early after a small accident. Other than that the wedding was (in Mum's words) 'a roaring success'. Even Aunt Angie overcame her fear of Romanians, taking her money belt off mid-way through the night. Oh yes, and Mihaela kissed her first foreigner – Vlad's Cantonese friend from UCL. Praise the Lord!

The sun was rising in the sky by the time I returned arm in arm with my husband to the hotel – to our marital bed and conjugal responsibility.

Vlad was raised on the mattress, only half out of his suit. 'Are you still thinking about it?'

'Yes, I can't help it.'

'It's our wedding night, Tessa. We are meant to be having sex.'

'I know but your mum was so unhappy.'

'Can you please stop thinking about my mum for one minute?'

'OK . . . Vlaaad?'

'What?'

'Do you think I'm a cuckoo?'

'Tessa for God's sake, it's five-thirty in the morning!'

CHAPTER FIFTEEN

London, June '07

'It's prostitution!'

'No, it's not.'

'Pretending you believe in ghosts, trailing around Egypt behind a psychic for a cable channel. That's prostitution.'

'It will be fun. Anyway, Derek Acorah's got a cult following.' Or at least so I'd discovered some ten minutes earlier on Google. 'Look Vlad, it's either Egypt or dinner with Nigel.'

'They're both prostitution.'

'It's called capitalism. Have you had any luck finding a job?'

In that moment, standing in front of me with his mind half on the beer in the fridge and half on the next day's 'Life in the UK' test, Vlad wondered if it was normal to so powerfully dislike the woman he loved.

'It's always so conditional with you.'

'At least I'm realistic. Who's going to pay the £800 for your visa?'

I'm not sure why I was so frantic about money. Being a fringe player in a whimsical industry didn't help. But at home pressures were easing. We'd been married for two years and Vlad was about to graduate – the final instalment of his fees had long since been paid. I didn't lack faith in him, but he lacked faith in himself and his disinterest in money was alien. I was, in comparison, acquisitive.

For Vlad it was simple; he'd never had any money and he didn't want to become another one of those people bent on a quest to run away from where they started. His brother Marcel was a case in point. He walked a tightrope with his wife thousands of miles away from home, this time Singapore, on a journey to earn more and more. They were neither Western Expat nor Asian native and privately Vlad wondered if they were really happy. Elena believed so but that was different; she had to believe losing her son to somewhere so far away was worth it. Vlad, on the other hand, saw all too clearly that the cards life had dealt him meant he could now earn decent money. But the process that would involve revolted him. He loathed the Careers Advice Centre at UCL with its corporate posters and felt helpless in front of a sea of jabbering application forms. He didn't like the *Milkround* sessions where the only keen recruiters worked in 'defensive' manufacturing. And I made matters worse, repeating that any job was better than no job, insisting on filling his applications with fabricated public school spiels.

Needless to say it was the one form Vlad filled in alone that got him a job. Not a particularly prestigious job, but a job in front of a computer with bar charts and numbers. After three years Vlad would be asked to go on his first business trip to Russia, the word 'Executive' inserted in his job title. Unfortunately his Romanian passport had just expired. The Russians would have to wait.

They didn't know it but Dad and Vlad shared a common disdain for money and status. My father lived his whole life without a credit card. He was gifted a greenhouse by the farm when he became too ill to work. It was, he said proudly, the only house he had ever owned. When Dad died and Mum had to move she made sure she took the greenhouse with her.

In 2007 Dad was still alive. He still didn't approve of Vlad, but he'd got used to him (maybe even a little fond of him, although he'd never admit to that). Anyway, he couldn't imagine me with anyone else.

'Ach daughter, now you need to get on and breed before you're yeld.'

'Dad! I'm not a sheep.'

'Tess, the most important thing in life is to breed.'

'Well I'm glad I'm so important to you. But Vlad's only just out of uni . . . '

'If it helps, when I die I'm going to leave you £20 000.'

This was the first time my father had ever offered me money.

'Thanks Dad, but sorry to disappoint you I won't be getting yolked – not anytime soon.'

'Don't mind me, I can't abide babies!' And he meant it. But the farmer in him wanted to die knowing his daughter wasn't barren.

I was yet to turn thirty-five, I wasn't maternal and I'd not married Vlad to have babies. That could wait. I'd married Vlad to make sure he wasn't taken from me by the system. It was a system that was meant to change overnight when Romania entered the EU in 2007 and in many ways it had. But, so appalled by the hordes of Poles, Romanians weren't granted an automatic right to work in the UK. They were quasi-EU members – poor second cousins.

Romanians were, however, now free to travel. No visa required. And that meant there was something I needed to do before any births (or deaths). It was something I'd intended to do ever since our wedding day. So I called Elena. And then I told Vlad.

'Hey, guess what? Your mum and dad are coming to stay in September.'

'What? Why didn't you ask me first?'

'Because you would've said it wasn't a good idea.'

Vlad stood still in the doorway of the flat, angry and faintly touched. 'What did Mum say?'

'To the Lord above, help us all!'

'So they're coming.'

'Yes. Of course they're coming.'

Marcel bought them their passports – he told me so down the phone. It wasn't a big deal but he wanted me to know that during his break from Singapore (he was the newly appointed head of Pan-Asian Mobiles) he'd done this for them. He felt frustrated. Why had he not thought to fly them first to his new world? It hadn't occurred to him that travel on such a scale might be for pleasure, that his old parents were mobile after all.

278

What Marcel didn't know was that I'd been motivated by a guilty conscience. It bore down on me, and was made worse by the accidental burble of Radio 4.

The mass departure of young Poles has left small villages almost desolate. The elderly gather in the evenings and talk of their loss. Never, they tell me, did they imagine they would lose their families like this. The local doctor has seen a sharp rise in anti-depressant prescriptions among the over-sixties.

I tried to imagine Elena swallowing a small white pill to take the pain away, a chemical haze that might dull the ache of her loss. But I could not. She would not. Instead I invited her to London and her pain was temporarily replaced with anxiety over the unknown and whether Tuca might show her up.

When Vlad had first got a supervisor's job in the university bar he rang his mum. He told her the news with a hint of pride in his voice. This was a definite step up from washing vats in a café.

Her response took him by surprise. 'Don't drink at work, Vlăduţ.'

'I'm sorry?'

'Don't drink behind the bar.'

'Of course not, Mum.' And he almost laughed at the ludicrousness of her suggestion. 'No one drinks behind the bar. It's . . . I mean, it's not allowed.'

Elena feared two things above all others: she feared dying alone, and the more she saw her husband's hands tremble, the more she worried about that; and she feared that one of her sons might go the way of their father and drink himself stupid. She didn't like the idea of Vlad being surrounded by alcohol.

When her daughter-in-law rang up all of a sudden and told her that she and Tuca were flying to London, naturally she worried about the flight. But she worried more about Tuca's drinking. He mustn't let the side down in front of their new family. She would make sure he didn't.

That night he came in wearing dark glasses and talking like a peasant. She smelt his breath, took him by the ear and smacked him neatly around the mouth before she pushed him into his chair and served his soup. Then she told him her news. 'We are flying to London.'

'Wayhey! Ha ha! Did I tell you about the time I flew to Syria! Hey hey, gypsy wife! We are going on an adventure.' He stood and lunged towards her.

She pushed him down. He got back up.

'Get out of my way woman!'

'Where are you going?'

'Eh. I'm off to Londra, Anglia. Did you hear? I'm off to Anglia.'

She listened as he clattered into the cold hole. He would find no wine down there, nor *ţuică*. Elena had hidden every bottle in a chickens' coup. She sat back and waited for the eruption, wishing all the while her daughter-in-law hadn't cooked up this hair-brained scheme. For the love of God's Lady!

September '07

Elena had not slept well. In truth she rarely slept well, her system long since broken by thirty years of rising well before the sun, leaving her little flat and her sleeping boys who took themselves to school. Children did as they should back then – thank the Lord for small mercies. Years on she still felt sick at the memory of those broken nights and the punishing eight hours on, eight hours off, eight hours on so that the women were too tired to work at their machines, too tired to thread their needles, too tired to satisfy their men and all because the Socialist State said so. Tired, very tired all the time, and that is how she felt as she lay next to her husband, clawing herself free of sleep's sickly grip to plunge immediately into the dawn of a truly terrifying day.

She shook Tuca awake on the Z-bed. They'd spent the night in Marcel and Silvia's empty flat. 'Tuca, get up, wake up – we must go! We must not be late for the aeroplane!'

She was focused now, every fibre alert and concentrated on catching her appointed metal bird. She wouldn't be able to recall exactly how the morning passed, the way they crossed the capital, why it was she kept snapping at Tuca, or even what happened at Otopeni with its bossy young people and noisy tanoy. She was oblivious, scared, her pulse racing, her lips blue – and it got worse, steadily worse all morning until finally they mounted the sky, her head bowed in prayer and her stomach in her throat.

Thank the Lord Tuca was with her. She would never fly again – never!

London

When Elena and Tuca came to visit we had sold my little flat and were renting in another unexceptional slice of south-east London.

I had got up early on the morning of their arrival in an effort to give the house some order. I put a bulb in the spare lamp, emptied a waste paper basket and hung the ceramic plates we received as a wedding present two years earlier.

I tried to prepare a soup for my in-laws but burnt the onions and it tasted bitter so I added a tin of Heinz Chicken Variety, feeling sure the packet aroma wouldn't be familiar to Elena. I scooped up the entrails of Vlad's visa application and stuffed the piles of paper behind the sofa. He had taken his Life test.

What percentage of children lives with both parents in the UK?

A. 40   B. 75   C. 65   D. 90

Vlad ticked forty per cent. Later I told him that was the wrong answer. Vlad shrugged – he'd made his own observations in south London.

Which UK country is home to less than one per cent of the ethnic minority population?

A. Wales   B. North Ireland   C. Scotland   D. England

Vlad guessed Wales. Had it been me I would have placed an asterix by my answer and explained, like most immigrants, I didn't have the money to travel extensively through Britain's Celtic fringes counting foreigners.

But Vlad wasn't a bolshy native. He passed the test. Now we just had to prove we'd lived together as a couple for the last two years when for the three before that we'd done everything we could to hide our relationship. Vlad didn't pay any bills; it was my name on the tenancy lease; it was my idea Vlad came to Britain; it was me who filled in the forms. £800 simply to ask for the privilege of staying in GB Plc. Oh, to be a sponging immigrant!

Elena and Tuca were not travelling to Britain to work; instead, as first-time tourists in Heathrow they stood, silently staring in a queue full of Britons, clutching their crisp new passports following the bold blue flag with a circle of stars, doing as they were told by voiceless, international symbols. They were holding hands in the same neutral way small schoolchildren do when they cross the road. On the other side of London I swung a Hoover around the sitting room and arranged some cut flowers. 'It'll be fun,' I'd reassured Vlad before he left for the airport. 'We'll give them the holiday of their lives!'

'Tessa, they've never been on holiday. Everything takes practice – you'll see! This is a very bad idea.'

Vlad (never late) saw his parents first – his father's neck out, forward and purposeful, his mother behind him, her eyes turned down, her mouth thin and pale with fright.

How much older they looked, thought Vlad, his worn-out and misplaced parents. Tuca carrying his felt hat, his black leather shoes a little too shiny, and their luggage dated and tied together with a bootlace. Vlad moved forward, pushing between the crowd, keen to reach and protect them.

'Welcome to London! Mamă! Tată!'

He took his mother in his arms and held her tighter than he had ever held her before, inhaling her comfortable smell.

'Welcome.' And more that he could not say.

*

'I feel like a rat! London makes me feel like a rat!'

Tuca began waving his arms above his head, knocking the shade off my lamp. Vlad told his father to sit down and be quiet in a manner only a son could get away with.

'Did Tuca say he feels like a rat? Have I heard right? A rat, Tuca?' I flushed pink, nonplussed by my father-in-law's first expressed sentiment concerning my adopted city. 'Why does it make you feel like a rat?'

'Just ignore him.'

But Tuca was not ready to be ignored. He had travelled thousands of miles to a country that was not Syria and after a (long) first day of sight-seeing he was ready to share.

'We spend all our time travelling underground. Like rats! And the streets are dirty here.'

'They are dirty in Bucharest!'

'But this is *London*,' said Tuca with a hint of triumph in his voice.

Elena chose not to listen. She was in the kitchen area of our open-plan living space, sorting through the cutlery drawer. I didn't look but I could hear her at her work; wiping and arranging, making good her daughter-in-law's mess.

Silently she marvelled (again) at the dishwasher and so, too, at the washing machine. And she wondered, not for the first time, what her daughter-in-law did all day that she should have so many modern appliances and such dirty drawers.

She bent down to tackle the skirting board with a wet cloth, Tuca began worrying about the animals he'd left behind in Romania and Vlad said, under his breath (twice), 'I told you this was not a good idea.'

I really wanted a drink but didn't like to open the bottle of Beaujolais in front of Tuca. Vlad and I weren't speaking and there was little appetite for the next day's planned activity.

I tried to hold on to their arrival in my head; the rush of love I felt as they stepped through the door, Vlad the proud custodian of his parents, ushering them in, cracking a joke about the paint work.

And they were smiling shyly, anxious to please, keen to relate stories from their journey. After all, had they not just crossed the world alone? Elena squeezed my hand, the blood only now returning to her lips. I kissed them both several times and made her a cup of Earl Grey tea with milk (later she would decide it gave her an upset stomach), and admired her perm. I was touched by the effort they had made and more so when she knelt beside her baggage and extracted gift after immaculately packed gift. A large hand-baked *cosonac* (walnut loaf) tied in a bread bag, several bars of Romanian chocolate, a heart-shaped wicker basket to hang on the wall, a lucky charm decorated in sunflower seeds with St Parascheva sanctimonious in the centre, a children's book of Romanian stories, a set of blue and orange bed sheets, a meat hammer, an egg whip and a plastic bottle of Tuca's homemade *ţuică* (also tied in a bread bag).

'Oh, thank you!'

Yes, it had all be so endearing and warm to begin with – I even found myself loving Vlad with an intensity I hadn't felt for a while, marvelling at the small involuntary gestures that linked him so intimately to mother and father.

In fact, things only started to go wrong (if that's not too strong a word) when I took them to their bedroom. (Well, more a dumping room with a pull-out double bed Vlad *had* promised to erect before they came.) We stood in a circle as eager son gallantly stepped forward to do what he should have done already.

'What a clever contraption,' exclaimed Tuca, as one mattress neatly slid from under the other.

And then, silence – a ghastly silence – as we all looked in horror at the artistic arrangement on the freshly exposed bed. Like small chocolate sprinkles in an astonishingly symmetrical pattern, almost good enough to eat. Mice shit! Mice shit everywhere – all over the mattress where my mother-in-law was to lay her head.

'Oh I'm sorry. I am so sorry . . . '

I had hoped things would improve the following morning.

(Elena assured me she slept very soundly – and no, she didn't dream of mice. Not once.) Tuca enjoyed his first grapefruit – very juicy, he said, wiping his chin with his sleeve – and Elena spent a long time in the bathroom where I ran her a steaming tub of hot foamy water she shared with her husband. Through the locked door I heard them giggle like teenagers. Yes, in fact that first bit of the morning was satisfactory; things only became strained when we set off on an excursion. This was meant to be a holiday, after all.

Elena did not gush. To be fair she'd had very little to gush about in her life. So it was with no visible enthusiasm that she'd greeted the idea of sight-seeing. To be honest she wasn't entirely sure what sight-seeing involved.

Undeterred and keen to show off my eclectic part of London we headed to Brixton tube in the rain, trotting in silent pairs along a busy road, Elena uncomfortable in unlikely, cream heels. She took my hand and stared at the long extraordinary street unfolding in front of her – at the foreign clothes, foreign food and foreign faces.

'You like?' I asked.

She gave a small nod. It was the most I got all day.

She didn't need to speak – I knew what she was thinking. My father, on a rare visit from the Scottish Highlands, had thought the same. 'By Christ,' he smiled in disbelief, 'you wouldn't know what country you were in.'

Elena spent her first twenty-four hours feeling overwhelmed. She'd breathed the air of nowhere other than her own small corner of Romania and here she was hobbling (I did recommend against the shoes) through the maze of inner-city London – staring at black faces, fat faces, brown faces, too, some faces almost totally covered; none of which even began to resemble her idea of England (pale, creamy, rich, shiny, green). None of it did – the noise, the colour, the stench (barbequed chicken, traffic, urine) and the children.

Thanks to the Good Lord above the babies were cute! And so many of them, too! Quite out of character Elena broke free of my grip at the entrance of the tube to stoop before a small girl, all brown eyes and beads with a jolly pink jacket, holding a sugar lollipop.

'Vai, drăguţ,' she cooed, only just able to resist leaning in to pinch the girl's plump cheek.

I gently pulled her away. (We had a programme to stick to and I was at an age where small children made me feel slightly panicked.) Reluctantly she left the bemused toddler and followed my lead into the rat-trap below, wondering (not for the first time) if her daughter-in-law had a problem. After all, our wedding had been two years ago and I wasn't young. But then, it wasn't Elena's style to comment.

Only much later when she was back in her own country would Elena be able to properly enjoy her time in London through the telling of tales, reliving the experience without the pressure of the here and now. When she saw Big Ben on Euronews she even called Tuca into the room, flooded with memories.

But in the moment it was too crazy and extravagant. She would've felt much happier and less exposed left to tackle the mess in my house. Even the barriers on the underground made her feel old and clumsy, and Tuca embarrassed her by talking too loudly when no one else was saying anything. And then there was the entertainment. What had possessed her daughter-in-law? (It was a listener who recommended the London Duck.) She felt upset I had spent such money on tickets for two old people; she simply didn't see the point. I'd tried to explain that the Duck was a famous amphibious military vehicle first used during the D-Day landings in the Second World War, but the story didn't resonate. The anecdotes were lost in translation and Elena struggled to hear what I said with her hood up (it was still raining). The Duck trundled past Buckingham Palace, Westminster Abbey, the Houses of Parliament, Trafalgar Square . . .

'Look, look! That is where our politicians sit. It's the Mama of all parliaments!'

Elena looked and nodded – she had seen Westminster on the telly. She thought it looked magnificent, even magical, but still she just nodded.

'Super!' said Tuca, keen to use his one English word.

Sploosh! The Duck performed its only party trick and entered the Thames. We were floating in the rain alongside the Houses of Parliament. Elena drew breath and briefly touched my arm. She had never floated before.

The next day it was London Zoo.

'Săracul. Sărac!' Elena sighed, peering through the webbing at a large black bear with a dry snout; round and round he went in one small demented circle. 'Poor things!'

I flinched – this was meant to be fun. Instead my mother-in-law was making me feel guilty about our animal husbandry. She from the country of chained howling dogs and orphans.

'Can you tell your mum that they're kept here mainly for the breeding programme?'

'No.'

'Why not?'

'Because it's not true.' And then, because Vlad couldn't resist it, 'I told you this wasn't a good idea.'

Elena didn't speak English but she had long since picked up on the tension between Vlad and me. They are like two sharp knives, she thought to herself, moving away from our bickering and the mad bears, and bending towards two small children who were looking at a giant snail. Tuca stayed as he had been all morning: with his neck cricked up, staring skywards.

'Come on, Tuca. We are going to the Butterfly Paradise.'

But Tuca wasn't listening. 'Vai, unbelievable! Unbelievable! There is an aeroplane in the sky every thirty seconds. How does a man ever get any peace?'

'You don't come to London for peace . . . '

But even Elena managed a smile among the exotic butterflies and steamy tropical plants.

'You like!'

She nodded, stretching out her arm to welcome a butterfly with transparent fairy wings. She liked. But she couldn't help feeling a twinge of regret that it was her and not Laura who was privy to such a spectacle. How her little granddaughter would have loved so much of what Elena felt too old for. What a waste!

'Please, Mum! Please!'

'Oh darling, your father's not been at all well, his legs are terrible. The place is in chaos.'

'I promise I'll help. Promise! It's just so difficult down here. I don't know what to do with them. Elena doesn't say anything and Tuca's obsessed with knocking down my damp wall. It's meant to be a holiday. I just know they'd feel more at home in Scotland.'

My mother was tired and she was living with half-a-man in our ramshackle house, which one day soon she must give up. She looked about the kitchen with its dogs' pots strewn across the floor and secateurs on the table. Dad was asleep in his chair.

'Well, they are darling little people. Oh, go on then! Bring them up at the weekend. I'll get Tommy to drop a pheasant off in the box.'

'Thanks Mum! Thanks. Totally owe you one!' I turned triumphantly towards my guests and husband. 'Guess what? The day after tomorrow we are going to Scotland! We are going to visit my parents.'

'Eh Scotland!' said Tuca and, quick as you like, he leapt to take me by the arm, simulating bagpipe playing with his pink cheeks and laughing out loud. 'I love Scotland! Whisky!'

Vlad and Elena remained where they were, sitting silently together on the sofa – one borne of the other and in so many ways alike.

'Tessa, how are we all going to get to Scotland?'

'We're going to hire a car.'

Romania has a word that is absent from the English language. That word is *cuscră*. It means mother of one's son or daughter-in-law. In Romania, the relationship is taken seriously between respective in-laws, where it's considered normal to share the burden of their offspring's family. But Vlad and I did not have a family. And the two *cuscre* had no common language. But still Elena had brought from Romania a series of small gifts for her *cuscră* on the off-chance they might meet, and so it was that she felt secretly delighted to hear we would be leaving London to visit her *cuscră*'s house and her handsome ailing husband. What a man he must have been! For the love of God that he should be ill.

And so, as is often the case when the end of an experience is suddenly in sight, Elena relaxed. Perhaps I did, too. We went together into town to buy Laura a present atop a large red double decker bus and she squeezed my hand in wonder. 'Tessa, if Tuca feels like a rat in London, I feel like a bird. A bird!'

I was the only driver. Actually, that wasn't strictly true; Vlad had in fact passed his test the previous summer. A week later we drove to Scotland together where he wrote off the car, steering up a bank into a Sitka spruce.

We didn't replace it. We were skint and I hated cars. So did Vlad, and he wasn't keen on me driving a Punto too fast up the motorway, aware as he was that I'd only had five hours sleep.

'Couldn't you have skipped the radio last night?'

'No I couldn't – anyway, I enjoyed the show. I told the listeners about having your parents to stay in London.'

Vlad said nothing.

'A couple of my regulars called and said I should write a book about it.'

'Tessa, concentrate on the road!'

A service station on the peripheries of Birmingham was our first stop on the long haul north. Vlad watched in silence as I tried to dig Tuca out of the Punto.

'Come on, Tuca. Pee pee!'

'No,' he insisted. 'No, I am not getting out until we get to Scotland.'

'It's a long way to Scotland . . . '

'No.'

The acute longing for a cigarette hit Vlad much less frequently now but on that close September day, as he dragged himself out of the car onto a slice of appointed grass, he cracked his fingers with desire. How he wished I'd drive a bit slower. He watched as his mother dutifully followed me to the loo. He never had much to say to his father, so he sat alone and stared in silence at the grazing customers who ambled slowly around the gigantic Moto complex masticating and talking. He was, he decided, surrounded by aliens and the thought briefly amused him. He couldn't help but wonder what his parents made of it all. For Vlad any journey out of London reminded him of our brief (alternative?) honeymoon. We'd wanted to visit the painted monasteries romantically hidden in the beech forests of Bucovina but there were time constraints – I had to film in Somerset – so we ended up returning to England and grabbing a weekend in the seaside resort of Weston-super-Mare.

And so it was that he finally saw a slice of England proper, something far removed from life in the capital or the anomalous feudal expanse of northern Scotland. We spent a night in a bed and breakfast where the landlady served strong milky tea and talked to us loudly over lukewarm eggs at 9.30am sharp (she didn't serve breakfast any later – not even to a honeymoon couple). The Victorian façade of her guest house promised sea views and access to the vintage pier. But there was no sand – just acres of mud chasing the tide – so we headed into the town and that was where Vlad first met those hard-working families he'd heard so much about; the mums and dads who'd driven their hatchbacks into Weston to do their weekly shop. There they were, all moving together in anoraks, slowly padding along the pavement carrying plastic bags, eating iced buns and sausage rolls. They were pale, wide creatures with forlorn faces.

Vlad put his hand in the air and started to wave. I thought he'd gone mad. 'Hello England!' he said. 'Hello.'

We drove back to London early the next day. Up onto the flyover that sucks you into the city; the GlaxoSmithKline building on the right and the Russian Orthodox Church on the left, cutting through the rush and buzz past Harrods, Harvey Nichols, Hyde Park, back into the underbelly of the city.

'Tessa . . . ' said Vlad.

'Yes.'

'If we must live in England, let's always live in London.'

We'd all got back in the car and were passing Birmingham (slowly), nose to tail. Elena said the tower blocks reminded her of home. She listened as I tried to explain how poor people lived in blocks like that in Britain and she nodded but didn't understand. She'd seen the people in my part of London with their puffy jackets and sporty shoes and she didn't think any of them looked poor.

Vlad was reluctant to enter the discussion. How do you tell your mother who has no running water and no spending money that she was better off than the puffy people in England? Elena continued to listen – this time as I attempted to explain about my father.

At our wedding only those closest to him had noticed a discernable change; the ubiquitous tweed jacket that was slack on his shoulders, his shock of once thick hair lifeless and dull and how he stood up last, when he thought no one else was watching. Otherwise his vast bulk more or less disguised his hidden killer.

Two years later, by the time our little party was travelling up to Rannoch, Dad had out-performed the most optimistic expectations.

'You're doing well,' said the specialist. He was dying more slowly than expected. (Mum believed it was her homemade soup.) He had a blood transfusion every fortnight. Gone were the days when he sucked a cut finger.

'I am grateful, but the idea of other people's blood revolts me.'

We would joke a lot (perhaps too much?) – I even brought him

291

a Dracula mug from Romania. It said *for blood only* and had gruesome red painted on the rim. Dad smiled but he never drank from it. We joked, too, about his funeral; if he bullied Mum we threatened the appearance of Claire's vegetarian canapés at the reception.

'Over my dead body!' thundered the carnivore.

He knew how to laugh at his fate, but we noticed he didn't whistle in the morning any more when he let the dogs out. He used to be a champion whistler.

I began trying to tell Elena that my dad's engorged spleen was the size of one – no two! – rugby balls. He did not have a pot belly; it was his cancer, but he never complained. Never!

'He looks pregnant,' I said, taking my hand off the steering wheel to draw balloons in the air. I wanted Elena to realise Dad wasn't just a sick man with a great kyte. He was remarkable.

Elena said nothing. What could she say? But she began to wonder why we were travelling so many miles to see someone so sick with whom she couldn't talk. If she'd been in Romania at least she could've made some borsch.

Vlad said nothing, but he placed his hand over mine on the steering wheel and gave it a squeeze.

It was Tuca who broke the silence. 'Vai de mine! I never knew Scotland was so far away from England.'

The light had gone by the time we crossed the border. There was less pressure to talk in the dark. Four hours later we'd left the A9 and were winding our way west to Kinloch Rannoch, the final frontier before the land of flood and mountain proper. An enormous loch with Rannoch Moor beyond – the last remaining wilderness in Britain, peat and sky and one small bothy – I'd never felt the need to cross it because I was born there.

Instinctively I swung with each loop and bend on the final road. *Home James, home!* I was going home with my precious cargo (the journey had softened us). I filled in the blanks outside the black windows

'Loch Tummel! To our left is Loch Tummel. There is a Scottish song about Loch Tummel . . . *by Loch Tummel and Loch Rannoch and Lochaber I will go –* '

'No Tessa, no singing.' Vlad was gentle but firm.

'There soon!' I could not be silenced. 'I did this journey every day to get to my school in Pitlochry. But in the end I went to boarding school because I was bus sick. I went to the same school as Vlad. Strathallan! Did I get the word for boarding school right, Vlad?'

'Yes.'

'Elena?' I turned my head, searching for a response.

'Tessa, keep your eyes on the road.'

'But I want to make sure she can hear . . . '

'She can hear, can't you Mama?'

'Da.'

Rannoch

Mum was making final adjustments in the house – she wound the grandfather clock, applied a little lipstick, lit the candles in the kitchen and adjusted the towels on the rail in the guest room, her eye catching once more on that darling posy of wild rose and red berries on the dresser. She couldn't help but feel a smidgen sad her guests would be arriving in the dark; the garden really was looking splendid.

'Donald! They'll be here soon! Could you keep an eye on the fire? Come on, wake up old man . . . '

The Punto swung along the road, passing the Home Farm and the Kennels. I pressed my foot down on the accelerator pad. 'Almost there now!'

'Steady . . . ' Vlad instinctively put out a restraining hand.

'Look, look! Here we are! We're here! Home again home again jiggety-jog.' I broke out in English. I beeped the horn. The dogs started to bark. We bounced up the drive.

'Darlings, darlings!' Mum was ready for us, running to the car, bony arms out-stretched. 'Well done! You've made it. Bine aţi venit. Bine aţi venit!' She had found the phrase book.

I watched as she clutched a speechless Tuca to a non-existent breast.

'Hello, hello! Bravo!'

My eyes swam. I didn't want to cry but there I was in tears. They welled up and spilt down my cheeks. Vlad, caught by the moment, looked away.

Tuca looked like he'd been spat on and polished when he arrived at the breakfast table the next morning. His grey shirt was neatly tucked into dark slacks held up with a black, silver-buckled belt. His hair was perfectly parted and his face shone with a stingy red of the recently scrubbed. His wire-rimmed specs were in place on his large potato nose and his lean frame was angled forward, ready for action.

'Morning, Tuca! Mum wants to know how you would like your hen's egg.'

But Tuca wasn't interested in eggs – Tuca was waiting to work. He'd woken to stare out at the staggering peaks and troughs of the glen and he saw the vast potential of a wild garden with a sick patron. He was here and ready to help.

'Dad, I promised Tuca he could help you in the garden. He wants to get stuck in. He felt useless in London.'

Dad looked green. He didn't look like he wanted to help anyone get stuck in.

'Please, Dad . . . '

'Darling, does Tuca want hard, tacky or runny?' That was Mum.

'Tell him to have his breakfast and then we'll see.'

'Thanks Dad.'

'Hard, tacky or soft?'

'Oh Mum, I don't know – just boil the egg!'

Tuca ate his egg and Dad sat with his head in his hands. Mum spun around the kitchen avoiding dogs, clearing plates and waving her arms at Elena who entered the kitchen with her head turning on her neck, moving from left to right. She looked like a curious dormouse. This wasn't like any house she'd ever seen in the countryside. This was an enormous, draughty (and, when she saw clearly in the daylight, slightly dirty) palace.

Mum harried her guests outside after breakfast, anxious for them to catch the garden in the early morning September sun. The dewy lawn was steaming gently and shafts of light picked out the green and grey in the trees and hills that framed the points of pink and blue in the garden, and even the greenhouse.

'Heaven on earth . . . '

Mum bobbed and hopped, and led the way through the patch-work quilt that was her lifetime's work. She was keen, very keen, that her Romanians should understand British people also knew how to live the outdoor life. Elena and Tuca stumbled to keep up. 'This is rocket.' *Tup-tup-tup*, Mum smacked her lips. 'Peppery.'

Tuca tasted and nodded.

'Smell this – heavenly . . . ' She pulled at a precious sweet pea and stuck it under Elena's nose. 'This rose has flowered and flowered.' She let her hands fall as if cascading petals beside a big fading yellow rose, and then lay down on the ground. 'We think it's because Chokkie is buried beneath it. Wuff!' She barked like a dog. 'Explain, Tessa. Explain Chokkie was our dog who did tricks. Wuff wuff!'

Elena and Tuca stood back, slightly unsure what to make of their *cuscră*'s unusual performance. Vlad caught us with the digital camera and I took Elena's hand, extending the other to Mum who was still lying on the wet grass.

That afternoon Vlad, exhausted (was it the heady air or his mother-in-law?), volunteered to play chess with Dad. So it was Elena and Tuca who came to the edge of the moor. We drove up the side of the loch and beyond the final hamlet to the railway station without a master. Elena looked out of the window; she'd never spent so much time in a car and seen so many changing scenes or a *cuscră* with so much energy.

'Bridge of Gaur,' I explained. 'It used to have the smallest school in Scotland. Only six pupils but now it's closed down. The triplets moved out of the area.'

At Rannoch station we crossed the tracks and walked on out to Loch Laidon.

'Take a picture!' Elena cried, standing on her tiptoes next to Mum.

(The captured image is grey and windy. The water looks like slate, the Scots Pine like a bent black broom and the sand damp and disappointing. But in the picture Elena's smiling.)

'Praise the Lord,' she murmured. 'I haven't seen the sea for forty years. This is my sea.' And she dipped a borrowed welly-boot into the water.

Tuca found Dad's chainsaw in the shed, hanging un-used, imposing and impossibly irresistible. He asked Vlad, who asked Dad, who said NO! With some relief Vlad translated this message to Tuca, who continued to stand in the shed looking lovingly up at the lethal orange toy. It was only a matter of time.

Down the years I'd never seen Dad wear protective clothing. Never. He bathed all summer in organophosphate sheep dip long since banned; he sprayed fields bare-faced with chemical pesticides; he chopped logs in welly boots. He didn't wear the recommended kit. But his cancer had changed things. He didn't even have the stomach to shoot his old dogs any longer. Instead he paid the vet.

'Tessa, if Tuca's going to chop logs he has got to wear Duncan's gear.'

'Are you crazy, Dad? His kit's far too big. Tuca'll trip over himself.'

'I don't care. We don't even know if he can use a saw. He has to wear the kit!'

With alacrity Tuca pulled on my giant brother's size fifteen steel boots. He wriggled into Duncan's vast gauze jacket and trousers. He giggled. He was a man in giant's clothes. Elena crossed herself. (Chopping trees – was this not how her uncle had lost his life almost before hers had begun?) Vlad shook his head. His father had never understood the word *no*.

He watched as his crazy old *tata* pulled and tugged the chainsaw into life, and winced as it started and stotted up and down the logs – there was no rhyme or reason to his movements. Tuca looked up at his audience and laughed with vigour. *Waaaaar waaaaar!* The blade waggled up in the air and down it bounced on the trunk. *Waaaaar* . . . like a crazed, screaming child.

I couldn't watch. Dad tried to hold still the logs he used to slice with cool perfection. He was too weak; Tuca too wild. *Waaaaar!*

Vlad replaced Dad. It didn't work. Vlad couldn't take his father's shakes and pokes. 'Bloody idiot! Show off!'

In the end Elena, the little loyal wife, bent over in her big round specs and held the dead trees steady. I took a photo of husband and wife against the odds.

'He shouldn't be cutting logs with his shakes,' grumbled Vlad, feeling frustrated (and inadequate).

Elena was still outside – patient attendant to her trembling husband. Finally, sweating and euphoric, Tuca re-entered the kitchen. Mum clapped; Dad smiled, scratching his head with his hand. I went to the fridge. Tuca had earned a large, cold beer.

'Eh foarte bun! Eh.'

I pummelled his wiry frame. 'Yes Tuca. Foarte bun!'

'A good communist worker!'

'All he needs now are the Hammer and Sickle on his chest!' Elena, sawdust spattered in her hair, looked across fondly at her game husband.

The chainsaw was the highlight of Tuca's holiday.

The abundant daily post that arrived in Scotland and recollections of her *cuscră*'s consistent correspondence with her own silent son would, on Elena's return to Romania, push her into writing a thank you letter to my mother. It arrived on our doormat in London. An astonished Vlad duly translated it down the telephone.

My dear Cuscră – From the beginning we want to thank you very much for the warmth with which you received us and all the same we apologise for the trouble you went to. For us it was something pleasant – we felt very well. To me it seemed like something from a fairy tale.

I liked very much Scotland, its mountains, its views and even in your home it seemed like a dream. We thank you again. We wait for you in Romania and may God let things be well for our children, for us and for everybody.

We wish you all the best in the world and we kiss you goodbye.

ELENA AND TUCA

Mum eyes filled with tears. There really was something deeply touching about that dear woman – if only she spoke the same language.

Several years on, Elena would fondly remember her Scottish visit. The deep browns and purples so very different from her Moldavian home, the enormous cattle and enormous dying caretaker and, of course, her over-active *cuscră*, the cooking magician. Never had she made so many wishes as she did in Scotland, where each meal was an edible first. A haunch of venison, roast parsnips, lemon meringue pie, thick whipped cream, chocolate biscuit cake, avocado salad and Scotch Broth – although Tuca was disappointed that we didn't distil our own whisky.

Mum, eager to please, rushed to the drinks cabinet to show off her sloe gin, with berries she'd picked and pricked herself. But that, too, caused confusion. How did she make the alcohol?

'Oh no, I buy the gin and add the sloes . . .'

What was the point of that?

Indeed, there was much about the Scottish trip that appeared topsy-turvy. Elena was filled with particular sadness that she left her specially purchased cream heels and embroidered shirt in London. In her world the countryside was a place of work, where the water is collected and the floors are stone. They got up with the light and went to bed with the dark. The countryside was not a place for scented baths and crystal glass, warmed towels and subtle lighting. And to think this was her *cuscră*'s way.

Vlad had indeed caught the leg of God. If only those two would get on and start a family.

Even Vlad was surprised the final departure proved so painful. In the end he was compelled to turn around in his seat. 'That's enough now! Come on, that's enough!'

We had started on the long road to London, winding through the glen. In the back of the car Elena sobbed openly beneath her glasses. Tuca rubbed his face with a large hand, dirty from his garden work. His cheeks were streaked and his nose wet. Vlad stared at his father over a shoulder, taken aback (impressed?) with this manly display of emotion.

'Come on now. That's enough!' Then, affected by what he'd seen, he tried a softer tack. 'It's OK,' he said. 'It's OK.' He reached across to place a hand on my knee, his silent way of conceding I was right. The trip had been worth it. It *had* been a good idea.

With no language they'd understood. I knew they would.

On the morning we left Dad had stood to say goodbye, unfolding his huge frame between heavy breaths.

Elena silently reached on tiptoes to kiss his cheek and hold his wrist. Then it was Tuca's turn. 'Come soon to Romania,' he said. 'Hai come soon to visit us!' Tuca liked what he saw and he knew that he would never see him again, that soon Dad would be dead. So he invited him to Romania.

'Yes,' said Dad. 'Thank you.'

But it was Mum who set them off. She ran to the road ahead of the Punto waving a white hanky and performing a curious routine of star jumps and shapes. Up and down she went, a hopping stick in the middle of the lane, her spindly shanks disappearing in the distance.

Beep beep! The car hugged the corner of the hill.

'Byeeeee!' We turned the corner and she was gone. The holiday was over.

London, March '08

'Mum's over the moon! You should call Elena and tell her.'

'Couldn't you, Tess?'

'You're her son. She'd like to hear it from you.'

Five months on from Elena and Tuca's British tour Vlad and I were sitting together on the sofa in London, toying with the telephone. In the end it was Vlad who dialled the number and broke the news and then promptly handed over to me, when his mother's voice cracked with emotion.

I could hear Tuca cry out in the background. Ecstatic, he leapt for the receiver across the sofa-bed. 'Eh Tay-sa! So you've caught the last train out of the station! Eh, bravo girl!'

Elena pulled the receiver back from her errant husband – that he should say such a thing, at such a time. *Vai!*

'So will you come back over, Elena? The baby is due in October. It would be great to have you here.'

'Yes, yes – I will come, God willing.'

'Great! I'm going to have the baby at home. I hate hospitals. They are for ill people.'

'Sorry?'

'You know, we call them home births here – when you don't go to hospital.'

Elena sat, silenced, astonishment gate-crashing her joy. With all their money why on earth was her daughter-in-law going to give birth like a gypsy? For the love of God! Foreigners!

CHAPTER SIXTEEN

Mara was born in our London bathroom on her due date with no pain relief, although apparently I nearly broke Vlad's little finger with the final push. His mother remained in the corner of the sitting room throughout my two-day labour, talking to God and longing for the midwife to stick a needle in me, if only I'd stop groaning like a cow.

Four days after the birth we all got on a train to Scotland. I wouldn't be put off by Elena's protestations about *microbi*. Dad had been in hospital with pneumonia – I didn't want to take any chances. He *would* see his first grandchild.

'Your mother never had one as small as that,' he grunted, but I could tell he was pleased to see us.

We left Scotland ten days later and I stopped in at the radio station on the way back home to assure them of my prompt return. It was then I was told my services would no longer be required.

At the time it felt like the end of the world. How would I manage without my late night listeners? Without my dad? Without my regular job? God forbid that I might have to be a stay-at-home mum! I cried huge tearful gulps on my bed as Elena watched over me and Vlad stood silently in the corner holding a very pink Mara. (My mother-in-law didn't believe in draughts, especially not anywhere near a new born baby.)

After Elena had returned to Romania I went back to Scotland with the baby and, as spring unfolded with its rude green shoots and perky bird song, Dad got progressively weaker. He took to his bed full-time just as Mara was learning to crawl, flapping her arms and legs on his bedroom floor like a stranded turtle. I lay next to him, inhaling his warm musky smell and together we laughed at her endeavours. He died at home a few weeks later. I would smell his jacket every day for a month until all trace of him was gone.

And then I went back to London with Mara, ashamed that Mum was coping better than me.

'I think you should go to Romania, Tessa. You know, it might help. My mum would love to have you both.' Vlad, my dear Vlad, was now suddenly the man of the family – the earner, the father, the sensible one. And I was lost. So I packed a bag and went back to the little blue house in Chicerea with Vlad's daughter.

On the night of our arrival Elena brought a small box into the room where we were sleeping, St Nicolas still hanging on the wall. 'I want you to have this.' She handed me a gold ring with Nefertiti's head stamped on it. 'Tuca brought it back from Syria. One day you must give it to Mara.'

'I will. I promise. Thank you.' Elena had given me her only ring and her favourite piece of treasure. I knew it meant a lot. (She would worry later whether she'd done the right thing, because I lose everything. But not Nefertiti.)

Baby Mara and the sun gave our hot dusty days their rhythm; that is, with the exception of one week when I announced to Elena I was taking her granddaughter on an excursion. She wasn't keen that I should leave with the baby. She didn't fully trust her foreign storm with such a precious bundle. But I was adamant.

It had taken the birth of Mara and with her an understanding of the minutia that we pour lovingly into our own offspring to jolt me into action, fifteen years too late. It was as if time had stood still in Siret – Doina, Radu, Irina, Valentin, Mariţa and Mihai were all there and so welcoming.

As for the orphanage, it was a ruin. The roof had fallen in and there was a dead wild dog in the entrance. The children grew up; some were living independently, some had even got married and had their own children and others, many others, had been moved to the adult institution in the town. There wasn't sufficient sheltered accommodation to house them. It was there, in a stone building with a familiar cloying smell and the same disturbed sounds, that I found Mariana and Vasilica.

'Hey blonda, what took you so long?'

We recognised each other instantly – I had some serious making up to do. Beyond their womanly frames and longer, dyed hair not much had changed; they were still imprisoned in a mad house. Vasilica ground her teeth and Mariana would keep crying. We all did. But so, too, were there vivid memories and moments of intense joy – they'd never had a visitor who asked specifically for them. What had taken me so long?

'It's Tessa! Tessa who we made pancakes with.'

'When are you going to fly away Tay-sa?'

I promised I would never disappear like that again. How could I? The visit left me feeling wretched – haunted, even. I returned to Chicerea and told my mother-in-law what I'd found.

'Poor things,' she acknowledged, and in the same breath asked if I had taken good care of Mara. Of course I had taken care of Mara! Every morning before I went into the hospital I walked up to the top of the town and handed her over to darling Marița, still fostering her gypsy siblings, overjoyed at the presence of my tiny daughter.

It was more than a year later, after another visit to Siret and more stories of my previous life in Romania, that Elena suggested a road trip.

'Next time you go, we'll all come with you. We can use Uncle Bogdan's car.'

And so it was that in the late spring of 2011 Elena, Vlad, Mara and I bundled into Bogdan's car. (Cousins Alin and Mihaela didn't come. They no longer lived in Romania; one a doctor in Ireland, and the other a student in London.)

The drive to Siret was slow and hot; Mara grizzled and Elena worried about dropping picnic crumbs in the car. Never a good traveller, I vomited in a lay-by. But it was worth it.

Finally the Romanian government had been shamed into coughing up the money to re-house the remaining 'children'.

'At last,' explained Tibi (the institute's director), throwing his arm out proudly, 'these young people have something to look forward to. In two months we move! A new chapter will begin!'

Surrounded by the crazy sounds and the sickly smells of the hospital my mother-in-law peered beyond her specs and said nothing. Mariana tried to pick up Mara who was having none of it, and Vlad joshed with the boys who tugged at him for attention. And I was eighteen all over again. Vasilica and I swapped bracelets and stroked each other's hair; we linked arms and laughed out loud.

'Tay-sa! Tay-sa! Tay-sa has come back again. Vai Tay-sa! Can we have a Coca Cola?'

It was later when we stopped in at Mariţa's tiny flat that Elena finally relaxed. She helped her hostess slice tomatoes and cooed over two newborn babies Mariţa had been charged to look after, her previous foster children having since grown up.

'I can't help but love them,' she explained, 'but it's difficult.'

Her allowance for two was twenty pounds a week and Mariţa was no longer young. Her weight had given way to severe diabetes.

'What can I do,' she smiled. 'Our economic crisis means lots of unwanted babies and Mihai has had his pension cut.'

Elena nodded. Her pension had been cut, too.

It was once we were safely back in Chicerea that Elena brought up the subject of the hospital.

'All those sick people in one room – how does the carer manage at night?' she mused.

I shrugged. I'd never thought what it might be like for the carers.

'I felt afraid in there,' she confessed. 'It hurt my soul. I've never seen anything like that. Didn't you ever feel scared?'

'No, never. I enjoyed being with them. You know me, Elena. I love an audience!'

She looked at me and smiled. Nothing more was said but that

night Elena had a word with God about the Siret orphans and impoverished Marița who sacrificed so much for others.

Vlad didn't say anything – I didn't expect him to; however, when I suggested that next time we might take the girls on an excursion to the little blue house in Chicerea, he didn't object, and nor did his mother.

Needless to say, for me our trip to Siret was huge. At last my two Romanias had collided – Siret and its orphans, who'd changed the course of my life together finally with Vlad and Elena, whose world was now mine.

And all of them from the country I love as if it were my own.

Epilogue

So I guess that's it – unless, of course, you want to know how the book came about.

It all started over four years ago, the day Elena and Tuca left London after their holiday. I held on to the image of them wide-eyed and scared at Heathrow, with avocados and whisky stashed in their bags, adamant they could find their own way to the aeroplane, and as soon as I got home that same afternoon I started writing.

Vlad, a very private man (hard though it is to believe given he's married to me), said I wasn't allowed to publish our story. So to begin with I just wrote for myself, and for Dad. I would read instalments down the phone to him, skipping the intimate bits to avoid his blushes and mine. I enjoyed sharing my latest efforts and he enjoyed tearing them apart. It took his mind off being ill.

I might reluctantly have left it at that. But then Dad died and I was back in Romania, where I finally revisited Vasilica and Mariana and Elena started talking. Under my persistent questioning she opened up in a way that had never been asked of her before. We often sat late into the night over cups of camomile tea, Elena flitting from subject to subject; secret pickling recipes, childhood memories, her father (here she shed a tear), even her army training under Ceauşescu (just one day at the end of which she had to sign a piece of paper confirming she'd fired a gun and was ready to protect the Socialist State). It was during these late night chats I confided in her about my book and she in turn gave me her permission to keep writing.

'If you can make money from our small lives, well done you!'

The following day she presented me with a large cardboard box full of every letter Mum and I had ever sent her son. Her acquiescence helped soften Vlad. After all, I had lost my job. *Purlease, Vlad!*

'Oh all right then – so long as you change my name and know that I don't think it's a good idea.'

'Thanks! I love you.'

'Why's it always so conditional with you, Tessa!'

I chose the name Vlad as it was the one Elena said she'd have gone for if she'd not been thrown by the arrival of a third boy. Friends said I couldn't possibly call my husband Vlad. It's a comedy name, they laughed. And so ugly! But to me it sounded strong and in Romania it's very popular. Vlad the Impaler's their favourite anti-hero, after all.

So that's my story, and to my relief Mum professed to like it.

'Darling, there's nothing to be ashamed of! It's a wonderful love story.'

But then, my mother has always been very loyal.